GOING DARK

ALSO BY JULIA EBNER

*The Rage: The Vicious Circle of Islamist and
Far-Right Extremism*

GOING DARK

The Secret Social Lives of Extremists

Julia Ebner

BLOOMSBURY PUBLISHING

LONDON · OXFORD · NEW YORK · NEW DELHI · SYDNEY

BLOOMSBURY PUBLISHING
Bloomsbury Publishing Plc
50 Bedford Square, London, WC1B 3DP, UK

BLOOMSBURY, BLOOMSBURY PUBLISHING and the Diana logo are
trademarks of Bloomsbury Publishing Plc

First published in Great Britain 2020

A catalogue record for this book is available from the British Library

ISBN: HB: 978-1-5266-1678-4; TPB: 978-1-5266-1677-7; EBOOK: 978-1-5266-1676-0

2 4 6 8 10 9 7 5 3 1

Typeset by Newgen KnowledgeWorks Pvt., Ltd, Chennai, India
Printed and bound in Great Britain by CPI Group (UK) Ltd, Croydon CR0 4YY

To find out more about our authors and books visit www.bloomsbury.com
and sign up for our newsletters

To my parents

Contents

Introduction   I

PART ONE: RECRUITMENT

1   Whites Only: Recruited by Neo-Nazis   9

2   Redpilling for Beginners: Undercover
with Generation Identity   25

PART TWO: SOCIALISATION

3   Trad Wives: Joining the Female
Anti-Feminists   53

4   Sisters Only: Introduced to the Jihadi Brides   75

PART THREE: COMMUNICATION

5   Info Wars: Confronted by Tommy
Robinson's New Media Empire   91

6   Meme Wars: Undercover in Europe's
Biggest Trolling Army   113

CONTENTS

PART FOUR: NETWORKING

7 Alt-Tech: Connecting Radicals around
   the World   137

8 Follow Q: Inside the Bizarre World of
   Conspiracy Theorists   153

PART FIVE: MOBILISATION

9 Unite the Right: Watching the Alt-Right
   Plot Charlottesville   173

10 Schild & Schwert: Attending a Neo-Nazi
   Music Festival   193

PART SIX: ATTACK

11 Black Hats: Trained by ISIS and
   Neo-Nazi Hackers   211

12 Gamified Terrorism: Within the Sub-
   cultures behind the New Zealand Attack   235

PART SEVEN: IS THE FUTURE DARK?

13 It All Started So Well   253

14 Ten Predictions for 2025   265

15 Ten Solutions for 2020   273

   A Note from the Author   283
   Glossary   287
   Acknowledgements   291
   Notes   293
   Index   337

Introduction

When I was seven years old, I wanted to study tornadoes. 'A storm chaser!' was my standard reply to the adults who bothered asking a first-grader what she wanted to become when she grew up. I had seen the movie *Twister* and was fascinated by the speed, force and unpredictability of storms. To fully understand tornadoes and create warning systems, my *Twister* heroes concluded, you needed to get to the centre of a storm.

Instead of chasing storms I have ended up chasing extremists for a living. In many ways this isn't too dissimilar. Like storms, extremist movements are fast, have strong destructive potential and can change direction at any time. In my day job at the London-based Institute for Strategic Dialogue (ISD), I monitor extremist movements across the UK, Europe and the US. My team works with cutting-edge technology partners and universities such as MIT to track and analyse harmful online content – ranging from extremist propaganda to pieces of disinformation. Based on this research, I advise governments, security forces, tech firms and activists on how to respond to extremist activities. There is no set recipe for this; sometimes we have to readjust our strategy on a daily basis to match the quick changes in the tactics of extremists. Beyond that, the problem is far too complex to focus on one stakeholder only. One day, I might brief a national intelligence unit about the cryptocurrency transactions of neo-Nazis, the next I could be advising Facebook on how to improve its take-downs of white nationalist materials. In the morning, I might find myself in a meeting with European policymakers to discuss the future of regulating the online space, in the evening at a radicalisation-prevention workshop in a high school in Saxony.

But even with all these different layers of engagement, my day job comfortably keeps me within the bubbles of those in charge of upholding the status quo rather than those attacking it. At the end of the day, the counter-extremism space offers only a feline view of the cat-and-mouse game between those who try to disrupt and destabilise our democracies and those who seek to protect them. To comprehend what is causing the havoc around us, I realised, one needs to be inside, where the engines of the movements can be observed and studied. How do the extreme fringes mobilise supporters and lure vulnerable individuals into their networks? What are their visions of the future and how do they plan to reach them? What are the social dynamics that keep members inside a group and how are they evolving?

To find answers I have spent two years undercover, adopting five different identities and joining a dozen tech-savvy extremist groups across the ideological spectrum – from jihadists and Christian fundamentalists to white nationalists, conspiracy theorists and radical misogynists. During my working hours I was the cat, but in my spare time I joined the mice.

This personal research has taken me to some bizarre, at times dangerous places, both online and offline. I have watched extremist movements coordinate terrorist attacks, launch disinformation operations and plot intimidation campaigns. I was in the channels where the alt-right planned the lethal Charlottesville rally, ISIS plotted cyberattacks on American infrastructure, German trolls coordinated online attacks on politicians and Italian neo-fascists carried out information operations to influence the 2018 election. From participating in a secret strategy meeting hosted by white nationalists in an Airbnb in south London to joining a militant neo-Nazi rock festival on the German–Polish border and receiving hacking instructions from ISIS jihadists, my time inside these movements not only taught me about extremists' strategies and tactics, it also exposed me to their human dimensions as well as to my own vulnerabilities.

The extent of the abhorrent content I came across during this project was sobering, and the number of young people involved saddening. On the surface, the movements I joined have little in common. But I would come to learn that on the inside they all operate similarly: their leaders create protected social bubbles to encourage antisocial behaviour in the wider world. Their members globalise anti-globalist ideologies and use modern technologies to put into practice anti-modern visions.

Going Dark exposes the hidden roots of life within extremist movements. Each part deals with a different stage in the radicalisation process. 'Recruitment' dives into the vetting procedures of an American neo-Nazi group, and the European white nationalist Generation

Identity (GI) movement. 'Socialisation' explores the brainwashing hotbeds for 'Trad Wives' and jihadi brides from within. 'Communication' uncovers the far right's media warfare strategies from the inside of hate storms and trolling armies. In 'Networking' I reveal how extremists create international hubs, using social networks and even dating apps, which lay the foundation for their growing global networks. 'Mobilisation' is a journey that starts in the chat rooms of the organisers behind the Charlottesville rally and ends at Europe's biggest neo-Nazi rock festival in Ostritz. In 'Attack', I receive hacking instructions from leading ISIS and neo-Nazi hackers before diving into the sub-cultures that radicalised the man behind the deadly attack in New Zealand in March 2019. And finally, 'Is the Future Dark?' reflects on the scale and nature of the extremism challenge that faces all of us, predicts its evolution over the next decades and features ten courageous initiatives with the potential to inspire a new generation of global agents of change.

The interplay between technology and society has long been key to radical change. In 1936, the German Jewish philosopher Walter Benjamin argued that the rise of fascism was propelled by inventions such as screen printing and early photocopying technologies, which changed the public perception of media, arts and politics. The birth of technologically progressive yet socially regressive movements shaped the power dynamics of twentieth-century Europe.

We are again witnessing a toxic combination of ideological nostalgia and technological futurism that might determine the direction of travel for twenty-first-century politics. The radicalisation engines that today's extremists are building are cutting edge: artificially intelligent, emotionally manipulative and socially powerful. They combine high-tech and hyper-social elements to drive counter-cultures that appeal to the young, angry and tech-savvy. When they are effective, they have the potential to become a dangerous force for change. They not only might fundamentally change the nature of extremism and terrorism but could also redefine our information ecosystems and democratic processes, threatening to reverse our biggest civil rights achievements.

My aim in this book is to make the social dimension of digital extremist movements visible. Extremists groom new members and intimidate new opponents around us every day. The results can impact our daily lives, sometimes in unexpected ways. In March 2016, printers across US college campuses spontaneously started printing neo-Nazi flyers. In July 2018, Hamas created a fake dating app to target hundreds of Israel Defense Forces troops with malicious software hiding behind the stolen profiles of young women. Throughout 2018, hardline Brexit campaigns were boosted by the international conspiracy theory networks of QAnon. By January 2019, far-right hackers had leaked the personal details of hundreds of German politicians. And March 2019 saw the livestream of New Zealand's most lethal terrorist attack go viral.

Recent policy reactions to extremism tend to neglect the group dynamics at play in today's loose online networks of extremists. Even though these are no longer traditionally organised groups, their cultural, anthropological and psychological aspects remain key to their allure and impact. By exposing emerging socio-technological challenges, I hope to make policymakers rethink their current tech- and law-heavy response. Ultimately, we can't always rely on our politicians, security forces or the private sector to resolve this problem for us. Neither guns nor censorship will affect the group dynamics that make today's extremist movements so successful. New laws and regulations resolve a tiny part of the puzzle, but temporarily and without the guarantee that they don't backfire in the end.

A more human-centred approach would mean that every reader could help to tackle the spread of misanthropic and anti-democratic ideologies. Having for several years watched extremist groups operate and perfect their tactical playbook, I am convinced that nothing is more powerful than arming people with the knowledge of how extremists seek to exploit our weaknesses in our online and offline lives. Learning about the tricks behind extremist activities was what kept me from being drawn into their radicalisation engines during my research. I want this book to help others protect themselves from being radicalised, manipulated or intimidated by extremists.

PART ONE

Recruitment

Whites Only: Recruited by Neo-Nazis

'Where the hell am I?' Bryan asks.

'This is a radical-right discussion group, mainly focusing on race, traditionalism, spirituality, philosophy, aesthetics and literature,' responds the administrator. His name is Aldrich. Aldrich ᛋ to be precise.

'To access the members-only channels, send a hand or wrist photograph with a piece of paper reading MAtR – your username – timestamp,' he tells all newcomers.

'Then answer this questionnaire:

Q1. What is your entire ancestral background that you are aware of?
Q2. How old are you?
Q3. How would you describe your political views?
Q4. What are your religious or spiritual views?
Q5. Are you a homosexual or any other type of sexual deviant?'

Bryan's hand picture soon appears in the chat room, accompanied by an apology for the bright-blue reflection his laptop casts on his hands.

'That's fine,' Aldritch writes. Bryan's hand is white enough to be accepted into the group. He claims to have Finnish blood, with a dash of European and American Indian influences.

Bryan is seventeen and describes himself as a national anarchist and a Finnish pagan, a so-called Suomenusko. 'But I was homosexual, due to my own degeneracy, sorry to say,' he writes. 'Occasional thoughts, it's a work in progress to purge my mind of such thoughts.'

A few days later Bryan is gone. Instead, Jason appears in the recruitment hub of the white nationalist channel.

'I'm already on a shit ton of watch lists,' he writes, 'and I'm only fourteen.'

'Ru white tho?;)' asks Aldritch, who himself is Anglo-Bulgarian with some German, Scottish and Croatian ancestry on the maternal side. Nobody in the group seems to care that Jason is a minor.

'2% nigger, 23andMe test into the trashbin,' is Jason's prompt reply. The boy posts a copy of his genetic test results into the group to prove his whiteness. 'Just kidding, I'm three-quarters German and a quarter Estonian.'

He gets a grinning emoji in response, as the second administrator, Deus Vult, enters the chat room. 'Did you know that Alfred Rosenberg, the leader of the NSDAP (National Socialist German Workers) during Hitler's imprisonment, was one-quarter Estonian?'

I down my glass of wine to dampen the chills this conversation is sending down my spine.

'Hello r u a girl?' Deus Vult approaches me with a direct message, as if he had seen the distress on my face through my screen.

I hesitate. For days I had been keeping a low profile, just lurking around in the entrance hall of the neo-Nazi chat group.

My username, Jen Malo, is suspiciously innocent. As I look around, it is hard to find names without references to either National Socialist or alt-right symbols. Deus Vult, a Crusader battle cry meaning 'God wills it', is among the more benign ones. Many names feature the letters WP ('White Power') or W.O.T.A.N. ('Will of the Aryan Nation'). Others carry the numbers 4/20, alluding to Hitler's birthday, 14 in reference to the Fourteen Words ('We must secure the existence of our people and a future for white children') and 88 referring to the initials HH ('Heil Hitler'). Aldrich is the obvious outlier, combining the runic insignia of the Nazi Schutzstaffel, the SS, with a rather random expression of admiration for the Cold War double agent Aldrich Ames.

'Yes, I'm a girl,' I respond finally. Did I wait too long?

'Don't worry, we also take girls,' Deus Vult writes. 'Got a few minutes for a chat on voice?'

I knew this would have to happen sooner or later, so there is no point in postponing.

'Ready?'

I try to imagine the face behind this voice: is he young or old? It's hard to say – there is no set profile for neo-Nazis these days. 'Sure.' As ready as you can be before chatting with a Nazi.

My hands on the keyboard are shaking, but I try to keep my voice steady. The letters MAtR are written across my wrist. The acronym stands for Men Among the Ruins, the most influential work of the Italian philosopher Julius Evola. An early ideologue of traditionalism and spiritual racism, Evola inspired Benito Mussolini's fascist regime and worked for the Nazi SS, whose head Heinrich Himmler he admired. He himself denied being a fascist, instead preferring the label 'superfascist'.[1] After World War II his vision of a societal and political order based on hierarchy, caste, race, myth, religion and ritual continued to be a major source of inspiration for Italian extreme-right terrorists[2] and neo-fascists.[3] Today, Evola's books sell well to the alt-right. Even President Donald Trump's former political adviser Stephen Bannon cites his works.[4] According to the Rome-based Evola biographer and head of the Evola Foundation Gianfranco de Turris, 'It's the first time that an adviser to the American president knows Evola, or maybe has a Traditionalist formation.'[5]

'You are vetted,' writes Deus Vult after a brief chat in which I tell him what he wants to hear: 'I am white, of Austrian nationality and European ancestry. I believe that our genetic and cultural heritage is under threat by foreign invading forces and am concerned about the future of my children who will have to grow up in a multicultural Europe.' Why do I want to be part of the group? 'To be honest, I'm not yet sure what to expect but I know that I want to connect with like-minded people and learn about the activities planned for the patriotic revolution in the US and in Europe.'

'Welcome in MAtR.'

As I enter the main chat halls I see Jason, who has changed his name to General Jason. The title appears fitting, considering that the channel is organised in tight hierarchies with military ranks. The server counts a few dozen members from across the world. I spot individuals who indicate that they are American, Canadian,

South African, European and Australian. A Canadian in his early twenties who was raised Christian but claims to be interested in 'Esoteric Hitlerism', a sixteen-year-old self-described National Socialist from Lithuania observing Romuvan traditions and a 'completely irreligious and agnostic' seventeen-year-old woman from New Zealand who currently resides in the US. The conversations are as diverse as the interlocutors, spanning from whether Jesus was a Jew or not to whether Trump and Kim will get along. Genetics and biology are among their favourite topics.

'So what do you know about genetic testing?' a so-called Mr White asks Jason.

Mr White is thirty-two and has been in what he calls the 'Movement' since turning fifteen. When neo-Nazis speak about the 'Movement' they usually mean Nationalist Socialist networks, but nowadays this can mean anything from specific group memberships to affiliations with loose online networks of individuals that have never met and maybe will never meet in real life.

'To be honest, not much. But I do really want to learn more about it.'

'That's understandable,' Mr White replies. 'I got into it because it would be extremely difficult to hold racial beliefs if my ancestry conflicted. At best I have a surface understanding on the genetics side,' he admits.

Mr White is not the only white supremacist who wants to know every single percentage of his ancestry. Many right-wing extremists have developed an obsession with genetics. Across the dozens of closed chat groups I monitored over the course of 2017–18, at least half of them asked their members to share detailed accounts of their genetic ancestry. Some even wanted to see the test results as part of the application procedure.

23andMe, Ancestry, MyHeritage and other DNA-testing firms recorded an unprecedented surge in their sales of genetic genealogy tests since the summer of 2016. More people had their DNA analysed in 2017 than in all previous years combined.[6] But white supremacists' genetic ancestry test results don't always match their own purity requirements, which can push them into profound identity crises. When your main scapegoats are Jews and Muslims, and you consider Blacks and Arabs biologically inferior, it can be a little discomfiting to find out you are a quarter Jewish and an eighth Moroccan.

New technologies tend to reinforce radicalisation dynamics, but genetic tests show that they can also have the opposite effect. The cognitive dissonance that arises when mono-ethnic ideals of the future meet the multi-racial realities of the past can set in motion profound attitude and behaviour changes.

Aaron Panofsky of UCLA's Institute for Society and Genetics and Joan Donovan of the Data and Society Research Institute analysed discussions around genetic ancestry on the white supremacist forums of Stormfront. They found that many individuals who had undesired test results employed twisted logic in an attempt to reconcile their ideological beliefs with their multiracial heritage.[7] 'You'd think that the members of this site would say, "Get out! We don't want you,"' Panofsky said. 'Instead, they find ways to support their community members and keep them as part of the group.'[8]

In some cases, however, repression mechanisms yield a reinforcement of the beliefs, or worse, an escalation to even more absurd conspiracy theories that allow them to deny all validity of their test results.[9] According to Mr White, genetic tests are purposefully distorted by the so-called 'ZOG', 'the Zionist Occupied Government', as part of their plot to wipe out the white race. 'To be honest, with the recent article about 23andMe being manipulated to show more Ashkenazi and Sub-Saharan African in customer reports, it's difficult to trust anything,' he writes. There is no reliable evidence to suggest that genetic-test data providers interfere with the test results they provide. But the white supremacist belief that every single aspect of their lives is ruled by Jews, the 'global elites' or 'cultural Marxists' sits so deep that it is hard to find in their minds anything that is not rigged. The genetic test providers 23andMe and Ancestry are not exempt from their universal distrust.

Distrust is one of the key constants that brings individuals to extreme-right channels, but fun, friendship and fulfilment are what keeps them there. 'This has been a lot of fun,' Mr White writes. 'I'm really shocked at the amount of intelligent people in here. I'm used to talking to baby boomers about their good ole days.' Others express their agreement: 'Lol. Yeah I'm enjoying this channel too,' one writes.

'Fun' and 'enjoying' are words that stick out in a chat room that starts with the words 'Gas the kikes. Race war now.' But the alliance of fun and evil are – just like the interlacement of inhumane and humane behaviour – neither new nor surprising. One hundred and sixteen photographs collected by the SS officer Karl-Friedrich Höcker during the Nazi regime show administrators of concentration camps enjoying themselves at the height of the exterminations. While hundreds of thousands of Hungarian Jews were being tortured and killed during the summer of 1944, concentration-camp staff are shown drinking, singing and having fun in their holiday resort Solahütte just thirty kilometres south of Auschwitz.[10] The Höcker Album is a painful reminder that even those that commit atrocities beyond imagination remain human on many levels: they enjoy sociable meals with their families, wild drinking nights with friends and occasional flirtations with colleagues they fancy. The American psychiatrist Robert Lifton called this development of two selves, one normal and one evil one, 'doubling'. Rather than a psychological disorder like schizophrenia or bipolar personality, this form of self-splitting is the result of an intense tertiary socialisation phase, which succeeds the early socialisation processes within family and education settings.[11]

The fun factor continues to be instrumental in the mainstreaming of extreme-right ideologies and conspiracy theories. Insider jokes, transgressive humour and irony helped far-right activists increase their appeal among young people in the run-up to the US election.[12] After spending a few weeks in the MAtR channel, observing the nightly discussions and listening to the voice chats, I start to understand how the pleasure of breaking taboos can kill boredom and how the sense of belonging can become an antidote to loneliness. Members are sharing their most intimate experiences, fears and visions, and are developing a common language, symbolism and even insider jokes. Gradually, these nameless, faceless strangers on the platform turn into virtual replacements for each other's families and friends.

At this point it may seem understandable that MAtR members spend multiple days per week in this little echo chamber. But how does a channel like this start in the first place? Does someone say 'Hey, let's create a neo-Nazi chat for gamers?' Are there discussions about whether to use the swastika or the Wolfsangel (an ancient runic symbol that was appropriated by the Nazis) as the logo, disputes about whether to use the runic alphabet or cryptic emojis to welcome newcomers?

Well, almost. A man nicknamed Comrade Rhodes created the server MAtR in the summer of 2017. While his friends were out barbecuing and swimming, he sat in front of his computer thinking about how to best slip his Nationalist Socialist ideologies into the heart of society. 'All right, we're going to get this to about 300 members as our first objective,' Aldrich ᚻ announced on Day 1 of MAtR.

'So where do we recruit people?' his virtual friend Comrade Rhodes asked.

'I'll set up a vetting channel and process when I'm on my PC. Then I'll start sending out invites at about 11 tonight.'

The first few weeks were easy for the initiators, as no one was watching them. Neither the security forces nor the tech companies were paying attention to the campaigns they were running both online and offline. MAtR was just one out of dozens of similar-minded channels on the encrypted gaming application Discord, and one of hundreds on the internet. But the weekend of 12 August 2017 changed the environment they were operating in.

After the white nationalist rally in Charlottesville ended in the death of civil rights activist Heather

Heyer, both public and encrypted messaging platforms started closing down multiple extreme-right channels. The MAtR administrators were not involved in the planning of the rally – in fact, they condemned the organisers for their blunt media strategy and premature efforts to 'unite the right'. To them, Charlottesville was an amateurish, ego-driven attempt to generate maximum media attention while lacking a thorough ideological and strategic basis. Despite keeping their distance from the Charlottesville organisation teams, the MAtR administrators became increasingly paranoid about being detected. Like other groups, they started introducing stricter entrance barriers and background checks and developed code words.

Many white nationalist groups resorted to framing their chat groups as safe spaces for freedom of speech, claiming to welcome members of all political leanings. A conspiracy theory about the creeping Muslim takeover of Europe would be sold as a fact-based discussion and a thread about why the Holocaust never took place as an attempt to test the limits of freedom of speech. But disagreeing with their views means being silenced, ridiculed and discredited as being 'part of the problem our countries have with censorship'. I have tried, and seen others try, to question the assertions and arguments made in extremist online groups, each time being called out as an infiltrator, labelled a traitor or kicked out of the chat room.

Other groups rely on humoristic and satirical illustrations to camouflage their extreme views. A joke about Jews being behind the global financial crisis? Satire. A derogatory picture of a homosexual couple? Transgression for the sake of 'triggering' the virtue-signalling left. And, 'If you don't get it, then you're either retarded or too woke, or both,' as they would say.

The goal of MAtR's leaders is to establish a white ethno-state, an Aryan nation. 'Which is not a new idea,' as Mr White stresses. 'There is already a plan for this and has been in place since the 90's.' He shares a link to the Constitution for the Ethno-State:

> Article IV. Residence and citizenship in the Northwest American Republic shall be restricted, absolutely and for all time, to those persons of unmixed Caucasian racial descent from any one of the historic family of European nations, who shall have no known or identifiable non-White ancestry, and no visibly non-White element in their genetic makeup.
>
> Article V. The race commonly known as Jews are in culture and historic tradition an Asiatic people, and shall not be considered White or accorded White racial status under law. No Jew shall be allowed to enter or to reside in the Northwest American Republic under any circumstances.[13]

The man who drafted this constitution, Harold Covington, has been an inspiration to many extreme-right activists. He was the founder of the Northwest Front (NWF), 'a political organization of Aryan men and women who recognize that an independent and sovereign White nation in the Pacific Northwest is the only possibility for the survival of the White race on this continent'.[14] Covington earned his money from selling sci-fi novels and T-shirts with AK47s printed on them.[15] But his Northwest novels 'are not meant to be mere entertainment', as Covington assured his readers; 'they are meant to be self-fulfilling prophecies'.

Self-fulfilling prophecies with real-world consequences they are indeed. The white supremacist Dylann Roof quoted the NWF in his manifesto before murdering nine African-Americans in the Charleston church shooting in June 2015. Roof, however, thought that expelling all non-whites from the Pacific Northwest wouldn't be sufficient because he didn't like the idea of moving to the Northwest. 'Why should I for example give up the beauty and history of my state to go to the Northwest?' he wrote.[16]

Mr White admits to empathising with Roof. 'The past 70 years has been so-called leaders speaking about problems forever, solutions never. And this kind of methodology creates guys like Dylann Roof. They hear nothing but problems and there are no solutions, so they make their own.' Like Roof, he believes that the Northwest Front's idea isn't going far enough. Their ideological disagreements are however rather cosmetic in nature: in the end, they all agree that racism is 'the purist form of patriotism'.[17] 'That's what people need to realise,' writes an MAtR member who calls himself Pretentieux. But he wouldn't use a gun like Roof. 'I think there is much more value in just trying to spread the knowledge, "redpilling" people if you will. It takes a lot of work and a lot of tact.'

Redpilling is a reference to *The Matrix*, the sci-fi blockbuster by Lana and Lilly Wachowsky that every teenager from the 2000s remembers. 'You take the blue pill, the story ends,' Morpheus tells the protagonist Neo. 'You wake up in your bed and believe whatever you want to believe. You take the red pill, you stay in Wonderland, and I show you how deep the rabbit hole goes.' Neo opts for the red pill and thereby discovers that he was living in a computer simulation designed by artificially intelligent robots to enslave humanity and harvest their bodies for energy. This cult scene has become a source of inspiration, hope and self-denial for the international alt-right. Recruiters use the movie's metaphor to persuade sympathisers that they are caught up in an illusionary world created by the 'global establishment'. In their obsession to 'expose the truth' some spend their late nights after work collecting 'red pills' that they store in large databases.[18] A red pill can, for example, be a piece of (mis)information about migrant crimes or a (distorted) statistic about demographic change that lends credibility to their world view. If redpilling is seen as a euphemism for radicalisation, then much of the internet has turned into redpill factories. By the way, the ultimate red pill for white nationalists is the conviction that the Holocaust never happened. *The Matrix* is part of an arsenal of internet culture references – from Japanese anime to pop star Taylor Swift – that the alt-right has co-opted and weaponised for its purposes.

Pretentieux is one of the teenagers from the 2000s, also called the millennials. Today he is thirty-one. He never cared about 'redpilling' until about five years ago when his niece was born. 'My sister is in prison and I'm helping my parents raise her, and I started to have to pay attention to things like how she will be treated, what she will have to face as she grows up.'

'I can't imagine what that would be like,' Mr White comments. 'The balloon is closer to going up now than it has ever been before.' Like many others in the group, he believes that the impeding race war is about to begin, and that the collapse of the democratic system is near. '[…] It wasn't until the past 4 years I started to see people who are under 40 and racially aware.' It is his first time on Discord.

Pretentieux admits that to him 'it's become an addiction'. He explains that it's the easiest way 'to find and communicate with people who are sane and honest'. After a brief pause, he admits: 'Well, not sure I am sane but [I am] honest […] I'm pretty blunt.'

'If you poke around a bit,' Pretentieux tells Mr White, 'over time you will find there are a lot of Discord servers with likeminded people. They all have their own particular flavor.'

This is precisely what cyber-security analyst Kevin Thompson warned of at the dawn of mass commercialisation of the internet. In his 2001 study of conversations on the white supremacist platform Stormfront he concluded that computer-moderated communication allows stigmatised and disenfranchised individuals to form alternative arenas to replace traditional neighbourhood and kinship communities.[19] That cyberspace could be leveraged by extremists to radicalise others and coordinate campaigns and violent acts became clear as early as the late 1990s, the internet's Stone Age. During the 1998 FIFA World Cup in France, German neo-Nazis and hooligans launched racially and ideologically motivated assaults, which they had planned on their mobile phones. At a match in the northern French town Lens, where Germany played Yugoslavia, ninety-six people were arrested, some of them performing Hitler salutes. They ended up seriously injuring a police officer, who fell into a coma.[20]

When it comes to the best use of the internet and new technologies, opinions differ even among white nationalists. Pretentieux is in favour of using it to win over the hearts and minds of young people. The democratisation of publishing and the distribution of (dis)information is seen as a substantial part of this. Northwest Front cites 'print-per-order publishing' as one example that 'has actually broken the back of a major Jewish monopoly in the arts and entertainment field'.[21] Users such as LifeOfWat, on the other hand, are convinced that circumventing traditional media won't be enough. 'War is the only way. Freedom by the Sword.'

What unites extreme-right actors across the ideological spectrum is the conviction that new technologies will be critical in helping them to expand and cement their political influence: 'The virtual battlefield needs to come first,' one MAtR member concludes. The far right's preparations for a virtual battle take place in hidden corners of the internet, like the Discord chat rooms of MAtR, and remain largely invisible to the average internet user. For me, entering this world of racialist discussions and genetic-test sharing felt surreal. But the far-right-inspired terror attacks that killed fifty people in New Zealand in March 2019 showed how quickly such virtual sub-cultures fantasising about white ethno-states can translate into real-world violence.

The pan-European movement I join in the next chapter does not openly endorse violence like MAtR. Unlike American extremists, its members would not even have access to guns. But the group's skilful use of new communication technologies and the social spaces these create has turned it into a top priority for national intelligence services. Its recruiters have been able to appeal to a wide audience of young, tech-savvy people across Europe and the UK. They have pioneered subtler and more innovative forms of group branding and outreach.

2

Redpilling for Beginners: Undercover with Generation Identity

'Hello Jenni!' A tall guy with rectangular glasses and short, gelled hair awaits me in the traditional Café Prückerl in the historic heart of Vienna. He looks almost too normal to be a white nationalist: no visible tattoos, not even a fashy undercut – the alt-right's trademark coiffure.

'Oh, hi! Are you Edwin?' It is a purely rhetorical question. I recognise the regional leader of Generation Identity (GI) from his various media appearances. After all, he is a prominent figure among European Identitarians. It took several months of setting up credible accounts within the various Generation Identity networks online and a couple of weeks of messaging with Austrian and British Generation Identity members to arrange this first in-person meeting.

An awkward handshake, a shy look around the neighbouring tables and I sit down next to Edwin Hintsteiner. My blonde wig matches the colour of the ponytail on the profile picture of my avatar Twitter account. Remember, I tell myself, your name is Jennifer Mayer and you are an Austrian philosophy student on an exchange semester in London. Adopting a fake identity is not unlike developing the character in a novel. If you don't know their past, present and future, no one will find your story credible.

It's the day of the Austrian general election, so most people around us are sipping their coffee and discussing the likely election outcome with their neighbours. The only pair of eyes watching us belongs to an elegantly dressed old woman, who looks up from her *Standard*, a centre-left daily newspaper. I doubt that she recognises either of us.

Little did I know then that Edwin would soon be infamous among Austrian pensioners. A few months later, on International Holocaust Memorial Day in January 2018, he would shock Austria's older generations by causing a media frenzy with his tweet: 'When you outlive your usefulness and never learned how to knit because you are so full of feminism.'[1] His tweet was a direct attack on the non-partisan movement 'Omas gegen Rechts' ('Grandmas against the Right') and their protest against the Akademikerball, an annual prom organised by Austria's far-right Freedom Party (FPÖ) that has become a popular meet-up for extreme-right influencers from across Europe. It was not just the indecency of attacking a consortium of grannies that made his tweet so controversial. Whether intentional or not, 'Life unworthy of life' ('Lebensunwertes Leben') was a phrase Hitler used in his decree of October 1939, which ordered the systematic killing of those considered too weak, impaired or inferior to deserve being alive. In addition to the 6 million Jews, 200,000 Roma and 70,000 homosexuals the Nazis slaughtered, they also murdered 300,000 disabled and elderly people in their euthanasia programme. The Association for Retired Persons of Austria joined the chorus of condemnation, criticising Hintsteiner for his 'disgusting choice of words'.

'So tell me about yourself. How come you are interested in Generation Identity? Have you been politically active at all?' Edwin doesn't do much small talk, I figure.

'Not really, just a bit of freelancing and flyering for the FPÖ,' I tell him and take out my phone, as if to look for a message. 'But I've been in touch with Martin, as you know.' The truth is that after I found out that GI was planning to open a UK offshoot, I applied to their British team. The movement's Austrian leader Martin Sellner immediately got in touch, suggesting we meet in Vienna.

But Martin is busy today; he is presenting his new book on Identitarians at the Frankfurt Book Fair. In the midst of 7,000 publishers from a hundred countries, it is his small far-right publisher Antaios that attracts all the media attention. So I meet Edwin instead and only learn later that, while we were having coffee, fights between Identitarians and counter-protesters at the Book Fair led to a few arrests and rumours of 'Sieg Heil' shouts.[2]

I order a cappuccino with soy milk, instantly regretting my choice. Edwin gives me a surprised look, though he is not as startled as the waiter. 'I'm sorry, miss, we are a traditional Viennese café. We don't do soy milk.'

Edwin laughs. 'How long have you been living in London again?' He ignores my sheepish smile. 'You know what I find interesting,' he resumes, twisting his spoon. 'It turns out that more and more people come to us who aren't actually that interested in politics.' Pride flickers across his face. 'We are the primary focal point for young people, they no longer go to the FPÖ if they want to change things, they come straight to us.' Edwin himself joined GI because he used to be active in the FPÖ's youth wing. 'There are a few things you need to know about us: we are not like the old Nazis, we are ethno-pluralist.'

A gay couple is sitting at the table across from us. Their conversation suddenly stops. Ashamed to be seen with one of the leaders of an openly homophobic movement I lower my voice. 'Ethno-pluralist…' I repeat.

'Right.' Edwin doesn't make an effort to keep his voice down. 'To us identity is about both culture and ethnicity. The only way to prevent the European civilisation from being replaced – ethnically and culturally – is to keep immigrants out,' he explains. Generation Identity's goal, according to the group's mission statement, is to create homogeneous societies – societies where different races and cultures do not mix. The first step for them would be to close off all borders. But since they perceive migrants as being a threat, even the ones that are already here, this wouldn't be enough. The second step would there-fore be to repatriate these migrants, including second- and third-generation migrants, whatever measures this may require in concrete terms.

Generation Identity sprang from Bloc Identitaire, a French nationalist movement founded in 2002 by anti-Zionist and National Bolshevik[3] sympathisers in Nice. A decade later, the youth wing of the group, Generation Identity, was formed and rapidly started expanding to Austria, Germany, Italy and other countries across Europe.[4] Today, Generation Identity is the European equivalent of the American alt-right, and the bridge between the European and the American far right. Martin Sellner, who is himself a former neo-Nazi, has become their most prolific figurehead in Europe and the US. In an attempt to rebrand himself, he has distanced himself from his previous mentor Gottfried Küssel, a notorious Austrian Holocaust denier.[5] Instead, he now talks about wanting to preserve Europe's cultural and ethnic identity, using terms like 'ethno-pluralist' instead of 'racial segregation' or 'apartheid', wearing Ray-Bans and T-shirts instead of jackboots and swastika tattoos.

Edwin looks me straight in the eye, as if he is searching for a sign of affirmation. 'You know, at the moment we are among the few movements that are resisting the Great Replacement.' I look down to escape his penetrating gaze, and up again to find the two men across from our table exchanging looks. Like most of Generation Identity's ideas, their notion of a 'Great Replacement' draws on the intellectual inspiration provided by the French Nouvelle Droite (New Right). One of their most admired ideologues and most enthusiastic supporters is Guillaume Faye, a French writer and journalist.[6] Faye claimed in a 2015 speech at the white supremacist National Policy Institute that Western countries are plagued by a 'mental illness', which he calls 'ethno-masochism'. His diagnosis is that the gradual replacement of white people, the so-called 'white genocide', is based on three phenomena: immigration, abortion and homosexuality. According to them, 'white genocide' is the result of a combination of pro-abortion and pro-LGBT laws that have lowered the birthrates of native Europeans, and pro-migration welcoming policies have allowed minorities to engage in a 'strategic mass breeding'.[7] 'It's a gradual takeover,' as Martin Sellner would say.

Demographic studies do not support these claims. A common logical fallacy in alt-right arguments is that if A came before B then it caused B (the *post hoc, ergo propter hoc* error). It is true that since the 1950s North America and Europe have experienced sharply falling fertility rates. It is also true that many Western countries abolished their sodomy laws and loosened their anti-abortion laws in the second half of the twentieth century. But the reasons for the declining birthrates over the past fifty years lie somewhere else. Research shows that rising living standards are responsible, with women's education, the availability of contraceptives and the enhanced health and well-being of children being the important factors.[8]

This idea of a Great Replacement has fed into many new variations of anti-left or anti-Semitic conspiracy theories that draw on older concepts such as the 'Hooton Plan'. In 1943, the US professor Earnest Albert Hooton published an essay that advocated a plan to 'breed war strain out of Germans' by crossbreeding Germans with non-German populations. Many German far-right groups have in recent years cited the migration crisis and their government's open-door policy to prove that the Hooton Plan is being carried out.

'Do you have any friends who are already at GI?' I shake my head. 'Interesting!' he cries. Those that aren't introduced by their personal contacts tend to stay the longest with GI, he explains to me. 'It's been happening more frequently in recent years that people join on their own initiative, mostly thanks to social media.'

Edwin's phone beeps. He apologises and responds to a message from a Belgian journalist from the daily newspaper *Le Soir*. 'It's been a little stressful with media interviews lately,' Edwin admits. Increasingly, there is international interest in Austria's swing to the right. He is not nervous any more, he tells me, he has done too many of them. And anyway, the mainstream media is fake news, he says, 'but we need them because they are free advertisement for us'.

Much more important for them, though, is social media. 'Which is why we are launching Patriot Peer!' With this new app, GI promises to 'connect the silent majority' and to 'turn resistance into a game'. Everything is gamified: you can even collect credits when you connect with other patriots, which improves your rating.[9] Edward tells me they want to get out of purely academic circles. 'We won't just advertise at unis but also carry out campaigns to recruit in schools, public baths and other public venues that young people may frequent.'

That's also why all of their offline activities are accompanied by slick online marketing operations, to maximise their impact and reach out among the youth. In the summer of 2017, they chartered a forty-metre ship, the so-called *C Star*, to prevent NGOs in the Mediterranean Sea from rescuing drowning refugees. The mission became widely known under the hashtag #DefendEurope thanks to their hyperactive social media feeds: each day they livestreamed their activities from the *C Star* to Facebook and Twitter, and posted pictures of their tanned bodies in trendy bathing wear on Instagram.

The support they receive on social media is global, with US alt-right vloggers and influencers playing a big role in making their hashtags trend. This is also reflected in their financial support. 'We've got donors from across the world for Patriot Peer,' Edwin tells me. 'But most important to us was all the support we received from the US.' He doesn't know that I spent the last few weeks investigating GI's funding networks. At the Institute for Strategic Dialogue we found that most of the €200,000 they received in donations for their #DefendEurope campaign came from US sources – despite its exclusive focus on European borders.[10]

'Why then aren't you expanding to North America?' I ask.

The US has the alt-right, Edwin explains, 'so we need to think very carefully about our strategy there'. Generation Identity did try to launch a branch in Canada, which didn't work too well. 'A bit of a fail,' he admits. No wonder, I'm tempted to say, selling the idea of a homogeneous society to a people that prides itself on hosting a cultural melting pot, and advocating anti-immigration in a country where few people don't perceive themselves as immigrants seems a little ludicrous. 'We'll need a rebranding there,' is Edwin's conclusion. Not this weekend, though. For now Austria is the priority.

'Do you have any plans for tonight? If you want to meet some other Identitarians, we are planning on going to the FPÖ's election party. Would you like to come?' I hesitate and when he adds, 'We've already cooled some Cokes and Club-Mate.' I choke on my coffee. Club-Mate, the Berlin-style energy drink, wasn't exactly something I would have associated with white nationalists. Apparently, my soy-milk request wasn't too hipster for the nipsters. (Nipsters, or Nazi-hipsters, are young neo-Nazis who have rebranded themselves and adopted elements of hipster fashion and culture.)

'Sorry, I have a family thing tonight.'

He nods. 'That's a shame, you'll miss out on a great evening and the opportunity to meet other members of GI.' Before I leave Café Prückerl, we agree that I will stay in touch and set up an initial call with the UK-based Identitarian leaders.

That same night, the FPÖ receives 26 per cent of the country's votes,[11] a shocking success for an Austrian party with links to neo-Nazi fraternities.

I log on to Skype. Thomas is waiting for our voice call; he joins me from Scotland. Although the new GI Scotland leader has been living in the UK for seven years, selling software, he has kept his Austrian dialect. He has a friendly laugh and a calm voice.

Thomas was on a family visit when he decided to go to one of Generation Identity's regular meet-ups in a Viennese café half a year ago. He didn't know what to expect. 'I was quite surprised, to be honest,' he tells me. 'I thought they had reserved one table but the entire place was filled with Identitarian activists and people interested in joining the movement.' Over the past few weeks he has been driving the development of the UK and Ireland offshoot and preparing for the official launch.

'Wow. They gave you so much responsibility so quickly?' I exclaim.

'Well, kind of, after I made Martin Sellner's videos accessible to a British audience by subtitling them.'

He asks me about my philosophy studies and seems happy when I express my admiration for Heidegger and Nietzsche. 'You should speak to Martin about this – these two are among his favourites.' Martin Sellner studied philosophy too. Special appreciation for the two philosophers is not uncommon among far-right figures: the Russian neo-fascist philosopher Alexander Dugin draws on Heidegger in his works, while alt-right figurehead Richard Spencer claims he was 'redpilled by Nietzsche'. Heidegger and Nietzsche both offer an intellectual framework for blaming today's perceived moral decline on modernism and liberalism. The alt-right uses this argument to denounce feminism, multi-culturalism and egalitarianism as products of the 'liberal corruption' of the Western world.

The political scientist Ronald Beiler would even go so far as to say that the 'incitements to genocide' by the two philosophers continue to inspire today's white nationalists, and their 'crazy ideological anti-liberal insanity'.[12] There is little doubt about Heidegger's ideo-logical leanings; he was a member of the NSDAP and never expressed regret about his support for Hitler, even after his lover, the Jewish anti-fascist student Hannah Arendt, had been forced to flee Germany. But when it comes to Nietzsche, opinions diverge; his biographer Sue Prideaux paints him as someone who was radic-ally misread and misappropriated, first by his own sister, then by the Nazis and now by the alt-right.[13] Maybe the answer lies somewhere in between. In an imagined conversation between Nietzsche and Hitler, the British comedian Ricky Gervais brilliantly pitches their rela-tionship: Hitler tells Nietzsche he loved his book, 'loved all that man and superman, not everyone is equal, so kill all the Jews ...' 'I didn't write that,' a shocked Nietzsche bursts out in response. 'Well, I read between the lines.'[14]

Thomas moves on to more practical matters. 'So now, which role could you imagine taking within the organisation?' I somehow hadn't expected that question.

'Don't know – organising events, helping with translations, building out the network?'

'Perfect,' he says. 'It's all still really in early stages here in the UK. If you ask me what we have achieved so far, I couldn't say anything specific, but believe me, it's been a lot of work. We get a lot of help from the Austrians, the Germans and the French. Martin Sellner's book serves as a guide – a friend is helping to translate it into English. Have you read it?'

'Subversion over confrontation' is one of the phrases that stuck in my mind from *Identitär: Geschichte eines Aufbruchs* (Identitarian: The Story of an Awakening).[15] The book argues that movements tend to be more effective when they don't go against existing power structures, but instead exploit the inner contradictions of dominating ideologies to reframe their notions and ideas. Words such as 'ethno-pluralist', 'repatriation' and 'conservative revolution' are carefully coined terms that don't radically overstep the boundaries of what is deemed socially acceptable rhetoric, and as such are perfectly 'mainstreamable'. I have to admit that Martin is probably right: creeping subversion is more effective than outright confrontation.

Thomas resumes without awaiting my reply: 'The idea is to give instructions on how to build something. We want the entire English-speaking world to be able to access it.'

'So you want to set up the UK branch as a bridge to the US?' I ask.

'Precisely.' He tells me that they have had 'lots of interest from people globally'. Apparently, Americans, Australians and even Asians contact them on a regular basis, as they want to found their own Identitarian offshoots. 'But we have to continue to be selective. We usually do interviews with all new members.' And they need new members, ideally bilingual ones.

'Oh, so this was an interview?'

'No, no. Not with you because you already know Martin Sellner. This weekend, Martin will be coming to London and we'll discuss the strategy. Are you coming along?' A few hours later, Thomas sends me the address, adding: 'I will make sure Martin sets aside some time to look after you! ☺'

That's how you get an invite to the New Right's secret strategy meetings.

Saturday night, I enter a pub called Ye Grapes in the heart of Mayfair's Shepherd Market.

'Hi, are you—?' A tall, fair-haired guy in his early twenties taps me on the shoulder.

'Ju-ennifer,' I stutter. 'You can also call me Jenni.'

'Fantastic, I was looking for you! I'm Jordan. They told me to watch out for a blonde girl.'

As Jordan leads me into the back room, forty eyes are staring at me. I thank God that none of them belongs to Anne Marie Waters. The self-proclaimed activist who started the nationalist, anti-Muslim 'For Britain' party after narrowly losing the UKIP leadership race in 2017 would have immediately recognised me from our many Twitter confrontations, even with my improvised wig and glasses.

'Hi everyone,' I say into the increasingly awkward silence.

'Take a seat.' An energetic short-haired guy walks up to me, smiling. He has a Nordic accent and a throaty voice. 'Good to meet you, Jennifer. I heard you were going to join us. Guess what? The UK branch of Generation Identity will be launched this weekend!' I soon learn that the man's name is Tore Rasmussen. He is a Norwegian entrepreneur and a prominent Generation Identity member who is in London to help set up the British offshoot. Only much later, when the *Observer* releases an investigative file on him, would I learn that he used to be a member of the Norwegian neo-Nazi movement Vigrid.[16] On that evening in Mayfair, he focuses on his future rather than his past.

'We were just talking about our next holidays,' Tore tells me, his hands resting on a pint of lager. 'The only place I go to for vacation is Hungary these days. Because I only give my money to free nations.'

While he sips his beer and his eyes drift into a daydream, I continue scanning the room. There are around twenty British GI members, many of them from Ireland. Thomas is here too, sitting among some older GI members from across the continent, some of them having flown in from France, Germany, Austria, Norway and Denmark to join the Traditional Britain Conference and launch the UK GI branch. The rest of the group ranges from members of the UKIP youth wing to outspoken neo-Nazis such as Mark Collett.

'Now Austria might become an option too,' Tore continues, suddenly resuming the conversation, before turning to me. 'What did you think of the last election?'

'Oh, erm, to be honest I thought that FPÖ would score higher.' My Austrian accent is thicker than usual, my voice slightly higher. 'From what I saw online they seemed to get so much more support.' He nods, smiling. 'You look so happy, your eyes lighten up when you speak about the FPÖ.' My stomach is cramping as I try to suppress the laughter. Tore takes a sip of his beer and looks at me. 'You know we need a public face for Generation Identity in the UK,' he says. 'So I actually lead the Norway branch but I'm too old myself to do the public-facing stuff.' I give him a surprised look. Tore is only in his mid-thirties. He adds, 'But we pay our leaders so they don't have to worry about work.'

Before I can think of an appropriate reply, a slim man in a suit on the opposite side of the table takes up the conversation: 'Jen, you missed a really good conference. Martin Sellner did a great job at presenting GI. People don't know about the movement here.'

'Yet,' Tore adds and puts a big grin on. 'They will know in a week.'

'Why is that?' I ask.

'You'll see tomorrow in the workshop. If you come. Even Hope not Hate won't be able to prevent us from doing that.'

'Oh I hate these guys,' the middle-aged man next to me bursts out. 'They tried to ruin my life.' His fancy suit, cuff buttons and the calculated expression on his face make him look like a banker, like someone who works in the City. 'They tried to dox me, give away my name and where I work. I could have lost my job and everything. Because that's what happens: you get fired here if you are a Nazi.'

'Hope not Hate, what's that?' I repeat stupidly.

Hope not Hate is the UK's most prominent anti-racist organisation and prevented the GI team from carrying out their 'Defend Europe' mission in the summer of 2017. Their researchers revealed the criminal past of the *C Star*'s owner and convinced the crowd-sourcing platform Patreon to block the payment services of the white nationalist activists.[17]

'All right, you know what? Let's go to their office – it's just a ten-minute walk from here,' Thomas says.

'No!' I gasp. I bite my tongue so hard that I can feel it start bleeding. 'I mean, I think that's a bad idea. It's the weekend, this will be a waste of time,' I add hastily.

'Oh don't be lame, this could be so much fun.'

I look at my phone, panicking slightly. Shall I text my friend at Hope not Hate to warn him?

But luckily some are hungry. I tell them I'm starving and suggest going the pub next door instead of Hope not Hate's office. The thought of filling their stomachs wins over the idea of causing trouble.

In the next pub, Tore introduces me to their future UK leader. 'Liam, this is Jennifer – she is Austrian but will help out with the UK branch.' Liam is a boxer, as I learn later. A good-looking, dark-haired guy in his twenties. His green eyes match his stylish North Face jacket.

'So how did you get involved with GI?' I ask him.

'I read Markus Willinger's book a few years ago and thought "Oh this is really cool."' The Austrian Identitarian Markus Willinger had been active in the New Right for five years when he published his book *Generation Identity: A Declaration of War Against the '68ers* at the age of twenty.[18] 'Then I did my first GI summer camp in France,' Liam says. He tells me that they are in the process of screening people for GI UK at the moment. 'So first we do a Skype interview and screen their social media profiles, then we meet them in person – we just go for a beer with them.'

Over a drink he tells me that he attended the march organised by the Football Lads Alliance (FLA), a group of English football fans who claim to be fighting extremism of any kind but have become increasingly associated with far-right activists.[19] 'They kept saying "*every* form of extremism",' Liam adds, bursting into laughter. 'As if there were other extremisms than Islamic extremism.'

Muslims are his main concern, he tells me as we walk up to Green Park tube station; he considers them inherently extreme. 'So do you tell your friends?' I ask just before our ways part.

'No.' He hesitates. 'Well, I try to redpill them step by step.' The nonchalance in his tone is striking.

'How do you do that?'

His walk slows but his reply is instant, as if he was doing it every day. 'Oh, I show them Rebel Media videos.' Rebel Media is a Canadian far-right media outlet best known for its provocative anti-immigrant and anti-Muslim features. To hide my shock, I quickly say goodbye, head towards the wrong Underground line and stop to take a deep breath once he is out of sight.

The next day, I get an idea of what redpilling looks like.

Generation Identity is very 2010s. When they hold a secret strategy meeting, they rent an Airbnb in south London. To be precise, in Brixton, one of London's most multicultural areas, known for its riots against police racism in the 1980s.

I am the last person to arrive at the Airbnb on Sunday morning. The Austrian leader of Generation Identity, Martin Sellner, stands outside next to his new girlfriend, the prominent American alt-right YouTuber Brittany Pettibone.

To my relief, Martin has left his glasses in the taxi. He might have recognised me otherwise, even with my blonde wig, as we had featured together in a BBC *Newsnight* report in late 2016. 'Good to finally meet you, Jennifer,' he says in German. A firm handshake, a charming smile, and we head to the living room. 'I'm afraid you missed the introductions. Could you please say a few words about yourself?'

I look around and recognise a few familiar faces from last night. Tore and Liam are there again, with Ray-Bans and T-shirts. There is a slightly surreal feeling about sitting in a holiday home surrounded by a dozen well-dressed white nationalists, sipping R. White's lemonade.

After I have finished telling Jennifer's story again – by now I am starting to feel more comfortable adding details and anecdotes – all newcomers, including myself, are asked to complete a questionnaire. This is part of the 'Identitarian brand risk management', as Martin explains. It involves questions ranging from favourite books and movies to more explicit enquiries about political leanings and ideologies.

I try hard to make up something credible while not opting for the usual suspects: George Orwell's *1984* would be a little too clichéd, as it is known to be the far right's regular metaphor for today's state of censorship and surveillance. *Fight Club* and *The Matrix* are also standard alt-right movies. Indeed, Hannibal Bateman, the managing editor of the white supremacist magazine *Radix Journal*, explained in an article entitled 'Generation Alt-Right' that 'for many alienated young White men our credo could be summed up in that most angsty of films, *Fight Club*', citing the following dialogue from the movie:

> We're the middle children of history, man. No purpose or place. We have no Great War. No Great Depression. Our Great War's a spiritual war ... our Great Depression is our lives. We've all been raised on television to believe that one day we'd all be millionaires, and movie gods, and rock stars. But we won't. And we're slowly learning that fact. And we're very, very pissed off.[20]

It is Bateman's belief that whites have been brainwashed into forgetting that they are 'the descendants of conquerors and settlers who brought a civilization to entire continents'. The migration crisis and Donald Trump, he thinks, may have led to 'the nagging search for what's been wrong since as long as we can remember', a sudden awakening that he equates with that featured in *Fight Club*.[21]

I settle for Kafka's *The Trial* and *Star Wars* – at least these are open to interpretation. In the next set of questions, I have to situate my political views on the axes along left wing–right wing, regionalism–nationalism, pro-Israeli–pro-Palestine and liberalism–socialism.

It is only when I reach the questions 'Why are you militating?', 'What does your family think of your commitment?' and 'Do you have siblings in the police or in the army?' that I put down my pen. I'm scared now. Militating is a strong word. And why would they care about the security forces, or my family? Although GI keeps repeating that it is against the use of violence, this sounds like I am about to join a militant group.

'Yeah … tough, right?' Tore whispers into my ear. 'But don't worry, there is no right or wrong. We just want to find out whether you are "full-fash",' he adds, grinning. I wonder, if this is a strange kind of humour that I don't get. 'Full-fash', a derivation of 'fully fascist', is their way of describing traditional neo-Nazis. They rejected one new member because he shared neo-Nazi symbols on Facebook, I later find out. 'We can't afford that. We don't want to harm the group's image,' Tore tells me. How ironic that he would soon be kicked out for his neo-Nazi links.

'Today we'll discuss the strategy for our new UK branch,' Martin Sellner begins. 'You've the Pakis, you have the indigenous Brits and you become a minority in your own country. It's the biggest crime ever.' After he has given us a briefing on how to deal with difficult questions from journalists – including 'Are you racist?' and 'Are you anti-Semitic?' – Sellner notes that GI does not declare the white race as superior to others and recommends emphasising the importance of keeping different races separate for their own sake. We discuss the concepts of 'controlled provocation', 'strategic polarisation' and 'meta-politics'. GI's social mobilisation strategies are rooted in a mixture of academic sociology findings and their own trial-and-error experience of what works and what doesn't.

Like the American alt-right, GI believes in the Breitbart doctrine: that you need to change culture first, if you want to change politics. 'Politics is downstream from culture. I want to change the cultural narrative,' said Andrew Breitbart, the creator of the website that has become the favourite source of information and commentary for today's far right.[22] To do so, you need to create provocative counter-cultures that attract young people to increase public pressure on mainstream politicians – 'metapolitics'. 'We need polarising action,' Martin Sellner explains. 'No one likes it because you are forced to choose sides, but it is needed to provoke change.' Over time this will normalise far-right world views, he believes, and move the 'Overton window'[23] – the range of ideas that are deemed acceptable in public discourse – to the right.

They have learned from the alt-right's transgressive and disruptive campaigns. For example, in 2016, the Austrian Identitarians simulated a terrorist attack in a flash mob in central Vienna and a few months later covered the famous statue of Maria Theresa in a burqa to attract the media's attention. Their media stunts are provocative enough to be turned into viral posts and tweets that are shared by key social media influencers – 'controlled provocation'. This in turn forces conventional media outlets to cover their activities and give them a platform. Once an online campaign reaches what Whitney Phillips, an American expert on trolling and new media, calls the 'tipping point', where a story extends beyond the interests of the community being discussed, the 'mainstream media' has no choice but to cover it.[24] The aim is to spread divisive content that makes it necessary for everyone who sits on the fence to take a side – 'strategic polarisation'.

That's perfectly in line with GI's redpilling manual, which is essentially a step-by-step guide on how to polarise and radicalise individuals from different ideological backgrounds. GI defines redpilling as 'the process of awakening from a deep slumber and leaving blissful ignorance'. I'm reminded of Islamist extremist calls on moderate Muslims to escape *jahiliyya*, the state of ignorance.

Brittany sits next to Martin, politely interrupting him every now and then to add comments on the US context – or to correct him whenever he mispronounces an English word or mistakes a v for a w. 'The alt-right is dangerous – we have to be very careful on how we associate with them,' she now warns. Compared to the alt-right, the Generation Identity leadership have done a good job at distancing themselves from overt racism, anti-Semitism and physical violence, at least publicly. Yet Martin goes on to reveal: 'I'm in touch with all the people in the US alt-right and all the big YouTube personalities.' I figure that this means everyone from cultural nationalists like Lauren Southern to the more extreme and overtly racist Richard Spencer and Identity Evropa.

'We have to be careful,' repeats Brittany, now more forcefully. 'I would never trust *anyone*. The alt-right is infested with infiltrators.' Just at that moment I spot my credit card, which has fallen out of my trousers pocket. I had been careful to leave at home anything that would give away my real identity, except for this one item. 'Oh, is this yours?' Brittany asks as she picks it up. I pray that she doesn't look at the small letters that say 'Julia Ebner'. But she hands it back to me without a word.

It's a surprisingly warm day for October in London, so we walk to an Italian restaurant not far from the Airbnb. Over pizza and beer, they discuss the next steps for the UK branch and the internationalisation strategy.

Again, this feels more like a casual chat about a business expansion than a plan to radicalise young people across the English-speaking world.

As I listen to their discussions, I understand how international GI already is. A girl from Denmark sits next to me, and on the other side of the table I over-hear conversations in French. Martin Sellner him-self switches between English, German and French. The group's banking and financial hub is in Hungary, while their annual training camps take place in rural France.[25] And the plan for the UK is to serve as the bridge between their European and future American branches, as well as between their offline and online activities.

Later in the week, they will meet with Tommy Robinson, the English Defence League founder who is now one of the world's most influential far-right figureheads. Robinson, whose real name is Stephen Yaxley-Lennon, has perfected his combined offline-online outreach strategy. 'Maybe he'll become the new GI leader for the UK,' one of the British members suggests enthusiastically. But some express a concern that he may be too old to be the public face. 'This is a youth movement,' Tore says. He and Thomas had opted out of publicly representing GI because they were considered too old. Martin nods, but they want to use Robinson's quasi-celebrity status and massive online reach to push the social media campaigns and advertise the new offshoot in the UK.

GI might be one of the most selective far-right movements: not only do new recruits have to be rela-tively young and decently trendy, they also need to be fairly well educated. 'Really?' I ask.

'Well. We don't say no to uneducated people, but they can't become the majority,' the girl next to me explains. All new members from across Europe undergo a training process: from lessons in literature and communications to martial arts and other physical exercises.

'So what's on the agenda for the UK over the next year?' one of the new English members wants to know.

'Social media campaigns, regular flyering on the streets, leaflet distribution on campuses and a breakthrough action every six weeks,' says Martin.

'What's a breakthrough action?' I ask.

Tore exchanges looks with Martin. It could be anything, they explain, as long as it's creative and taboo-breaking. The goal is always the same: to attract media attention and generate interest in the movement, from journalists and from the public. The concept is borrowed from marketing, where breakthrough activities are used by small and medium-sized companies with limited advertising budgets. To create a buzz for their product they will launch an innovative, sometimes provocative, campaign that makes their market share look bigger than it is and enhances their power position vis-à-vis bigger competitors. A terrorism flash mob in Vienna, Maria Theresa in a burqa … I understand now. 'The next one could be about acid attacks in London,' Tore says.

'Or the new mosque they are building in York,' the girl next to me throws in. 'We'll all head to the bridge later for our first breakthrough. Surely it will be in the news tomorrow.'

This is going too far. I wouldn't want to feature in GI's propaganda materials, so I excuse myself and head home. A few hours later, Martin sends me a picture of their first big breakthrough, a twenty-metre banner saying 'Defend London. Stop Islamisation' over Westminster Bridge. 'Our media stunts are so successful because no one knows about it,' he had explained to me in the strategy meeting. 'We are there before the police arrives. No one can stop us, not even Hope not Hate.'

This was the beginning of the group's UK and Ireland branch and the end of my undercover experience in GI. A few days after the official launch, they found out that Jennifer Mayer was in fact Julia Ebner. 'We have been doing our research on you since yesterday;),' Martin texted me. 'I hope it was at least interesting for you.' After I had spoken to the *Independent* about GI's secret strategy meeting and their plans for the UK this was inevitable. They put one and one together and linked my avatar profile to my real profile. I knew that, as always, there would be an expiry date to my undercover experience; it had happened to me before, at a rally organised by the far-right English Defence League, as well as at a conference hosted by the Islamist organisation Hizb ut-Tahrir.

Finding the right approach to warn about the sophisticated online mobilisation of groups like GI can be tricky. When they came to the UK with the goal of recruiting young people into their networks, I found myself in a dilemma: how do you raise awareness and expose their distortive and manipulative tactics while avoiding giving them an undeserved platform? To me, it was clear that their new members would soon make it into the headlines of the British press in any case, especially after learning about their 'breakthrough' strategy. Indeed, since October 2017, they have managed to live up to their goal of receiving English news coverage every six weeks. In May 2018, the *Sunday Times* even ran an article under a headline that labelled them 'hipster fascists' who are 'middle class and well spoken', accompanied by a large photograph that made them look a bit like a new boyband.[26]

Exactly one year after my infiltration, in October 2018, I am back in the Generation Identity UK and Ireland chat group on the encrypted messaging app Telegram. Little has changed – they are still actively recruiting, campaigning and training their new members: 'Activists in the North West met in #Manchester on Saturday to conduct a study session, bringing our new members up to speed and covering topics such as Heroes, the Will to Survive and Discipline. They did some leafleting, receiving many positive responses. #GenerationIdentity #DefendEurope,' reads their latest post. What has changed is that their many media stunts have made them grow significantly: their Telegram group has over 300 members, and their Twitter followership has surged from a few dozen when Jennifer Mayer first followed them to over 7,000 one year later.

The internet and new technologies have rendered recruitment a great deal easier – outreach can be amplified, branding adjusted and vetting gamified. And there are many pathways into extremist networks. Some members join for ideological reasons, others are entirely apolitical when they first get involved. Sometimes their number-one incentive is to become part of an exclusive community, a cool counter-culture. A recurring theme among recruits, however, is identity – a troubled self-image, a broken self-esteem. To lure vulnerable young individuals into their networks, extremists use the whole spectrum of technologies – from aggressive recruitment campaigns on social media to intense testing phases that involve live voice chats, DNA tests and meme competitions in encrypted apps. Spectacular real-world stunts are livestreamed and turned into trending topics on Facebook and Twitter to attract attention beyond traditional audiences. Different online communities are targeted with youth culture references and gaming vocabulary, while new members are asked to submit genetic test results and join live voice interviews. Recruitment into extremist groups isn't just a tedious testing process any more, it's in itself a way of attracting and engaging target audiences, of creating the illusion of exclusiveness for new members.

After recruitment comes socialisation.

PART TWO

Socialisation

3

Trad Wives: Joining the Female Anti-Feminists

'Where do you think you fall on the SMV scale?' Kim asks me.

'Um.' I google SMV. Sexual Market Value is 'a measure of desirability for sex in the eyes of a person of the opposite sex', according to the online male supremacist community Men Going Their Own Way (MGTOW).[1] 'Don't know,' I confess. 'How would I?'

'Well, it's hard to judge yourself and often we don't know exactly how we are perceived. It's not uncommon to inflate or devalue one's attractiveness. But as a woman it is often said our SMV goes up if we control our weight.' She adds: 'Ultimately, your SMV can only really be told to you by men, and even then it's subjective. You might be an 8 to one guy and a 5 to another.'

'I see. So do you know yours?'

Kim tells me that she went from size 20 to size 14 in one year after joining the Red Pill Women, a female anti-feminist community on the discussion platform Reddit. 'I am sure it helped, since I am treated differently. But I am not stopping traffic or anything. My face is average or even below average, which probably keeps my SMV low even though I'm skinny now.'

I stare at her brutal self-evaluation. This is a typical discussion in the forum. Kim is one of roughly 30,000 self-described Red Pill Women or Trad Wives (short for Traditional Wives). Like the MGTOW men's-rights activists, these women perceive gender roles as the result of 'sexual economics'.[2] The heterosexual community, they believe, should be seen as a market place, where women are sellers and men buyers of sex. A woman's single most important resource is therefore, according to them, her SMV.

This radically simplistic view of gender relations is used to legitimise the objectivisation of women; to make it acceptable, even necessary, to rate, trade and replace women – like market goods. This is now my third week talking to the Trad Wives and I have started to get used to their endorsement of openly misogynist statements. 'Women's highest value to men is her sexual value, and she's most valuable when she's in her sexually pristine state,' I am repeatedly told. To see where you stand in terms of sexual value, Kim recommends trying some apps that allow you to get rated anonymously: from the old-school Hot or Not to a more sophisticated attractiveness rating service on Photofeeler.

'Okay [...] but what about other factors like being funny, educated or having exotic passions?' I ask, half knowing the answer.

'Oh come on. Health, age and femininity are the single most important qualities that appeal to men,' Kim says. 'Education, career or workplace don't influence a woman's SMV. Think about it, they don't enhance the sexual satisfaction of her male partner.' This is in line with MGTOW's assessments: 'The SMV of a woman is given by birth and her achievements in life do little to increase it,' they claim.[3]

'Oh and your SMV also goes down if your N-count goes up,' a woman named Marie adds.

'The what count?' I ask her, starting to feel a little stupid.

'The N-count. You know, her cock count,' Marie explains. 'While being sexually experienced may increase the physical pleasure of her male partner, being sexually inexperienced actually increases satisfaction.' Marie is in her early thirties and married. Apart from being a 'good wife', she sees her mission as giving tips on dating, relationships and marriage to fellow Red Pill Women on Reddit. She appears to be one of the most frequently consulted coaches in the community. Many women drill her with questions ranging from 'How do female duties change upon pregnancy and childbirth?' to 'Is chastity before marriage necessary?'

Marie is convinced that feminism has brainwashed men and women into believing that the N-count doesn't matter. 'But human nature will always prevail sooner or later,' she tells me. 'And human male nature is to have less and less desire for a woman as her N-count rises. Eventually, this lack of desire will turn to out-right disgust.' She gives the example of 'a smoking hot, 10/10 bombshell beauty' who has had sex with a thou-sand men. 'How many men will want to marry her? Very few. Why?' Before anyone can respond, she con-tinues: 'Because women are the gatekeepers of sex. Sex is the main thing that men need from women. Therefore, it's the prime value that a woman has. Each time she gives this value to a man, her value is diminished.'

The Trad Wives movement is a small but growing internet phenomenon that developed as the female equivalent of The Red Pill (TRP), a Reddit community that the New Hampshire Republican state house member Robert Fisher anonymously founded under the nickname pk_atheist in 2012.[4] TRP promised 'discussion of sexual strategy in a culture increasingly lacking a positive identity for men' and counted roughly 300,000 subscribers before being banned by Reddit in 2017 for its toxic, dehumanising and threatening content.

But TRP is only one part of a much bigger misogynist online community, the so-called 'Manosphere', which played a key role in the creation of the alt-right and is made up of a range of sub-cultures: from the secret seduction community of the Pick Up Artists (PUA), who seek to learn how to manipulate women's minds to get them into bed, and the anti-marriage community MGTOW, which teaches men to stop caring about women, to the male supremacist Men's Rights Activists (MRA) and the vengeful Involuntary Celibacy (Incel) movement of men whose main goal is to punish the women they make responsible for their sexual frustration.[5] While these groups pursue different strategies to 'reconquer' male power, pride and privilege, they all share an outright hostility towards feminism, liberalism and modern gender roles. They ridicule movements like #MeToo and denounce women's-rights activists as 'feminazis'.[6]

After reading *Angry White Men* by Michael Kimmel I was convinced this was an almost exclusively male phenomenon. But the more time I spend immersing myself with the Red Pill Women, the more I understand that anti-feminist movements aren't just made up of men. Female men's-rights activists who want to return to traditional power roles and exaggerated notions of masculinity and femininity have adopted the rhetoric of the Manosphere. 'Feminism is attacking the white male,' the Russian-American alt-right activist Lana Lokteff claimed on the white supremacist Radio 3Fourteen.

The Red Pill Women community is 'open to all women wanting to improve themselves and their relationships', but it does have a few official rules, most notably:

Rule Five: No feminism. This is an anti-feminist community, and as such, we are not interested in being 'saved' by feminism. Anybody stopping in to weigh-in with the feminist perspective will be shown the door, as it is off topic.

Instead, conversations should be based on traditional evolutionary psychology or an anti-feminist premise.

'I've been learning and growing, becoming more virtuous through God's grace and learning to follow my husband and submit instead of making demands and arguing [...] It's beautiful, really. The biggest thing I've done is to just say "yes". Yes to what he asks for or wants [...],' one woman writes after having been indoctrinated by the Trad Wives for several weeks.

I start to understand that this is a forum of unconditional self-deprivation. The single most important goal is to learn how to please men. 'If you want to keep a man, you have to put femininity over feminism,' our coaches keep telling us. 'Here we don't shy away from embracing a feminine, humble and submissive position in life.' Books such as *The Surrendered Wife* by Laura Doyle or *The Proper Care and Feeding of Husbands* by Laura C. Schlessinger feature at the top of the reading list.

SMV is one of the core concepts underlying the Red Pill Women ideology. Another is the 'STFU' (Shut the Fuck Up) method. 'Men prefer women who don't talk too much' is how Marie summarises the not-so-hard-to-guess concept.

As the Trad Wives start sharing stories of how they have successfully applied the STFU method in daily life, I can feel my stomach turn. It feels almost surreal to be watching women get excited about the idea of being literally silenced. 'Last night, girls, he gave me the cold shoulder all night and I was getting more and more frustrated,' one of them tells us. 'But then I realized that I did it to myself. In fact, if I had STFU we would have had a lovely night like we always do. I feel like I actually needed something like this to happen to really learn the STFU method, because I saw real, immediate consequences to it. I'll make sure to watch my mouth a lot more often from now on.'

STFU is part of a bigger idea about 'Domestic Discipline'. Marie says that it applies to wives and girlfriends as much as to children – all of whom are in a man's power and are supposed to obey him. Her recommendation to men is: 'Sit them down, explain what rule they broke, explain why it's a rule, calmly apply the prescribed punishment, and then hug them because it's over.' Although the Trad Wives wouldn't encourage the use of fists, many believe that 'men who spank their women are doing it right'.

To my surprise there is no typical profile for Red Pill Women. The majority of women I've come across appear to be between seventeen and thirty. Some are married, others aren't even dating. Their financial background varies just as much: while some ask how to save money on kitchenware, others want to know where to get the most glamorous dress to meet Donald and Melania in the White House. Even their educational background is diverse. 'I just finished my PhD and figured that it gets you nowhere with men,' one woman confesses. Whatever their life journey looks like so far, most women arrive here in shock or fear of losing the person they love. A few of them join because they haven't found anyone yet and are blaming themselves for it. Similar to the men joining the Manosphere, the search for love is what radicalises most Trad Wives.

'What you are really asking for is RMV = Relationship Market Value,' Kim explains to a woman who calls herself Liz and seems obsessed with optimising her SMV in an effort to regain the love of a guy who ditched her after several weeks of dating. It's painful to watch in real time how Kim skilfully takes all her fears and insecurities, inserts them into the Red Pill formula and gets a Trad Wife out of it.

I am not in the most mentally stable state myself. Having just come out of a painful break-up, I begin to question myself, my approach to relationships, my role as a woman. Just focus on the research, I keep telling myself. But as I start spending hours, days and weeks in the forum, I can sense that this is becoming more than an undercover experiment. For the first time, I don't have to pretend to be vulnerable – the insecurities that I write about are real, the fears I express are authentic.

'You know what distinguishes the average girlfriend from wife material?' Marie asks.

'I have no idea,' Liz replies, speaking my mind.

'Well, you know what the womanly duties are?' Marie continues. I notice that she keeps referring to her husband as 'Captain', as if to stress his role as an alpha male, as the one who steers her on her life journey. 'One of the things I love about my Captain is that he tells me exactly what he expects and exactly what he wants. I take care of the house, watch our kids and tend to his sexual needs.'

Again, Liz expresses the doubts in my head: 'But I thought that being an independent woman is attractive to men.'

'Have you ever read *Fascinating Womanhood* by Helen Andelin?' Marie asks. Helen Andelin, the anti-feminist who started giving marriage-enrichment classes in the 1960s, is one of the key references for the Trad Wives. 'What kind of life would a man get when he chooses you?' she continues. 'Can you deliver the care and nurturing a man wants and needs? If not, then why should any man pick you?'

No reaction.

'Don't blame yourself, blame it on feminism, blame it on modernity,' Marie insists. 'We have been brainwashed; it's normal that it takes you some time to go back into the natural state.'

Is it? I mean, have we? *What if* she's right? *What if* I was trying to fulfil too many roles at once? *What if* I have to choose between being respected and admired on the one hand and being loved and desired on the other?

'Just focus on what's important for a healthy relationship,' she says, as if replying to the words I never typed up. My hands, still resting on my keyboard, are now trembling. 'Forget your career and just concentrate on the things men look for in a woman: make sure you always look great, are family oriented, cook very well, and show submission and respect.'

Should I? I mean, would I? *What if* I had been doing everything wrong? *What if* these women are right about the things that men are looking for in women?

Am I in the process of getting redpilled myself? Stop the *what ifs*, I tell myself. I can see how easy it would be to get drawn into this community. These redpillers first make you question everything, then radically twist your world views. Don't let them do that to you. But. *What if?* I have to get out of here. Now.

I log out of Reddit and shut down my computer. It was far too easy to get drawn into this strange place, a radical online community like most others I'd joined before, yet entirely different: the hatred wasn't directed towards others but towards oneself. There was something weirdly comforting in the self-blaming, self-denigrating language that connected its members – a certain kind of consolation in the offer of collective self-optimisation.

I want to see the other side, so I decide to create a male avatar account. I sign up for MGTOW and dig into the archives of the banned Incels and The Red Pill forums.

Here is a random sample of talking points I found in archived discussions of The Red Pill:

1. How to get laid like a WARLORD: 37 Ways of approaching model-tier girls
2. The most important part of game is not being emotionally invested
3. Three ways to consciously manipulate women before they subconsciously manipulate you

These are not the redpilled men the Red Pill Women were painting, the glorified alpha males who are taking natural leadership roles in relationships. These are men who reduce women to their reproductive and sexual functions to compensate for their own ego complexes.

In the 1990s, a Canadian statistics student called Alana created a website to connect anybody – man or woman – who was still a virgin, felt lonely or unable to find a sexual or romantic partner.[7] She called the platform 'Alana's **In**voluntary **Cel**ibacy Project', which was soon abbreviated to Incel. It was a well-meaning initiative: the idea was to give individuals suffering from low self-esteem and loneliness the confidence and consolation they needed. But in less than two decades the Incel movement evolved into something quite different: a predominantly male community started classifying women into attractive 'stacys' and less attractive 'beckys', and men into hyper-masculine 'alpha males' versus undersexed 'zeta males' or 'soy boys'. While Alana had introduced terms such as 'love-shy' or 'FA (forever alone)', the use of dehumanising and misogynist language became more common over time. Women were referred to as 'femoids', a merger of 'female' and 'humanoid'.[8]

Alana's positively framed self-help community had effectively turned into a dangerous echo chamber of women-hating and self-loathing loners. When Reddit finally banned Incels from its platform in November 2017, the community had attracted 40,000 members. Most Incels migrated to other corners of the internet such as Voat, where men continue discussing their 'unfuckability' and the injustice of being denied what they see as a basic right – the right to have sex with attractive women. To escape 'inceldom' some would impose strict diets and workout programmes on themselves or undergo plastic surgery, something they call 'looksmaxing'. Others reach more radical conclusions: for example, that the only solution is to kill themselves, other people or both.

'The Incel Rebellion has already begun!' the twenty-five-year old Alek Minassian posted on Facebook before driving a van into a crowd of pedestrians in Toronto, killing ten, in April 2018.[9] Four years earlier, a similar incident had happened in California when Elliot Rodger massacred six people and injured fourteen others in a mass shooting. In his manifesto he referred to himself as a 'supreme gentleman' and vowed to punish all females for depriving him of sex. 'You girls aren't attracted to me, but I will punish you all for it,' he wrote.[10]

It is true that the average man has a harder time getting laid than the average woman. Research shows that it is more difficult for men to achieve matches on Tinder than for female users: while male users matched with only about 0.6 per cent of the profiles they had liked, their female counterparts had a matching rate of around 10.5 per cent and managed to collect over 200 matches in just one hour.[11] Another study revealed that women have a response rate of over 50 per cent on their first messages, while the average man received replies on only 17 per cent of their messages.[12]

Over the past few years, anti-feminist thinking has penetrated large proportions of the millennial generation. Mainstream figures like the psychologist and bestselling author Jordan Peterson, the popular British YouTuber and UKIP member Carl Benjamin (aka Sargon of Akkad) and University of Toronto academic

Janice Fiamengo have been fuelling a sense of male victimhood. They often cite the high suicide rates among men[13] but fail to mention that although more than three-quarters of suicides in the US and the UK are male, women are actually more likely than men to attempt suicide – a phenomenon known as the 'suicide gender paradox'.[14]

The Manosphere has a love–hate relationship with women. Even men's-rights advocates acknowledge that movements that lack female support don't last very long. 'It's time to get women on our side, and in my opinion one of the best ways to do this is by slowly exposing them to Red Pill women YouTubers,' the dating coach and founder of the men's advice forum Masculine Development Jon Anthony wrote.[15] The Swedish alt-right influencer Marcus Follin, a muscular man with long golden-blond hair and bronze-tanned skin better known as The Golden One, argued in a video entitled 'The Women Question' that white nationalist movements needed to get more women involved. He cited statistics from the 2016 Austrian presidential election in which the Green Party candidate won by an extremely narrow margin over the far-right Freedom Party candidate thanks to his support from female voters. 'You might not like that women have the right to vote, you might not like that anyone has the right to vote, but it's about winning a long-term political victory,' he concluded.

Female men's-rights activists tend to attract a wide male followership on Twitter and their YouTube accounts often count over 10,000 subscribers. Their vintage swing dresses, matching lipsticks and heels reflect a strong nostalgia for the hyper-feminine images of the 1950s.[16] One of the most popular Trad Wives on social media is Ayla Stewart, who goes by the nickname A Wife with a Purpose. The self-proclaimed 'Alt-Right Mormon' rose to worldwide notoriety after calling for a 'white baby challenge' to preserve the white race. 'I've made six,' she wrote. 'Match or beat me.'[17]

DeAnna Lorraine, an attractive brunette with full lips and carefully applied make-up, sits at her desk; in the background you can see a copy of her book *Making Love Great Again*. She is a 'redpilled relationship coach' and I am about to join her livestreamed YouTube coaching session for men. Today's topic: 'How To Redpill your Girlfriend'.[18] 'Remember: she is BRAINWASHED and has been indoctrinated to be a sheep, blindly following an irrational, dangerous herd. It is not entirely her fault if she doesn't "get it" right away.' Lorraine's male listeners send her hearts and kisses via the live chat as she starts to encourage them to deal with their girlfriends as they would with someone who has a mental disorder. 'Thank you for the love, thank you for the hearts, guys,' she responds, her face beaming at the camera with a seductive smile, before walking us through her detailed step-by-step redpilling guide:

Step 1: Laying the groundwork for her paradigm shift
Ask her if she is open to having an honest discussion, putting emotions aside and looking at actual facts
Ask her questions like 'What do you think about men these days? Do you think they are masculine enough?' and 'What are your biggest complaints in the dating world with

men? Do you feel like most men just want
to hook up and are sex-focused?'

Step 2: Exposing the hypocrisy, lunacy and lies of
feminism and liberalism
Give her assignments such as listing 'REAL
differences between men and women'
and researching 'Cultural Marxism', 'The
Frankfurt School' and '11-Step Plan'.

According to DeAnna Lorraine, all three waves of
feminism – the battle for voting rights in the nine-
teenth and early twentieth centuries, the fight for equal
legal and social rights in the 1960s and 1970s, and the
continued efforts in the 1990s to break through the
glass ceiling and challenge biased gender perceptions
in the media – are part of a plan of cultural subversion. The Frankfurt School, she explains, was plotting to
destroy society with the so-called 11-Step Plan, which
included steps such as 'the creation of racism offences',
'the teaching of sex and homosexuality to children',
'huge immigration to destroy identity', 'the promotion
of excessive drinking' and the 'emptying of churches'.

Step 3: Walk her through the frightening future –
future pacing
Get her to read studies on women's primal
nature and discuss MGTOW

The steps in this manual follow a familiar radicalisation structure:

Step 1: exploit fears and grievances to cast doubt on
the current system

Step 2: blame a demonized out-group (e.g. feminists, liberals) for these societal failures by linking them to conspiracy theories

Step 3: provide a radical solution to all existing problems (e.g. The Red Pill)

Having seen how Red Pill men are encouraged to manipulate and mortify women, I decide to go back on Red Pill Women and type in 'abuse' in the search function. Katie is one of many women who share their experiences of verbal and physical abuse. She gives a sample of things her husband said to her that same day:

- *Fucking whore! This is none of your goddamned business!* [About the family business that he expects her to work at for free.]
- *You're the stupidest fucking person on the damn planet! How the fuck can you have not gotten the fucking strawberries from up there in the fucking field, you fucking dumbass whore! Fucking God Damnit! I should have told you long ago to fuck off, with your bastard kids!* [Speaking about his children with her.]
- *Fuck off! I fucking don't ever want to see you again in this fucking room, and if you come near me I'll fucking make you wish you never married me, you* [insert racial slur for Asian people that doesn't translate easily to English] *hooker!*

The responses she gets from other Red Pill women are hardly comforting: 'Respecting your husband will end the abuse' and 'abuse is very rarely a one-way street, and is often a man's way of protecting himself against ongoing insults and emasculation'. They often resort to citing *The Surrendered Wife* by Laura Doyle, who has made the case for verbal abuse as a legitimate measure in the male leadership toolkit.

Taking the blame for verbal abuse is common-place among the Trad Wives, but even physical violence is frequently relativised or justified: 'There are some bad qualities because of me such as when I cry he would slap me,' one woman confesses. Another one offers advice based on Jolynn Raymond's book *Taken in Hand: A Guide to Domestic Discipline, Power Exchange Relationships and Related BDSM Topics*. 'In some more traditional relationships (but not all) the man disciplines the woman either physically (like spanking) or with things like writing lines or standing in the corner,' she argues. 'It's the same way people use to discipline children (well, and wives) just done with grown women. It works for some, doesn't for others.'

Taken in Hand (TiH) is the preferred relationship model of Trad Wives. The Urban Dictionary defines it as a 'monogamous, heterosexual relationship which is male-led, and in which the female defers in matters of everyday life, as well as sexually, to her partner'. An anonymous self-declared female TiH provides the following tips to men:

> Don't delay discipline any longer than is absolutely necessary. If you think she should be spanked for a sarcastic remark, it is infinitely more effective if you take her by the arm, and lead her to the bathroom, the bedroom, the garage, and administer the swats right then.

Learn how to use your authority in public. Subtle signals between the two of you can be very powerful in a public setting. A raised eyebrow, a gentle squeeze, a pointed finger, even a code word can send the message that although she might feel safe at the moment, she is still under your jurisdiction. If nothing else is working, don't be afraid to physically remove her from the situation.[19]

Several Trad Wives complain that the feminist anger-management industry has defined anything a man does to get or maintain authority in a relationship as abuse. 'Raising his voice, refusing to give her money, hitting a wall, leaving, using logic in an argument, sticking to his guns, calling her names even if they are true, like telling a fat girlfriend she's gotten fat,' Marie writes. 'It is now illegal abuse for men to exhibit dominance outside of hilariously phony BDSM games,' she continues, 'and the media is trying to make every relationship the story of a cruel man and a terrorized woman.' This 'insane extension of the concept of abuse', the Trad Wives argue, is preventing men from keeping 'Domestic Discipline', and from ever winning the dominance struggle.

Confusion about changing notions of masculinity and femininity, and about the delicate balance between submission and dominance, has pushed men and women into fundamental identity crises. 'Everything you had been taught and told was based on a lie. The lie that you can have everything, self-fulfillment and a happy family life. It just doesn't work that way,' one Trad Wife tells me. Blame it on the hook-up culture, as Brittany Pettibone would say, the product of modernity, social progress, feminism.

Millennials are increasingly fed up with the fast-speed dating culture of the techno-sexual age, where apps like Tinder and Bumble mess with its users' brains. The instant gratification, the dopamine that gamified dating sends through our bodies to manipulate our desires and twist our perception of reality. But – perhaps most worryingly – the illusion of unlimited choice can lead to a spiral of endless self-optimisation and partner-optimisation.[20] Research suggests that Tinder users are less satisfied with their bodies and faces and male users suffer from lower levels of self-esteem than non-users.[21]

'We are in the middle of a romance apocalypse,' some Trad Wives would say, citing declining marriage and fertility rates in the US and Europe. It is true that more Americans are single than ever before,[22] birthrates have reached a historic low in the US,[23] only one in six Brits in their twenties are married or in a civil partnership and the average relationship duration of British couples aged twenty-something is 4.2 years.[24] Women in the UK now have on average around eight sexual partners over a lifetime, twice as many as in 1990. For men this number has increased from roughly nine to twelve.[25]

No wonder the idea of going back to traditional power relations, old-fashioned gender roles and a clear division of responsibilities can be appealing to men as well as to women. Was it all easier back then? With well-defined roles and behaviours on both sides? Women who are trying to find out why their relationship isn't working out the way they imagined it, the way Hollywood made them imagine it, flock to the Trad Wives community. The Red Pill offers an easy explanation and a straight way out of an increasingly complex socio-psychological labyrinth: when the woman takes up too many responsibilities and powers that aren't supposed to be hers, she erodes those of the man, making him feel redundant and humiliated as his traditional role of the provider and protector is being stripped away.

In the Trad Wives community, confusion meets insecurity before turning into guilt and self-doubt. The redpilled start to believe that relationships break down not as a result of mutual failures and mistakes but when the woman isn't woman enough. 'She wasn't embracing her female part in the relationship,' they would argue. Submission is sold as emancipation, traditional femininity as empowerment. 'She was abused or punished because she wasn't disciplined or well behaved enough.' Female anti-feminism is rife with inherent contradictions: although a happy marriage is the declared number-one goal of the Trad Wives, they endorse concepts propagated by the anti-marriage MGTOW community such as SMV.

The redpilled would argue that the community is taking men and women back to their roots, back to the 'real' nature of the sexes. But in the end the red pill appears more like a drug that makes its consumer get addicted to the endless chase of an ideal self – whether it's Red Pill Women desperately trying to be the storybook wife, bending and twisting themselves and suppressing their desires, or Red Pill Men attempting to become alpha males, adopting techniques to manipulate and seduce women.

The Red Pill communities act as socialisation hubs for male supremacists and alt-right influencers to redpill normal users, whom they call 'normies'. Unlike other online advice and counselling forums, most users who enter the platform to seek help with a specific problem end up sticking around in the medium or long run. They are gradually indoctrinated and internalise the norms and ideologies of their coaches and peers. The change in their identities, attitudes and behaviours illustrates how effective and dangerous this online socialisation machinery is. My own exposure to the Trad Wives taught me that even ideological opposition is no reliable shield against extremist manipulation tactics. I could not have been further away from the ideological leanings of the Trad Wives. And yet I was close to getting drawn in by their powerful group dynamics. I never believed in extremist profiles; neither class, gender or race, nor political or religious views, determine if someone will be groomed by extremists. Everyone can be exploitable in moments of weakness, and vulnerability can be a highly temporary concept. The only effective guard is information. As with other unconscious processes, such as depression and panic attacks, being able to recognise the different stages, trigger points and thought distortions is a crucial tool for disrupting the cognitive vicious circle kicked off in ourselves.[26] What ultimately helped me to walk away from the Trad Wives was knowing the steps and signs of radicalisation before joining the Red Pill Women forum.

The Trad Wives are just one example of a recurring group dynamic in extremist gateway communities. Socialisation into jihadist sub-cultures isn't dissimilar. Gender-segregated forums that discuss the role of men and women in society are a powerful tool for linking the group ideology to personal questions. The next chapter looks at a sisters-only ISIS chat group. Despite its religiously inspired ideology and higher willingness to commit acts of violence, the social dynamics within this jihadi bride group resemble those under way in female-only alt-right spaces. Counselling and advice among its members are important pillars that strengthen in-group cohesion and ensure loyalty to the values and norms of the organisation.

4

Sisters Only: Introduced to the Jihadi Brides

'Brother, what are you doing here?' asks one of the sisters. 'This chat is for sisters only, no men allowed in here.' The small but international 'Terror Agency Sister chatting group' on the encrypted messaging app Telegram is for female ISIS supporters only.

I wouldn't usually chat with the sisters while sipping a Bintang beer and watching surfers on a Balinese beach. But just as I decide to give in to the street vendor who desperately wants me to buy rice cakes wrapped in banana leaves, I receive a push notification from Blue Sky, the administrator of the ISIS sisters chat. 'Three martyrdom operations killing 11 people and at least 41 wounded from the guards of the churches and Christians in the city of Surabaya in the province of Java in east Indonesia.' If the news about the neighbouring island is true, it hasn't hit the headlines yet. The joyful faces around me on the beach mirror the celebratory mood that is spreading in the sisters' chat.

A few minutes later my phone beeps again. '52 dead and wounded from the Crusaders in three martyrdom operations east of Indonesia.' Blue Sky adds the hashtags #IslamicState and #Wilayah East Asia, as if to prompt us to share the statement of the ISIS Amaq news agency on social media. Once the news breaks on BBC and CNN, I can see tourists on the beach beginning to check their phones for updates. The beach bar is located just a few hundred metres from the 2002 Bali bombing memorial and brings back memories of the jihadist attack that claimed over 200 lives. This time, though, something is different: it soon emerges that the attacks were carried out by families. Six family members, including two teenage boys and daughters of twelve and eight, blew themselves up.[1]

Kinship has been a recurring theme in Indonesian jihadism; two of the central figures in plotting the Bali bombing were brothers and four of the perpetrators of the 2009 Jakarta bombing were members of one family. But entire families involved in martyrdom – in fact 'ordinary-looking' families, as their neighbours emphasised[2] – that is new.[3] The radicalised family members were part of the pro-ISIS network of Jamaah Ansharud Daulah (JAD) and had been exposed to preachers and videos in the group.

ISIS recruiters plan every step of the socialisation and integration of new members and their families into the group's circles. Once recruited, newcomers are familiarised with the organisation's expectations, rules and norms – usually in gender-specific channels. To become a full member, a new recruit has to intern-alise, accept and obey the values and practices of the group. Part of this transition phase is to ensure that new members remain loyal to their 'fellow travellers' at all times and under all circumstances – even when their close friends or relatives challenge their new beliefs or behaviours.[4]

Dahlia, one of the higher-ranking members of the Terror Agency Sister group, urges us to 'stay away from anyone and anything that tries to stop you from Jihad even with arguments that sound Islamic'. She tells us that it is normal to stand out and appear strange in the beginning. 'The more I increased in my adherence to the Sunnah the more I became distant from my family members, old friends and society in general.' According to her, feeling different and alien in the land of unbelievers (Kufr) is part of being a Muslim woman who is steadfast in her creed (Dīn). '[Her] external appearance, statements, character, and daily routine distinguishes her from those who have embraced the social norm.' She calls this process 'situational estrangement' (Ghurbah). It is the desocialisation from known environments that lays the ground for socialisation into an exclusivist group like ISIS.

No one among the fifteen women in the group questions the concept of 'situational estrangement'. Dahlia tells us that she began to hate those who did not accept the guidance of the Prophet, including her close relatives. 'At this point I became concerned,' she says. She was asking herself what was happening to her and she heard the Shaytan (devil) whisper: 'You're becoming extreme.' But the female jihadist warns us that is necessary to silence this inner voice, that you have to tell yourself: 'No, sister, you are only feeling what every true believer should feel: hatred of Kufr and its people.' The goal of this rhetoric is to erase all doubts that new recruits may experience in the early stages of the radicalisation process – whether they are caused by suspicious relatives, their own scepticism or aggravated external circumstances such as tightened security measures.

Compared to the Trad Wives, I'm finding it much harder to grasp the allure of the Terror Sisters. I do not share any of the grievances they discuss, nor do I understand what it means to live in a war zone. I have never had a child or husband taken from me, I have not even been victim to a discriminative law or a racist rant.

But the longer I am part of the Terror Sisters, the more I start to realise that susceptibility to the jihadist ideology doesn't mean immunity to the stress caused by terrorist attacks. Especially for new members who have not yet fully subscribed to life within a terrorist organisation, the first exposure to violence from within the group can be a deeply shocking experience. It can also put them under severe fear of being the one weak link in the chain. If one member gives in to police pressure, this may backfire against the entire group as well as their own families.

In most countries, security and surveillance measures are much higher for jihadist groups than for far-right terror groups: their propaganda materials are removed more quickly, their Telegram channels monitored more comprehensively. 'So hard for Indonesian IS fighter and their family now,' complains one of the sisters a few days after the Surabaya bombing. 'Policemen and government block anything including their bank accounts.'

Traditionally, Jemaah Islamiyah was the terror organisation most feared in the region, especially after carrying out the Bali bombings. According to Professor Kumar Ramakrishna, the coordinator of the National Security Studies Programme at Nanyang Technological University of Singapore, ISIS has gained significant traction in recent years and transformed the operational terrorist-threat picture in South-east Asia. 'Daesh has tried to leverage regional troubled waters,' he tells me over coffee at a counter-extremism conference in Melbourne. Their attempt to take over the Filipino province of Mindanao and their intensified activities in Indonesia are part of a bigger strategy to expand their influence in South-east Asia.

Indonesian security agencies have long been concerned about the returning fighters from Syria, Iraq and the Philippines, as well as home-grown lone wolves. ISIS has a strong ideological reach in South-east Asia, especially in Indonesia. Indonesian pro-ISIS ideologue Aman Abdurrahman and online publications available in Bahasa, like Dabiq, Rumiyah and An-Naba, inspired a range of highly coordinated attacks as well as lone-wolf ones. I'm familiar with some of these documents from my time spent in the chat with the Terror Sisters. Instructions on bomb-making were shared via Telegram along with calls to target iconic buildings.[5] Whenever I came across such materials or concrete calls to action, I would flag this to the responsible security and intelligence agencies. Although they are monitoring most ISIS Telegram groups, the infrastructure of the app and their own limited resources make it difficult to have full visibility.

In recent years, ISIS-aligned terrorists carried out coordinated suicide bombings and shootings in Jakarta[6] and captured the southern Philippines city of Marawi in a surprise attack.[7] In August 2016, Singaporean security services foiled a terrorist attack against the Marina Bay Sands Hotel. Militants of the ISIS-linked cell Gigih Rahmat Dewa had planned to fire rockets at the iconic skyscrapers from Batam Island. But the ring-leader of the attack, Bahrun Naim, was not even based in the region; he was directing the plot from somewhere in the Middle East via his mobile phone. A combination of Facebook, YouTube and Telegram enabled the prominent foreign fighter to orchestrate the attack from thousands of kilometres away.[8]

Long-distance relationships between jihadist recruiters and jihadi brides often start on Facebook but are quickly taken into encrypted chat rooms. In marketing, these channels are referred to as 'Dark Social', as they are hard to track and analyse. 'Let's talk in private' is the typical phrase you would read before receiving an invite to a closed Telegram or WhatsApp group. For example, a sixteen-year-old Indonesian girl was targeted by ISIS recruiters on Facebook, according to documentary filmmaker Noor Huda, who has interviewed dozens of jihadists. 'She ended up radicalising twenty-six of her family members,' he tells me. This is not an isolated case in Indonesia, which is among the countries with the highest social media usage rates in the world: nine out of ten smartphone owners in Indonesia use Facebook.[9] Noor Huda blames the traffic jams: 'In urban areas like Jakarta you may be stuck in the car for hours, so people end up spending a lot of time on Facebook.'

Researchers at the University of Maryland collected social media data of close to 500 US extremists, finding that in 2016 alone online social media platforms played a role in 90 per cent of all radicalisation cases. Not only has social media facilitated extremist relationships, it has also speeded up the radicalisation process. When extremist groups like Al-Qaeda first started experimenting with social media in 2005, the average radicalisation period was eighteen months. At the time, Facebook counted only 5.5 million users – compared to over 2.2 billion today. YouTube had just launched and Twitter was still in development. It was only a decade later that ISIS started revolutionising online jihadist messaging by spreading sophisticated propaganda content in a highly coordinated manner across Facebook, Twitter, Tumblr, Ask.fm and Instagram. In mid-2014, when ISIS released the videos of the beheadings of US journalists James Foley and Steven Sotloff, its Twitter army counted at least 14,000 supportive accounts.[10] By 2016, the percentage of US foreign fighters using social media had surged to 90 per cent, while the average radicalisation duration had decreased to thirteen months.[11]

At the dawn of social media, members of a jihadist forum put it this way:

> This [Facebook] is a great idea, and better than the forums. Instead of waiting for people to [come to you so you can] inform them, you go to them and teach them! God willing, the mujahedeen, their supporters, and proud jihadi journalists will [use the site, too].[12]

'Assalamualyaykum. My town is still so dangerous. Police sirens every 5 minutes. 4th crisis level,' one of the Indonesian sisters writes. Danger, it seems, is in the eye of the beholder. I decide to stay out of the area because I fear another terrorist attack, while the sister deems it too risky due to the high presence of security services. Both online and offline, she has taken precautions to avoid detection: 'I told my fellow Indonesian IS supporters to change or delete their IS profile pics and change their account names to something funny.'[13]

But just a few days later she informs us that intelligence officers have come to monitor her. Although our leader, Blue Sky, is based in Germany, she gets more and more concerned that the Indonesian sister might be under control of the domestic anti-terror division. If the Indonesian and German intelligence agencies exchange information and make the link, this could pose a risk to the entire group. In Germany, she explains, the police just need to be in doubt about you to put you on their watch list and intercept your communications.

'I have to remove our Indonesian sister,' Blue Sky finally decides. I am surprised; instead of offering to help, the group abandons the sister at this critical moment. This exposes a basic truth about extremist groups: they can be ruthless in their exclusion of members. Group loyalty and ideological adherence are one requirement if someone is to be granted membership, but there is a second one: the net value a member brings to the group. If the risk and potential damage exceeds the value a member adds to the network, the verdict is usually expulsion.

Despite recent security concerns, Blue Sky tells me that she still considers Telegram safe. Indeed, 'more safe than any social media', she writes. In a private message she advises me to delete the chat history after I talk to anyone else who supports IS. I'm surprised that she trusts me, but I guess I've been in the group long enough – since its earliest days when they thought nobody apart from IS members knew about it. 'And please tell to your good friend (IS supporter bro/sis) to delete their profile pic in their account to avoid that any intelligence official is monitoring us.' What a funny thing to tell a counter-terrorism researcher. To escape detection new members are advised to use identity-obfuscation methods such as virtual private networks (VPNs), Tor browsers and fake phone numbers on Facebook and Twitter.[14]

One of the biggest challenges for the security services is to monitor all the new channels ISIS cells create to indoctrinate and initiate new recruits. Online chat groups exist in multiple languages and use protected notes on content-sharing webpages such as JustPaste.it. ISIS runs its own news channels with live updates from war zones via radios, photo series and videos. It provides theological lectures and courses on hacking by identifying security loopholes in webpages and circulating default router passwords.

Telegram has stepped up its efforts to crack down on ISIS channels. 'Hundreds of Bots, Channels and Groups of #IslamicState are banned every day. Thousands are every month. Millions are every year,' an official Telegram statement reads. But, as some ISIS members proudly point out in reply, 'hundreds [of] bots, channels, and groups are created everyday. Thousands are every month. Millions are every year.'

The fact that ISIS members have started to program their own secret chat applications has made this task even trickier. For example, new tools like MuslimCrypt enable them to privately communicate with members across the world. It encrypts all messages and hides texts in pictures, a technique called steganography. While encryption is the practice of cyphering a message itself, steganography is the art of storing a message within another message.

Encryption and steganography are hardly new techniques. In the fifth century BC, Histiaeus, the ruler of the Ancient Greek city of Miletus in Anatolia, allegedly warned of Persian invasion plans by tattooing the message on the shaved head of a slave and waiting for the hair to regrow before sending him to the Greeks.[15] But modern technologies have revolutionised the creative concealment of information.

Osama bin Laden was reportedly a master of digital steganography. A few months before the Twin Towers collapsed in New York in 2001, *USA Today* reported that he was hiding maps and pictures of terrorist targets within pornographic websites and sport chat rooms.[16] Ghost Security, a group of cyber-security analysts that helped intelligence agencies to foil attacks in New York and Tunisia, discovered in 2015 that ISIS had developed an encrypted messaging platform, the Nasher App.[17] Since then there have been various in-house creations that facilitate socialisation, indoctrination and attack-coordination activities.

In June 2018, Blue Sky forwards a message from the 'The United Cyber Caliphate':

IN THE NAME OF ALLAH,
WE ARE ISLAMIC STATE
A MESSAGE TO THE WORLD
From UNITED CYBER CALIPHATE
Soon, soon, you will see the wondrous sight, A fierce conflict.[…]
We have come, we have come, we have marched with determination, In earnest we have striven to ascend the peaks, We embark on the deaths, we close ranks.
We die standing, as lions of courage, expect us!

'#Unitedcybercaliphate!' one of the sisters repeats, adding an enthusiastic emoji. The Terror Sisters appear excited by the prospect of a cyber caliphate. Now that the physical Islamic State – which once equalled Britain in surface area and Austria in population – has dissolved, a virtual jihad seems to be the logical next step.

Female ISIS supporters have been especially active in cyberspace, engaged in activities such as posting propaganda materials on social media, encouraging and recruiting men for jihad or persuading their families to go to Syria. The 'Terror Agency Sister chatting group' is a good case in point. 'Kindly help us reach out to more Muslims by sharing Anti-Nusayris' post [sic] and enlighten them about shirk [idolatry] & kufr of Nusayris,' Blue Sky writes.

Day and night, the sisters post about worldwide events, ranging from pictures of beheaded hostages, injured civilians and war-zone scenes from Syria and Iraq to President Trump's retweet of anti-Muslim videos posted by the deputy leader of Britain First, Jayda Fransen. These posts have a clear message: we, the jihadi sisters, are all in the same boat. It reinforces the sense of a collective struggle against shared injustices, strengthens the group identity and creates closer bonds between its members.

In their efforts to build a global community of female cyber warriors, the Terror Sisters go beyond circulating the usual ISIS propaganda materials, unedited war footage and theological justifications for a violent jihad. They also provide advice to fellow jihadi brides who have questions about their role as a woman. For example, they address questions such as: What is your role in the global ummah, the Muslim community?

What are your duties and responsibilities? And how do you best support your husband in jihad? The questions themselves sound strikingly similar to the ones I encountered in the Trad Wives community. Despite their realities and ideologies being miles apart at first sight, they share the same concerns and questions around identity and responsibility. Some women are attracted to the Terror Sisters not because they want to become female suicide bombers but because they are looking for female solidarity and support.

With the waning power of ISIS and its defeats in Iraq and Syria, the tone in sisters-only groups has changed, however: many of the interactions are now about dealing with difficult emotional situations. The sisters offer solace to the sad and a sense of belonging to the lonely, direction to those that lack perspective and encouragement to those that need confidence. Some share poems to mitigate the suffering of jihadi widows. Others try to turn the anger of those women who lost their husbands or children to jihad into a desire for revenge.

Blue Sky encourages us to take on primary roles in jihad. 'Sisters need to realize their importance to Jihad and Islam today,' she writes. I am surprised by the direction the conversation is taking. Had this not been an ISIS chat, I could have easily mistaken it for a feminist forum: 'Time for playing with Barbie dolls is over. Time for make-up is over. Time for fairy tales is over. Time for Cinderella stories is over. Time for selfies is over. It's time to grow up, mentally. You are not weak as people make you believe. You are stronger than men.'

Since the summer of 2017, ISIS has significantly changed its policy on the role of women in jihad, from seeing them as *muhajirat* (female emigrants) to accepting them as *mujahidat* (female fighters).[18] Despite its initial opposition to female combatants, the July 2017 edition of its Rumiyah magazine encouraged women to follow the example of Umm 'Amara, who took up arms to defend the Prophet Muhammad at the Battle of Uhud. In October 2017, ISIS went as far as to formally declare women's participation in jihad an obligation – an unprecedented step.[19]

The fact that jihad no longer needs to come in the form of physical violence has enabled women to play a key role on the virtual front lines, as online recruiters, virtual honey traps or even hackers. In June 2018, a Wisconsin-based sister called Waheba Issa Dais hacked multiple social media accounts for the cyber jihad, Blue Sky tells us. The forty-five-year-old Arab woman with an Israeli passport and residency in the United States allegedly used the hacked accounts of her victims to recruit attackers and facilitate attacks.[20] According to the FBI, she created a virtual library of instructions on how to build bombs, biological weapons, poisons and suicide vests to help would-be ISIS terrorists stage attacks in the US and beyond.[21] The Terror Agency Sisters applaud her when the news breaks and share detailed accounts of her story.

'The struggle for the cyber caliphate has only just begun,' one of the ISIS sisters tells me. Sooner or later, we should expect a massive cyber war against the 'evil Jewish–Crusader Axis led by US, Israel and coalition of friendly governments'. The struggle starts with battles over the hearts and minds of young Muslim men and women receptive to the ideational and social offers made by a new tech-savvy generation of ISIS recruiters.

The rise of online echo chambers has heavily influenced the ways in which extremist movements can indoctrinate newcomers, foster their dependence on the group and strengthen their identification with its values. Platforms that offer advice on how to deal with hyper-personal questions around identity and anxiety provide common gateways into toxic ideologies. Both explicit dating advice forums like the Red Pill Women and incognito female counselling chats like the Terror Sisters act as a soft entrance point into extremist networks. What is more intimate than one's sexual and romantic life? These forums not only facilitate recruitment, they also create powerful lock-in effects by establishing close in-group bonds and tying their ideology to the members' identities. The goal is to emotionally chain fresh recruits to the group and make it as difficult as possible for them to reach the exit door.

Once new members are familiarised with the internal workings of an extremist group, they can focus on effective communication with the external world.

PART THREE

Communication

5

Info Wars: Confronted by Tommy Robinson's New Media Empire

Stephen Yaxley-Lennon (aka Tommy Robinson), the founder of the English Defence League and international anti-Islam figurehead, is pointing a microphone at me. 'Why did you call me a white supremacist?' he keeps asking.

The man's voice is calm and he doesn't have a gun or a knife. His only weapon is the camera that is livestreaming every word I say to his hundreds of thousands of social media followers. But the prospect of being embarrassed publicly can be scarier than the thought of dying. The cameraman next to him, far-right activist Caolan Robertson, visibly takes pleasure in filming the shock and intimidation registered on my face.

It's a mild day in May 2017 and we are underground, supposedly in a secret location. My bosses at the anti-extremist organisation Quilliam Foundation, former Hizb ut-Tahrir recruiter Maajid Nawaz and former Libyan Fighting Group leader Noman Benotman, both have bounties on their heads from groups like ISIS and Al-Qaeda. It is not exactly an atmosphere in which unannounced visitors are welcome.

After I had infiltrated the English Defence League and published an article in the *Guardian* about the internationalisation of ultra-nationalism,[1] I became an opponent to Tommy Robinson. But I'm not his primary target, neither is my employer. His main goal is to denounce the 'mainstream media' as fake news and to drive views and clicks to the 'alternative news' content of the Canadian far-right news outlet Rebel Media.

Having watched YouTube videos of the English Defence League founder barging into the Wales Online office and visiting a *Guardian* journalist in his home, I know his game. Now I would become the third journalist to feature in his popular 'Troll Watch' series. I am painfully aware that every word I say will not just be shown on Rebel Media but also shared across multiple social media platforms.

This new sensationalist form of reporting is part of the far right's ongoing information battle against traditional media outlets. To Tommy Robinson, the 'Troll Watch' format is a power game as much as it is an entertainment stunt. He picks any journalists who associate him with racism, white supremacy or far-right extremism. In my case the following lines of my *Guardian* piece prompted him to confront me:

That the far right has moved from the fringe into the mainstream demonstrates the massive support that white supremacist movements have attracted from digital natives. Their online followership often exceeds that of mainstream political parties: with over 200,000 followers, Tommy Robinson's Twitter account has almost the same number of followers as Theresa May's.

'So I'm literally gonna walk in there and ask her to justify her accusations,' Tommy tells the camera before walking into our office. 'It's about time that any journalist writing stories across the UK to demonise and silence criticism coming out of the working class have to deal face to face with the person they are talking about.'

The video shows Tommy Robinson making his way past reception in the building and sneaking down the stairs into our office space. 'Julia?' As I see Tommy Robinson walking toward me with his cameraman filming every step, at first I can't believe it. Informing him that he breached our security does not seem to help. Telling him that I did not personally call him a white supremacist only makes him angrier. As my colleagues try to physically force Robinson back through the door and attempt to get hold of the camera, things get more chaotic. Fights break out and Robinson accuses my colleagues of breaking the camera and stealing the microphone pack. In a desperate attempt to keep them from hurting each other, I offer to go upstairs with Robinson and repeatedly say: 'I'm happy to engage in dialogue.'

But Robinson wasn't looking for dialogue, that much I know. He was seeking conflict to entertain his watchers and boost his monthly subscriptions. He was hoping to get footage that would help his smear campaign against the 'mainstream media'. 'Let's at least do it in a fair way. Let's have this interview with an independent media outlet that does not cut every single line.' I propose this knowing it is doomed to fail. We couldn't even agree on a definition of 'independent media'.

'The *Guardian* is a propaganda machine,' Robinson tells me, and laughs at my suggestion that we involve the BBC.

After the police arrive and Tommy Robinson leaves, the real information battle starts. What follows in the next few days is a chain reaction of reporting across alternative media outlets in the US, the UK and Europe. Breitbart, JihadWatch, GellerReport and Gates of Vienna all run headlines such as 'Tommy Robinson vs Quilliam Shows How the Establishment's Grip on Political Narratives is Slipping'.[2] Their shared goal is to denounce the 'mainstream media' as an unreliable source of information.

Raheem Kassam, former editor-in-chief of Breitbart News London, writes that 'the dynamics are shifting between the establishment media, be it the *Guardian* or the BBC, and alternative ways of combating what Tommy referred to as "fake news" about himself, that he has been subjected to for years'.[3] The Troll Watch video itself attracts hundreds of thousands of views, millions of impressions and dozens of comments:

> Got to start calling him 'Tommy Gun', he truly is a machine gun of truth!
> We're just people who are fed up with the lies the MSM has fed us.
> Well done Tommy standing up to them scumbags for spreading fake news!!!!
> I LOVE IT!!! STAND UP TO THESE LIARS!!!!!!

Two weeks later I find myself in the fancy Crowne Plaza café in central London, sitting opposite my CEO Haras Rafiq to discuss the next steps. Our office is closed and the police are investigating a series of threatening calls and messages my colleagues and I have received. As we wait for the coffee we ordered, I check my Twitter for new death threats and insults. 'Message to journalists, if you LIE in the media about us, there will be NO safe space for you. You will be called out to justify your lies,' one of Tommy Robinson's tweets reads.

'So what happens if I don't make the public statement?' I ask five minutes into the conversation.

'You won't be doing any research into the far right any more and I'll make sure your book doesn't get published,' Haras replies. Without my knowledge or consent, Quilliam promised Tommy Robinson in a private meeting that I would release a written public statement to retract my claims and apologise for having associated the English Defence League founder with white supremacist movements. In return, Tommy Robinson would 'pull back his dogs'.

'But I wouldn't want to stab the *Guardian* in the back like this. I stand by my analysis,' I say. 'I can prove that his support base overlaps with that of white supremacist movements. And we both know that all Tommy Robinson wants is to discredit traditional news outlets.'

'Think about it this way: if something happens to your colleagues, you'll have to live with that responsibility. It's your choice.' I swallow hard: how could I possibly look myself in the mirror again after releasing a statement that goes against all my principles? 'He gave us twenty-four hours,' he concludes before getting the bill. Tommy Robinson's tactic of intimidation appears to work: he is able to leverage his social media megaphone to effectively silence critical voices.

Less than twenty-four hours after I refuse to make the statement, I receive an email from my boss. It says nothing but contains two disciplinary warnings as well as my dismissal note:

Unprofessional Conduct – Refusal to Follow Chief Executive's Instructions
[...] you have had two weeks to think about the written statement requested from you.[...] You have left me with no alternative but to write to you this second disciplinary letter. It seems from the conversation at today's meeting your view on this area of work conflicts with those of this organisation, and once again you have left me with no alternative other than to take the following course of action.

It was hard to believe. I had lost my first job because of a far-right extremist.

As I am in the middle of typing up a response to Quilliam, minutes after receiving the dismissal note, my email system unexpectedly logs me out. All my organisational accounts have already been terminated, all my accesses ended.

Looking back at these events, I am unsure what I find more shocking: the extent of harassment I received for what seemed like an innocuous opinion piece, or a world-leading counter-extremism think tank bowing to the demands of the harassers. The experience was an example of the power that far-right media influencers can exercise over entire institutions. It showed how fear of losing face and support can make organisations and individuals give up everything they stand for, how a think tank combating extremism might end up appeasing extremists.

Few far-right figures in England have been as savvy in playing with the media as Tommy Robinson. Having grown up in Luton – according to the latest census, one of three places in the UK where whites are in the minority (the others being Slough and Leicester)[4] – Robinson has framed himself as the hero who risks his own life to expose the media's lies about grooming gangs, criminals and terrorists, according to him all by-products of the growing Muslim population in the UK. To his fans, he is a brave patriot who defends his country and the white working class. To his critics, he is a dangerous far-right influencer who drives societal polarisation.

Regardless of one's view of Robinson, there is little doubt that he is a charismatic and powerful narrator. Former Metropolitan Police counter-terrorism chief Mark Rowley compared him to the Islamist hate preacher Anjem Choudary, whose speeches have inspired jihadist attacks: 'While Choudary became the de facto spokesperson for Islamism in the UK, mouthpieces from the far-right wing such as Tommy Robinson also attracted notoriety and attention.'[5] The police estimate that Robinson's toxic rhetoric and angry rants against Islam and immigration have acted as an accelerator for radicalisation in the UK and beyond. In 2016, the far-right terrorist Darren Osborne drove a car into pedestrians standing outside Finsbury mosque announcing that he would 'kill Muslims'. The jury at Osborne's trial heard that he had acted after reading email newsletters and tweets from Tommy Robinson, and conducting numerous online searches about grooming gangs, the murder of Lee Rigby, and terror attacks.[6]

Although Robinson argues that he is neither racist nor anti-Semitic, he used to be a member of the British Nationalist Party (BNP) and his supporters include neo-fascists who perform the Hitler salute and chant racist lines.[7] Some 65 per cent of his followers on the alternative social media platform Gab also follow at least one prominent white nationalist account. His own fans regularly 'outradicalise' him, but he makes little effort to distance himself proactively from the more extreme ends of his support base. In 2018, he helped to fundraise for the court fees of the Scottish vlogger Mark Meechan (aka Count Dankula), who was charged with a hate crime after publishing videos that show him teaching his girlfriend's dog to perform Nazi salutes in response to the phrases 'gas the Jews' and 'Sieg Heil'.[8]

Tommy Robinson is a central figure in the international far right's war against the media. In early 2019, he launched his own UK media empire called Bubba Media[9] and staged demonstrations against the BBC's investigative programme *Panorama*. Around 4,000 protesters gathered outside the BBC headquarters in Manchester on a Saturday afternoon in February 2019 to watch his 'Panodrama documentary' and call for the BBC licence fee to be scrapped.[10]

Just days before the 'Panodrama' premiered, a Trump supporter attacked a BBC cameraman covering a rally in El Paso, Texas.[11] Tommy Robinson is just one of many self-framed journalists who are confronting the 'lying press' with innovative and transgressive means. Alternative news outlets and right-wing YouTube vloggers are increasingly well networked – with initiatives like Steve Bannon's The Movement attempting to empower and connect them,[12] and right-leaning donors such as the Horowitz Foundation and the Mercer Family Foundation supporting them financially.[13] But a big proportion of alternative media's funding sources, as with all popular websites, comes from advertising.[14]

When German brand strategist Gerald Hensel sat down one Saturday morning in 2016 to pen a blog piece about brands buying ads and banners on far-right websites, he did not expect that this would set in motion a life-changing series of events.

'I saw an ad on the German Breitbart site and wanted to get brands to think more carefully about where they place their ads and who benefits from it,' he tells me. 'We knew how important the internet would be in politics at least since the second Obama election in 2012, but we didn't foresee the Frankenstein's monster it would give rise to by empowering anti-democratic and hateful grassroots movements.'

He realised that the big institutions hadn't kept pace with digitalisation, while the fringes were miles ahead. 'For someone in advertising, it was almost surreal to see how backward big institutions were when compared to a few frogs on the internet. They didn't even know what memes are.' Richard Dawkins coined the term 'meme' in his 1976 book *The Selfish Gene*, as an idea, a thought or a behaviour that can easily be reproduced in a new host.[15] As such, memes, in the age of the internet, are visuals that have a high potential to go viral. They are not inherently political. Memes can be about anything, from animals to food (or both at once, as the 'Puppy or Bagel' meme demonstrates). One of the first viral memes was the Hamster Dance, which spread like wildfire on the World Wide Web in 1998.

Gerald Hensel's blog piece immediately sent the hashtag #KeinGeldfürRechts (#NoMoneyForTheFar-Right) trending. The campaign became the German equivalent of the anonymous Sleeping Giants initiative, which was launched shortly after Trump's election victory to convince US brands to remove their ads from far-right news outlets.

Within hours of the campaign starting, a damning article about Hensel appeared in Achse des Guten,[16] a far-right German news outlet, and triggered a series of organised intimidation and coordinated hate campaigns. 'I remember being in a six-hour meeting when it all kicked off,' he tells me. He only realised what was happening when his girlfriend phoned him up to ask what was going on.

From that moment, he would find at least one article about him per day in every German far-right news outlet – from Tichys Einblick and Junge Freiheit to Breitbart – as well as thousands of hateful and threatening messages in his social media feed. 'It was incredible how interconnected this alternative media space was.' He calls it collective storytelling. 'They didn't know who I was, but within a few days they curated everything that my digital signature gave away about my past to construct a story that would fit their narrative. One day I was an arrogant advertiser, the next an agent of Merkel. One day I was an anti-Semite, the next a Stalinist. It didn't make any sense, and it didn't have to.' When he learned that his address had been leaked, he decided that it wouldn't be safe to head back to Berlin, so he went to Frankfurt instead.

In the weeks that followed, his employer received massive amounts of hateful messages and threatening calls. Gerald Hensel had been in advertising for twenty years and was the executive strategy director at Scholz & Friends, one of Europe's largest advertising agencies. 'I didn't really fear losing my job but I did feel sorry for my colleagues. I didn't want them to go through all that stress,' he tells me. The campaigns caused him to leave the company and to found the initiatives Fearless Democracy and HateAid to help other people who undergo similar experiences.

Neither Gerald Hensel's story nor my experience with Tommy Robinson are exceptional. They are examples of a much wider phenomenon that increasingly concerns journalists, activists, artists, data analysts and researchers who engage with politically controversial topics. In the US, at least 250 university professors reportedly became victims of right-wing online campaigns between early 2017 and mid-2018.[17] 'Those of us in higher education increasingly find ourselves the target of hostilities,' Joshua Cuevas, a psychology professor at the University of North Georgia, wrote. He himself was targeted in a sophisticated public trolling campaign for his liberal leanings and received racist messages from far-right trolls.[18]

Those covering far-right-related news events are particularly in the crosshairs of malicious actors. Lizzie Dearden, the *Independent*'s home affairs correspondent, always wanted to become a journalist, even when she was too young to write articles about crime and terrorism. At the age of ten, she wore a badge saying 'editor'. Now, eighteen years later, we sit in an Italian restaurant celebrating the mere fact that the extreme right didn't leak her real address. It's 1 p.m., a little early for a glass of wine on a normal working day, but Lizzie has just come back from the trial that freed Tommy Robinson from custody.[19]

'The first and worst wave of threats started as I reported on the Finsbury Mosque attack trial,' Lizzie tells me. 'It's interesting that I've been covering various Islamist groups for years but the most threats I've had are from the far right.' After her article on the anti-Muslim terrorist Darren Osborne had been released, the website Right-wing Dox Squad leaked pictures of her and her boyfriend, an old address of hers, as well as details of her boyfriend's social media accounts.

To dox, short for 'dropping documents', refers to the publication of a person's personal information – usually address and phone number – against his or her will.[20] It is 'a common first-stage tactic of mobs of anonymous online groups looking to intimidate you and start digging up information on your life', according to the Crash Override Network, an organisation made up of former cyber-bullying victims.[21]

Doxxing first emerged in the 1990s as part of hacker culture but has become one of the alt-right's favourite revenge tactics in recent years.[22] In 2014, the so-called Gamergate controversy was a large-scale coordinated doxxing and harassment campaign against fem-inist reporters who had reported on misogyny in the video-game industry. Zoë Quinn, who was among the journalists at the epicentre of the Gamergate hate storm, was attacked with half-truths, lies and private-information leaks from her own Twitter account, which the hackers had taken control of.[23]

The goal of the malicious intrusion into people's private lives is to intimidate, silence and publicly discredit critical voices and political opponents.[24] Doxxing campaigns do not just fuel online hate but also increase the likelihood that these people are attacked in real life. Post-doxxing consequences have extended from undesired subscriptions and deliveries to threatening phone calls, prank anthrax hoaxes and in-person visits. Doxxers sometimes use social engineering and hacking to extract information from non-public sources. But in most cases a simple open-source intelligence (OSINT) search provides them with all they need. From our social media profiles, public records and online phone books to third-party info sellers such as Spokeo, Pipl and Intelius, the internet is a treasure trove for doxxers.[25]

Erasing these traces from the internet can be tedious and time-consuming. Some of the white-pages listing companies, it seems, made removal-request applications as difficult as they possibly could. Ironically, some of the most cutting-edge people-search engines work with the most outdated means of communication in their opt-out processes. PeopleLookup.com, for example, requires you to send them a copy of your driving licence via postal mail or fax to prove your identity. The removal of all personal data can then take several weeks.[26]

'Luckily, I was careful to not leave my current address anywhere on the web, but my boyfriend was really freaked out when they found out where he lived,' Lizzie Dearden tells me. It was strange, she continues, as they have no online relationship, don't share the same name, are not married and all of their social media chats are private. 'The amount of effort that went into these guys' research was shocking – this wasn't simply a Google search. I assume it must have taken a long time.' They had screengrabbed conversations between her and her boyfriend from Twitter. 'It was very private. The tweets that they were citing as evidence of our relationship were from 2014.'

Lizzie's doxxers did not just target her but also threatened to expose details about her family members. 'Within the next week I'll find her close relatives online, so watch this space,' said one of the messages. She reported them to the police, but the investigations didn't go anywhere, as most accounts were anonymous. So the Right-wing Dox Squad site was removed and Lizzie took the necessary security steps to protect herself and her family. This was different from her previous experience. 'I'm used to writing about nasty things that other people do to other people, not to us.' She adds, 'There seems to be a trend in journalists becoming the target rather than the people and issues we are writing about. I don't really understand why that's happening now.'

A second wave of harassment, this time with many threats of rape and sexual violence, kicked off after Tommy Robinson shared a picture of her holding a 'refugees welcome' sign from 2015 while accusing her of misreporting evidence from the Finsbury Park trial. 'There are still memes and photoshopped pictures out there that are circulated every time I report on him.' Lizzie's male colleagues covering the same stories were called 'cuck' and 'pussy' but did not receive the same amount of violent and direct threats. 'Everyone receives abuse, but the character of the abuse is different,' she concludes.

The *Guardian* analysed 70 million comments left on its website between 2010 and 2016 and found that articles written by female journalists have consistently attracted a higher proportion of blocked comments than those written by their male counterparts. Eight of the top ten abused writers were women and the remaining two were black men. The top ten least abused writers are all male.[27]

The International Federation of Journalists released a groundbreaking study in December 2018 which found that 66 per cent of all female journalists who suffered online harassment in the previous five years faced attacks based on their gender, from sexist insults and humiliating misogynist comments to rape threats. The online anonymity of most harassers meant that although half of the cases were reported, just 13 per cent of harassers could be identified or brought to justice. The consequences are often severe: 63 per cent of victims reported severe psychological effects, 38 per cent said it led to self-censorship, 8 per cent lost their jobs and 6 per cent left their jobs as a result.[28]

Discrediting formerly respected news outlets and their reporters is just one part of the information battle. The other part consists in spreading disinformation. Disinformation doesn't necessarily mean outright lying; it can also include information that is misleading.[29] Inaccurate information, severe biases and logical fallacies often reinforce misleading narratives. In the tradition of the Soviet strategic-deception technique of *dezinformatsiya*, modern-day disinformation campaigns seek to obfuscate, distort or conceal facts.[30] The founding counter-intelligence chief of the CIA, James Jesus Angleton, claimed that their goal is to create an information landscape 'where fact and illusion merge, a kind of wilderness of mirrors'.[31]

In October 2018, I enter a plain white house in Riga, Latvia that looks like a detached family home. Only the high-security gates would suggest that rather than being a private property this building hosts the world-leading information warfare analysis unit: the NATO Strat Comms team.

'We had a crazy weekend,' Donara Barojan says after leading me through the various security controls. On the day of the Latvian election, a Russian troll hacked Latvia's top social media network Draugiem. 'We are still investigating who was behind this hack,' she says. 'Actions like this can have a strong psychological impact on voters.' Donara is what some call a 'Digital Sherlock'. Her team at the Digital Forensic Research (DFR) Lab at the NATO StratCom Center of Excellence in Latvia exposes the tactics and narratives used to spread disinformation and follows influence campaigns in real time.

'There are four tactics to spread disinformation,' Donara explains to me 'Dismiss the opponent, distort the facts, distract from the central issue and dismay the audience.'[32] This '4D approach' is used both by state actors, such as the Russian and the Chinese governments[33] and by non-state actors such as alt-right trolls. The Kremlin's tactic of flooding the media space with so much content that it becomes impossible to distinguish between right and wrong pieces of information has increasingly been copied by non-state trolling networks. Many of today's far-right operations are, however, amplified by state-backed bots and media networks. For example, the Russian news outlets Sputnik and Russia Today (RT) frequently help far-right campaigners to spread their messages by amplifying their themes and hashtags.[34]

Some accounts pushing disinformation campaigns operate like cyborgs – semi-automated, human-operated accounts. For example, a Twitter account that operates under the handle @thebradfordfile tweets over 300 times per day, has a network of more than 100,000 followers and a core group of hundreds of amplifiers. Its messages, which reach from far-right propaganda to conspiracy theories, have been retweeted by Donald Trump and quoted by major US media outlets to illustrate the alt-right's social media successes.[35]

There are too many elections for the few people at the DFR Lab to monitor. 'An estimated 100,000 websites spread disinformation,' Donara tells me, 'but there are only a few dozen fact-checker websites.' In other words, we are constantly outnumbered. The Oxford Internet Institute found evidence of formally organised social media manipulation campaigns in forty-eight countries in 2017. Since 2010, over half a billion dollars have been spent on psychological operations and public opinion influence campaigns over social media. Tactics ranged from the use of automated accounts and commentary teams to targeted online advertisement campaigns. Most campaigns involved the circulation of misinformation in the run-up to critical junctions such as elections, referendums and crises.[36]

The disappearance of trust in independent information sources is a slow poison that threatens to undermine the fundamental pillars of our democracies. The erosion of civil discourse, political paralysis, alienation and uncertainty are among the most severe consequences of the 'Truth Decay', as researchers of the RAND Corporation have called it.[37] Trust doesn't vanish overnight, but over the past few years we have watched its gradual erosion on different levels.

First came the distrust in the political and financial establishment. The 2008 global financial crisis and its various connected scandals fuelled fears that national and international political and economic bodies were not acting in the public's interest and had secret agendas that might at any point afflict the average man's bank account. Many suffering from real losses or fear of losses in its aftermath felt betrayed by those who they thought had sold them a whitewashed idea of globalisation. This frustration was funnelled into growing distrust in the most powerful and suspicion towards the weakest. A 2013 survey by Public Policy Polling showed that almost three in ten US voters thought that a 'secretive power elite with a globalist agenda is conspiring to eventually rule the world through an authoritarian world government, or New World Order'. Republicans were more than twice as likely as Democrats to believe in this conspiracy theory.[38]

The second stage brought an escalation of distrust in the establishment media and academic institutions.[39] In Europe, the establishment media's reporting around the migration crisis, terrorist attacks and rape scandals gradually chipped away its undisputed credibility: the media's late response to the rape crisis in Cologne on New Year's Eve in 2015 was a watershed moment that prompted many on the far right to resurrect the historically tainted term *Lügenpresse* in Germany.[40] Originally coined a hundred years earlier by the German author Reinhold Anton,[41] the term was first used to denounce enemy propaganda during World

War I. But it is better remembered for its extensive use by the Nazis in their campaigns against Jewish and communist media. In the UK, the media's failure to report on grooming-gang scandals in Rotherham, Rochdale, Telford and Oxford[42] was exploited by figures like Tommy Robinson to decry the 'mainstream media' as complicit with the rapists.

In the US, polarising events such as 9/11, Obama's presidency and Trump's election victory were critical junctions in heating up the nationwide information battle. The investigative journalist David Neiwert powerfully explained in his book *Alt-America* how the aftermath of 9/11, the racist backlash against the first black US president and the growing popularity of far-right media figures has led to the emergence of a 'mental space beyond fact or logic, where rules of evidence are replaced by paranoia'.[43] Far-right and conservative social media influencers were quick in promoting the idea that the media's coverage of Trump was biased, one-sided and unfair. In tandem with Trump himself, these emerging alternative news figureheads helped to popularise the terms 'lying press' and 'fake news'.

A 2017 Pew Research Center survey found that two in three Americans get their news from social media.[44] In the competitive, fast-paced twenty-four-hour news ecosystem, traditional media outlets are struggling to strike the balance between speed and accuracy of reporting. This difficult reporting environment is exacerbated by malicious attempts to trick and manipulate the media. Trolls sometimes plant misleading or inaccurate information into credible sources, such as think tanks or local media, which are then frequently quoted by journalists. For example, less than an hour after the Parkland high-school shooting occurred in February 2018, far-right trolls made plans to hijack the public narrative. 'Start looking for [Jewish] numerology and crisis actors,' one wrote on the image board 8chan. This disinformation and obfuscation technique is called 'source hacking'.[45]

In December 2018, *Der Spiegel* revealed that one of their award-winning journalists, Claas Relotius, had freely invented major parts of his stories, including quotes, places, scenes, even entire characters.[46] This scandal gave far-right actors such as Martin Sellner across Europe ammunition to paint all journalists as dishonest and unprofessional.[47] One month later, in January 2019, members of Generation Identity launched a nation-wide campaign against journalists, attaching posters on the façades of media outlets across the country and attacking a journalist of the newspaper *TAZ* in Berlin.[48] A similar wave of scepticism towards scientific studies took root when three scholars published a series of hoax papers called 'Grievance Studies' with the aim of exposing flaws in the academic review processes of journals in 2017 and 2018. Even though the Relotius scandal and the 'Grievance Studies' affair are isolated cases, far-right influencers such as Martin Sellner have used them as the ultimate proof that we cannot trust any news articles and scientific studies.

As a result, trust in the democratic system itself is dwindling at high speed. In 2018, German far-right activists spread panic over rigged election processes, calling on their followers to become election observers in the German 2018 state elections in Bavaria and Hesse.[49] At the same time, Swedish alt-right figures propagated allegations that the national election was fraudulent and designed to disenfranchise the far-right parties in the national election.[50] The German-American Harvard University scholar Yascha Mounk showed in his book *The People vs. Democracy* that people living in Western democracies are not just increasingly suspicious of their political representatives and institutions. With stagnating living standards, fear of multiethnic democracy and the rise of social media, their belief in the system of liberal democracy itself is gradually fading as well.[51]

This democracy trust crisis has led to an atmosphere in which anti-democratic movements thrive, as their calls for radical change become louder and their public protests more widespread. The Tommy Robinsons of this world are getting louder, and their fan boys are multiplying. Had Robinson come to my office ten years earlier, the media stunt likely would not have worked. Not just because Quilliam didn't exist then, Robinson still attended BNP events[52] and Twitter counted only around 5,000 tweets per day (as compared to 6,000 per second today),[53] but because there wasn't a big enough audience that wanted to see news outlets dismantled and journalists disgraced.

6

Meme Wars: Undercover in Europe's Biggest Trolling Army

'It's a real shame,' O says. 'In people's heads, trolling is now associated with the spread of hate and toxic narratives.' O is one of the few left-leaning trolls out there.

'So what do you think: are many trolls politically motivated or do they just participate because it's fun?' I want to know.

'That is a good question,' O says. 'I'm sometimes wondering if they have always been latently far-right or if they are being turned into xenophobes, racists and conspiracy theorists because they are exposed to these brainwashing materials all day. Many far-right YouTubers host AMA ['Ask Me Anything'] sessions on Discord, so that might have played a role in the radicalisation of the trolling community in recent years.'

I first met O when we were working together to expose the activities of alt-right trolling armies by leaking their internal discussions via a Twitter account called 'Alt Right Leaks'.[1] For a few years now, O has been part of the YouTuber networks, which are strongly intertwined with the trolling world. Many YouTubers become trolls and many trolls become YouTubers, he tells me. The YouTuber community is like the world of journalism, according to O. 'Everyone knows everyone.'

YouTube is one of the internet's top breeding grounds for far-right extremism.[2] With over 1.8 billion unique visitors every month, the platform attracts almost a quarter of the world's population.[3] The fact that its algorithms do not distinguish between 'conservative' and 'far-right' does not help.[4] Zeynep Tufekci, a techno-sociologist at the University of North Carolina, powerfully exposed how YouTube's algorithm fuels radicalisation by prioritising extreme content. In a self-experiment, she went down the rabbit hole of the autoplay mechanisms. Although she was searching mainstream content, YouTube started suggesting and automatically playing 'white supremacist rants, Holocaust denials and other disturbing content'.[5]

Whether you start with a Clinton or Trump video, you are always more likely to end up with a Trump video. This does not only apply to inherently political topics. Often the gateway drug is apolitical: for example, a gaming video might pave the way for radical content. 'Intrigued, I experimented with nonpolitical topics. The same basic pattern emerged,' Tufekci wrote. If you start with a video about jogging, for instance, you can be almost sure to end up seeing extreme Parkour or ultra-marathon videos. And when you watch a vegetarian cooking lessons, you might get suggestions for militant veganism at the end of the day.[6]

Trolls, unlike YouTubers, have been around since the dawn of the World Wide Web. In the mid-1990s trolls were simply mischief-makers in the digital sphere. In the early 2000s the first organised trolling networks and internet cultures developed around the image board

4chan and the Anonymous collective. Most trolls were just in for the taboo-breaking, pranks and jokes. The early days of the trolling communities were fun and lightsome, and pleasure was an end in itself. Even if their activities sometimes took place at the expense of others, the main motivation was to kill boredom rather than to vivify political action.[7]

This has changed quite dramatically over the past few years. Since the 2016 US election, political warfare in the form of trolling has become the new normal. Between 2015 and 2017, the divisive social media content disseminated by troll accounts linked to Russia's Internet Research Agency (IRA) reached one in three Americans. The US House Intelligence Committee published a list of 3,841 Twitter troll accounts linked to the IRA. Researchers who analysed these accounts identified five types of trolls, all with different behaviour patterns: right trolls, left trolls, news feeds, hashtag gamers and fearmongers.[8]

Europe's biggest trolling army, Reconquista Germanica, has clear political goals. 'Do you think they are dangerous?' O asks me.

'You tell me,' I say.

'Well, I wouldn't want them to have my name,' he says. For fear of being targeted by neo-Nazi trolls, most people – even some of his friends – don't know his real name. On WhatsApp, he uses two fake names.

This is not unusual. Trolls do everything to keep their real identity hidden, even from their closest online allies. Die Vulgäre Analyse (TVA), a popular German YouTuber and troll known for burning the Quran and releasing Islamophobic and misogynistic content, even uses two VPNs. The worst nightmare for any troll is when their online identity is matched with their real identity.

'Doxxing?'

'Precisely,' O says.

I promise to not leak his name, and enter the war rooms of Reconquista Germanica on the gaming application Discord.

My avatar account is among 7,000 virtual soldiers who are obeying the daily orders of Supreme Commander Nikolai Alexander. I am called Isabella I, in reference to the Queen of Castile in the late fifteenth century. She and King Ferdinand II of Aragon ordered the conversion or exile of Muslims and Jews living in Spain and are known for completing the so-called Reconquista, the Christian reconquest of the Iberian peninsula. After all, Reconquista Germanica claims to be a big LARP, a Live Action Role Play.

'Welcome to the official Discord-Server of Reconquista Germanica, Germany's biggest patriotic server. You are now part of the resistance,' a bot greeted me on my first day. According to the official selection criteria, 'an authentic description of your patriotic identity is key to getting access'.

'Hi, what do I have to do to join the LARPers crew?' I asked the recruiter.

'Good evening. Tell me something about you. What brings you here? How old are you? Do you have any experience in LARPing?'

I quickly type up my application:

Hi, I came here from Krautpol, the link sounded interesting. I am 19 and don't have any previous experience in LARPing to be honest but I think I can be helpful. I am from Oberammergau and currently live in Munich, where I work as a marketing assistant at an insurance company. My Facebook account was blocked for the second time in a row last week and Facebook still hasn't replied to my messages. I'm on Gab though. I live in Pasing next to a refugee camp, which probably explains why I'm here.

'All right, do you have a headset?'
'Sure'.
'Okay, let's do a voice call tonight.'
My preparation time is rather limited, but I do some speedy research on insurance companies based in Munich, write a quick list of words and phrases of marketing jargon and open a Google Earth map of Pasing on my laptop.

As the recruiter called Gardes du Corps (Bodyguard) is awaiting me in the voice chat, I calculate the chances of him being Bavarian. Bavaria counts just over 12 million citizens; the entire German population is currently at roughly 82 million. About 15 per cent. I think of my grandmother's dialect before switching on the microphone.

'Hello. So you want to join Reconquista Germanica.' A northern German accent, thank God. His tone is controlled but not unfriendly. I wonder how old he might be.

I decide to go with a thick Bavarian accent. '*Grias di*,' the Bavarian 'hello'.

'What does it mean to you to be a patriot?'

'To be aware of my cultural heritage and to want to preserve my nation,' I reply, wary of the pronunciation of every single word.

'Are you active in any patriotic movements?'

'No, not currently.' I pause. 'I'd like to see what it's like though, which is why I'm here.'

'Have you heard of the books *Mein Kampf* and *Das Kapital*?'

'Well, I remember discussing them in school.'

'But have you read them?'

'Not entirely. Should I reread them?'

'That would be good. But remember: whatever you make of them, we don't want you to share any citations or references to these books in this channel.'

'Ah, okay.' They are afraid that Discord might have adopted trackers alerting their security teams whenever National Socialist keywords are used. Indeed they have: the gaming app's public policy manager Sean Li told me in the San Francisco office in January 2017.

After the recruiter with the northern German accent has interrogated me about my family background and political leanings as well as my marketing skills and the value I could add to the movement, he asks an unexpected question. 'Would you describe yourself as exclusively conservative or progressive?'

The German conservative revolutionary movement in the inter-war period springs to my mind. When the German cultural historian Arthur Moeller van den Bruck wrote *The Third Reich,* his idea of a new state would rebrand conservatism by combining right-wing nationalism and left-wing socialism. Like fascism, Islamist extremism combines conservative and progressive thinking. For instance, the Iranian revolution of 1979 was a careful and cunning attempt to reconcile fundamentally different leftist and rightist values. The resulting ideology under Iranian Supreme Leader

Ayatollah Khomeini was therefore an innovative merging of socialism and Islamism,[9] often described by oxymorons such as 'pragmatic fundamentalism'[10] and 'illiberal democracy'.[11] The direction of many radical movements is 'forward to the past', or at least to a reinterpretation of the past.

'I don't think that one precludes the other. I am conservative in that I want to preserve our national identity and cultural heritage, but progressive in that I am in favour of radical change.'

'What do you think?' the recruiter asks into the silence. Only now do I realise that we are not alone on this call. Two other recruiters were listening the entire time, which increases the chances that someone might have noticed my amateurishly imitated dialect.

Silence. 'Are you still there?' No one replies but I can hear someone typing.

'Okay, you are accepted.'

The recruiter explains the rules of conduct and the hierarchies to me. 'Neo will be your main point of contact. Whenever you have questions or ideas you can write to him.' Neo is on the call too but hasn't said a word.

'Sounds good.' I enter Reconquista Germanica's 'virtual army'.

Since the prominent far-right YouTuber Nikolai Alexander founded the group in September 2017, it has declared an all-out war against the political elites and left-wing activists. After just a few days, his troll army counted a few thousand members who were accorded military ranks.

'First you need a way to recruit people, second you need a space to connect them, third you need a clear mission,' Nikolai explains to another of my avatars, the French Claire, via email. (I have half a dozen different avatars – but some are more credible than others, and I use them in different contexts.) 'Since I am a YouTuber I used that pool to recruit people. But, of course, there are many other ways: you could also recruit on campus and connect in a café.' Building a good team of people around you that you can trust and absolutely rely on is essential, he says. The absolute numbers are less important than the individual qualities of the members. 'Ten creative, hard-working, courageous people count more than a hundred slackers.' He also warns of the downsides of starting a neo-Nazi trolling army. This is all kind of risky, he says. 'So I recommend you stay anonymous – at least at the beginning.'

Although Discord has removed the channel multiple times since I started flagging it to them, it has reappeared over and over again under different names. In the meantime, its application procedures have become stricter and its membership has grown. 'Current army strength: 10,845, among which 4,200 private first class,' reads a message from the Supreme Commander.

Reconquista Germanica's first major milestone was to influence the online discourse in the run-up to the German parliamentary election in September 2017. In the weeks preceding the election the trolls managed to catapult hoax stories, anti-Merkel memes and far-right hashtags into the top social media trends. Manipulating computational systems in ways that maximise the reach of content and elevate a topic's perceived importance is fairly easy. For example, the 'trending topics' functions on Facebook and Twitter allow individuals and groups to create the impression of widespread public interest in a topic or content regardless of its accuracy or intent.[12]

By spreading disinformation and sowing discord, they were able to shift the online political discussions in favour of the far-right populist party Alternative for Germany (AfD). Seven of their hashtags reached Germany's top trends: #TraudichDeutschland ('Dare Germany'), #nichtmeinekanzlerin ('Not my chancellor'), #merkelmussweg ('Merkel has to go') and #reconquista were among the most successful ones. Even official AfD accounts ended up sharing some of the hashtags and content, which additionally boosted the campaign's reach, effectively bringing it into the mainstream. The YouTube channel AfD-Television, which appeared to be run by a Bavarian AfD member, even advertised the server of Reconquista Germanica by linking to the group's Discord channel.[13]

In spring 2018 they are planning a new offensive:

Good morning, comrades.[…] it's time to start this year's summer attack. In a late-night discussion the high command has decided on all necessary steps.[…] The first step for me is to record a 'Blitztotalstvideo' […] to attract maximum attention, to recruit new troops and to go on to the offensive both online and offline. Now is the perfect time of the year to start filling Germany's walls with posters, the official Reconquista flyers arrived just in time.[…] the Reconquista Germanica will have the opportunity to finally write history in 2018.

The group's members range from neo-Nazis and sovereign citizens to simple patriots and AfD enthusiasts who are looking for a way to help with online campaigning. Some don't try to hide their extreme mindsets. Nazi symbols, Holocaust-denying literature and announcements of a race war feature on the channels. 'This is why I keep urging you: do get yourselves a knife,' wrote one of the users in their so-called 'crisis prevention centre'. Instructions on how to build your own electro-shocker and recommendations for guns and other arms were circulated in the group. But most activists also know that they have to be careful now, especially in the context of strict German hate-speech laws. 'We should take this video down,' one of their members says after finishing a YouTube livestream session in May 2018 – its live chat had been flooded with Nazi symbols and racial slurs.

Other users, especially some of the younger ones, do not appear to be there for political reasons, though. Community, friendship and a sense of belonging play a big role for most of them. Many members, such as Neo, write that they are here because of 'the community and sociability among all comrades'. Others even say things like 'this movement has had such a positive impact on my life. You guys are simply great.' The hierarchies and military language provide a framework for this community that many find appealing: 'I like the structure of the server, which is not trying to hide the hierarchies instead of lying to us about alleged freedoms, as well as our noble Supreme Commander. Long live the Supreme Commander!' Wahrheitskampf writes, whose username translates as 'Struggle for Truth'.

As I watch the members get excited about the strict rules and chains of command, I can't help but be reminded of 'The Wave', the social experiment that turned a Californian high-school class of around thirty students into a fascist movement in 1967. The history teacher Ron Jones wanted to demonstrate how the Nazis managed to impose their ideology on the masses, and used the motto 'strength through discipline, strength through community, strength through action, strength through pride' to create a movement that got out of hand after just a few days. The movement gained hundreds of supporters from outside the class and students started bullying those that did not adhere to its rules.[14]

Reconquista Germanica appears like a game at first sight, a fun experiment, LARPing, nothing more. Clear targets are set, successes celebrated and rewards given to particularly good virtual soldiers. You can move up the ranks and become an officer and even a general by performing well. The environment is competitive, but still there is a sense of mutual solidarity thanks to common enemies and shared goals. All members' successes in conquering the online world will be reflected in their real lives one day, Nikolai Alexander promised them. But first, they need to change the existing power structures. Like many extremist movements, Reconquista Germanica has found a way of gamifying its propaganda, recruitment and mission.

Psychological studies show that specific gaming designs such as badges, leaderboards and performance graphs can be powerful tools to maximise customer participation and brand loyalty.[15] Over the past decade most corporate brands and media outlets have adopted interactive gaming elements to boost human motivation and performance. Political movements, including extremist and terrorist organisations, have done the same: they increasingly use competitive scoring and reward systems as well as gaming language and imagery. Most Islamist and far-right hardline forums use points-based rating systems: on the white supremacist forum Stormfront users could attain various statuses from 'will be famous soon enough' to 'has a reputation beyond repute', while the British Islamist site Salafi Media adopted a 'fundamentalism meter' to rank its users' engagement level.[16]

Back in 2003, Al-Qaeda reversed the roles in the video game 'Quest for Saddam' to turn it into their own version, 'Quest for Bush'.[17] ISIS made reference to computer games like 'Call of Duty' in their urge for a jihad, mixed gaming terms with Quranic references and programmed its own video game 'Salil al-Sawarem' ('The Clanging of the Swords'). Likewise, far-right gamers have created racist modifications (mods) for their favourite video games. For example, the neo-Nazi website Daily Stormer designed its own mod for the game 'Doom 2' with the header 'Fight against the Jewish Supremacy'.[18] The game 'Hearts of Iron IV' allows players to reshape the political landscape of the twentieth century – for example in Hitler's favour. One user commented that he found the alternative style mod of its twenty-first-century equivalent 'Millennium Dawn' 'awesome', as 'you can focus on Racial Superiority'. Another commented: 'lots of genocide options, great fun'.[19] Some 4chan trolls even photoshopped the head of Luca Traini, the Italian neo-fascist terrorist who carried out a gun attack on African migrants in spring 2017, on to the cover of the video game 'God of War' and renamed it 'God of Race War'.[20]

Social media researcher Ahmed Al-Rawi calls this gamification strategy 'troll, flame, and engage'.[21]

Despite Reconquista Germanica's game-like character, their impact is real. Using leaked materials from GCHQ, the British spy agency that focuses on signals intelligence and cyber threats, to optimise their information warfare against the political establishment,[22] the trolls decide on new targets each day – their victims range from refugees to television presenters. Then the generals and more junior officers announce a series of hashtags and time slots, so that they can launch coordinated campaigns that manage to trick the algorithms of social media platforms into prioritising their content. This allows them to make their provocative posts and comments visible to a wide audience that goes way beyond their traditional support base. To maximise the circulation of their content, they work with fake accounts and infiltration tactics: 'Just pretend to be a normal account that posts about football, BBQ, parties, Karl Marx or similar stuff.'

Their strategy of change is based on psychological warfare, as Supreme Commander Nikolai Alexander explains:

> You cannot get rid of everyone that gets into your way, and even if you could, that wouldn't be smart. No, it's best to beat your enemy without firing a single shot. This means you have to beat him with legal or at least semi-legal means.[...] Through demoralisation, subversion and infiltration. This means you need to undermine the morale of your opponent by spreading defeatism. For example, by saying this doesn't make any sense, this doesn't

lead anywhere, just leave it. Ideally, in combination with smear, for instance by claiming that you work for the enemy. Then of course denigration, so that everything will be questioned, picked to pieces and decried. You sow discontent, impatience and doubt about the leadership. The word for this assault tactic is 'constructive criticism', a concept of the Frankfurt School. Then you try to pit members against one another, stir up disputes, create coteries, promote traitors and expel loyalists. Install levers to influence everything in your interest, outsource relevant structures, etc. And of course, spying, disinformation, lies, smear – the entire set of approaches. These are the tactics and mechanisms to sabotage and destroy a movement.[23]

Some of their activities draw on the so-called 'Handbook for Media Guerrilla Warfare', a playbook for information operations in the digital space the Identitarians released a few weeks before the 2017 German parliamentary election.[24] 'We all love to troll victims on the internet. There are a multitude of words to describe this activity: troll, shitpost, fuck with, use memetic warfare against or just take the piss out of someone,' reads the introduction. The book speaks of 'massive air strikes' and 'sniper missions' in cyberspace. For example, a sniper mission would be a targeted verbal attack on a 'big enemy account', which aims at embarrassing or discrediting the person behind it. The instructions for the 'massive airstrike', on the other hand, recommend that one 'directly target enemy accounts: politicians, celebrities, mainstream media, etc. and spam the comments sections'. To avoid removal mechanisms for hyperactive behaviour they advise all trolls to change accounts after two to three tweets.[25]

Memes are a central element of the online manipulation toolset of far-right trolls, who often claim that 'the left can't meme'.[26] Over the past decade, units of national security bodies and intergovernmental military alliances have increasingly grasped the powerful psychological potential of memes in information warfare. In 2011, the military robotics expert Dr Robert Finkelstein even suggested the creation of a new US military unit, a so-called 'Meme Control Center'. While this seemed like a ridiculous idea back then, memetic warfare has in the meantime become a common tool to influence attitudes and behaviours and to win the competition over narrative and social control in online battlefields – for state and non-state actors.[27]

In the 2016 US election campaigns Trump supporters weaponised internet culture for political propaganda to sway the election.[28] They launched several meme campaigns against political opponents with the goal of influencing public perceptions of truth and power. 4chan called this 'The Great Meme War'.[29] The legendary #MAGA (Make America Great Again) hashtag sprang from the same communities.

The Stanford graduate Jeff Giesea who got 'bored being nice to people all the time' and saw 'Trumpism as the only practical and moral path to save Western civilization from itself' organised MAGA meet-ups and effectively helped to create an army of pro-Trump meme trolls.[30] A 2018 analysis of 160 million archived visuals showed that far-right trolls on the internet were highly effective in spreading racist and anti-Semitic memes from fringe forums like 4chan's /pol/ board and the subreddit /The_Donald to more mainstream platforms.[31]

Socio-demographic research showed that men were 1.76 times more likely than women to produce and spread hateful content online.[32] Another study concluded that men have a higher tendency to engage in anti-social Facebook activities like trolling due to elevated levels of narcissism.[33] Women, on the other hand, are more likely to become victims of online hate. A Pew Research Center study showed that women experience online stalking and sexual harassment much more frequently than men.[34] The conclusions that researchers from Amnesty International and Element AI reached were even more shocking: female politicians and journalists became victims of hate speech on Twitter every thirty seconds in 2017. A total of 1.1 million hateful tweets reached high-profile women in the UK and US, including all British female MPs and female members of the US Congress.[35]

The GI media guerrilla handbook specifically recommends the targeting of 'young women who come straight from uni. These are classic victims and not used to putting up with much. You can easily take them apart.' The handbook goes on to advise: 'Use all available means, don't leave out anything. Their family is often a weak spot. Be prepared to have a repertoire of insults, which you can adapt to your opponent.'[36]

Across Europe and the US, many prominent female artists, activists and politicians have been repeatedly targeted by online trolls. The English singer Lily Allen even decided to leave Twitter after suffering multiple waves of online harassment, including over the stillbirth of her son.[37] British Conservative MP Nicky Morgan became the victim of a series of death threats and insulting tweets after taking an anti-Brexit stance in 2017.[38]

But such campaigns are not just reserved for prominent figures. Whenever I publish a report or article about the tactics of the far right, I know that my social media accounts and email inboxes will be filled with hateful and abusive messages a few days later. I received a range of death and sexual-abuse threats after reporting Reconquista Germanica to the security services and warning publicly of their activities. 'You should be careful, Julia,' one tweet said, showing a picture of a woman who is raped by an octopus. 'Our tentacles extend to London, in fact to anywhere in the world.' In the days that followed, the ISD office was put under police protection and we significantly upgraded our security measures. Threatening messages against the entire team included anonymous posts like 'Hey ISD: I'll give you a pro-tip of my "psychological driver". I want every one of you dead and I don't care how it happens.'

Overall, 40 per cent of online users have suffered mild to severe online harassment and over 70 per cent have witnessed it.[39] One doesn't need to spend much time reading the comments sections of newspaper articles to succumb to the illusion that hate speech is an omnipresent phenomenon of the digital age. But the hate that is visible everywhere on social media is profoundly misleading. In many cases it is not the average user spreading hateful content but rather far-right extremist fringe groups that hold a quasi-monopoly on hate comments in the news sections.

In fact, a tiny minority is responsible for the bulk of hateful speech online. In a study undertaken with the Facebook community #ichbinhier, ISD found that 5 per cent of all active accounts were responsible for over 50 per cent of all likes of hateful comments in the comments sections of German news articles on Facebook.[40] This distorts reality in the minds of millions of Facebook users, impacts the online discussion culture and puts pressure on politicians and journalists. Reconquista Germanica are perfectly aware of the disproportionate impact they can have on social media. 'The best thing about the server is that we can connect and are no longer isolated from each other. A great strategic advantage,' one member of the trolling army writes.

Reconquista Germanica is only one of dozens of online trolling groups that are inciting hate, fuelling divisions and spreading hoax stories in Germany, and just one out of hundreds internationally. The alt-right has been strong in building global networks and content-sharing platforms and has strengthened international ties. For example, Reconquista Germanica teamed up with the Scottish alt-right vlogger Millennial Woes and reached out to the American white supremacist editor Jared Taylor, who was moved when he heard that there was a German equivalent movement to the alt-right. When Alt Right Leaks started leaking content that exposed their connection, Millennial Woes was quick to remove all public chats with Reconquista Germanica.[41]

The tactics used by European troll armies resemble those of the US alt-right, whose playbook can be found across obscure data-sharing platforms and serves as the international far-right trolling community's bible for election-manipulation campaigns. For example, one popular tactic is to pair trending hashtags with extremist ones to link mainstream discussion points to more extreme ones. Another common technique is to hijack opponents' hashtags, so called 'hashtag stuffing'.[42] European neo-fascist trolls campaigning in the run-up to the French, German, Italian and Swedish elections also used the same ecosystem, vocabulary and imagery as their American counterparts.[43] The trolls usually recruit and mobilise sympathisers on image boards such as 4chan, 8chan and Reddit before moving the conversations into encrypted chat rooms on Discord, Telegram or WhatsApp, where they get organised and coordinate their campaigns without detection. Finally, they launch them on the more mainstream social media platforms like Facebook, Twitter and Instagram to reach a wide audience.

Far-right activists are not the only ones trying to influence online discussions and mainstream their views, even if they are the most frequent.[44] Islamist groups have in the past also been successful at launching influencer operations on social media to expand their audience and attract media attention. In April 2018, a controversial debate on whether to ban the headscarf for girls under the age of fourteen broke out in the German Ministry for Integration. The German Islamist group Generation Islam, linked to the global Islamist movement Hizb ut-Tahrir, called for a 'weekend of indignation' and a 'Twitter storm' in response. They launched a coordinated campaign using the hashtag #NichtOhneMeinKopftuch (#notwithoutmyheadscarf), which ended up being used in over 100,000 tweets in just one day, as our research at ISD showed.

Russian media outlets such as Sputnik and Russia Today and alternative news outlets magnify the voices of trolls. But traditional media outlets also share responsibility, they unwittingly gave rise to alt-right accounts, language and memes as a result of their race for clickbait stories. In 2018, alt-right trolls created hundreds of Twitter accounts with grey avatars as profile pictures to mock liberal activists. They called them all 'NPCs' ('Non-Playable Characters' in gaming lingo). After Twitter removed 1,500 such accounts and various international news outlets reported the story, the new NPC meme rose to worldwide prominence. Something similar happened with the OK hand gesture: far-right internet trolls managed to turn it into a white-power sign in the public perception by generating huge amounts of media attention for what was essentially a hoax.[45] These cases show how reporting on hyper-niche phenomena can lend oxygen to fringe communities.[46] Knowing the dynamics of media sensationalism, alt-right activists purposefully design sexy headline stories.[47]

It's partly the generational divide among journalists that can be blamed for the growing notoriety of the alt-right between 2016 and 2018. There is a fundamental disconnect between the generation of those (mostly younger) journalists that grew up with the 4chan board language and memes and those that did not even know what a troll was – the troll-trained vs the not troll-trained reporters, as the Data and Society Research Institute calls them. While the former highlighted the funny and bizarre sides of trolling, the latter approached it with hysterical sensationalism. This has led to grossly inconsistent and exaggerated reporting on far-right trolling in the past and impacted the perceived credibility of traditional media outlets.[48]

The new media ecosystem has given rise to online wars over truth and power, and the internet has turned into a battleground for information. Those that see themselves as combatants on the front line, like Tommy Robinson and Nikolai Alexander, invest their time and resources in developing and implementing strategies to win the war against the 'mainstream media'. Step by step, they discredit traditional sources of information, intimidate journalists of independent media outlets and disseminate their own twisted versions of the truth.

But they are not just learning to launch sophisticated influencer operations, they are also looking to maximise their reach and impact by building international networks and coalitions – taking their ideas on to a global stage.

PART FOUR

Networking

7

Alt Tech: Connecting Radicals around the World

'Finally! The dating site for those wishing to preserve their heritage.' I stare at the announcement of what appears to be the world's first white supremacist dating site, WASP Love. On this obscure site, white Anglo-Saxon Protestants (WASPs) can find fellow 'white people of diverse religions, nationalities, political ideology, and backgrounds, united in one cause for the benefit of our race and children'. I can't help but wonder: what kind of people do you find on WASP Love? How do they present themselves and how do conversations differ from normal dating apps?

To access WASP Love you need to create an account. WASP profile descriptions are much longer than on the more mainstream dating platforms such as Tinder, Bumble or Happn. To create a profile you have to complete a lengthy questionnaire and provide details about your political and religious views. 'Conservative and patriotic' is the standard answer but some are a little more forthright: 'The 14 words are my goal. Trying to build a nuclear family with a loving and loyal-as-she-is-humble stay-at-home wife. Wanting many kids to bring honor to my family name and legacy' or 'The

Church and Lord are essential to keeping society from becoming the degenerate shell it is today.'

All right, let's have a go.

'My name is Claire and I'm a French flight attendant. I was raised in a traditional, conservative Christian household, so I want my children to grow up with these values too.' I search for WASP men aged between twenty-five and thirty. I have 371 matches.

After just a few weeks on WASP Love, Claire has received over thirty messages from men across the US and Europe. The ice-breakers and pick-up lines are not dissimilar from more mainstream dating apps. Except that you can be sure that your date will be a 'Reformed Christian, Quiverfull,[1] Confederate, Homeschooled, Christian Identity, white nationalist, alt-right, Sovereign Grace Singles'.

At first sight, many profiles look nondescript. But you get the little hints: 'All my ancestors were of Celtic background,' writes a Galician ex-soldier of the Spanish army. 'I like European music only. The more foreign influences there are, the less I like it,' a Romanian based in the UK tells me. It quickly becomes clear that all of their lifestyle choices and hobbies are determined by their whiteness. As other layers of their identity are erased, their white identity becomes all-embracing and serves as the single most important point of connection with other people.

According to most white nationalists I've been following, the white genocide is imminent. But each has their own ways and strategies of reversing the alleged eradication of the European race and culture. While some demand the closure of all borders and remigration, others focus on the fight against pro-LGBT rights and abortion laws. And then there are those who concentrate on the essential: reproduction. White nationalist dating websites clearly fill a niche here.

Some WASP Love users confess that they have received negative feedback on the 'mainstream' dating apps. I am not surprised; imagine that awkward situation when you sit with a Tinder date who tells you that Jewish policymakers, bankers and journalists have been plotting to wipe out the white race. But then others have different reasons for no longer using Tinder and the like: what if these apps were controlled by the global establishment too? One user I chat with tells me that he would never want to give his data to Tinder or other 'mainstream dating platforms that serve as spying tools for the Zionists'. He goes on, 'It's great to see another patriot here.'

For a site with the motto 'Love your race and procreate' I find this pretty unsurprising. 'Yes, absolutely,' I write back.

I scroll through the groups:

National Socialism. 'Asserting the interests of the Indo-European (Aryan) people through the cultivation of unity on grounds of race, language, culture, religion, tradition and tribal structure'. 123 members.

Breed Them Out. 'You are 9% of the world's population, this group is for people to discuss and meet with people whom [sic] want to reverse this trend, this group is anti-birth control, pro-polygamy'. 7 members.

Others include 'Christian Identity' and 'GamerGate Veterans'.

Some users appear to be bored, others lonely. One messages me, 'I want a family too, I live off grid in Canada on 120 acres,' and gives me his exact ancestry. 'I am English Acadian French, Scottish, Belgian, Irish and Norwegian.' Others are more straightforward with their political goals: 'My dream is to create a social movement for the formation of a "European Israel". I would love to see it grow from secret society to social club, to political party, to nation.'

Lucas from southern California is in his mid-thirties, likes sailing and bluegrass music, hates football and techno beats. He calls his political views 'hardline' but also thinks he is a 'classical liberal'. He says he likes 'serious women, certainly women [sic], very feminine'. Lucas addresses me as 'sister' and explains that 'women of French extraction' disproportionally capture his interest. To him, the most valued feminine character trait is 'demureness'. 'I do admire French and honor French culture,' he says and asks me if we can convert the conversation to text messaging.

Benjamin from the US is less impressed with France and asks me how I can possibly live there. He tells me about his last visit to France, how he saw 'tons of immigrants from Africa and the Middle East in Paris all trying to sell trinkets and stuff near the tourist spots'. He read history, so he likes looking at current events from the perspective of history. 'I see a lot of parallels with the modern western world and Rome just before Rome fell,' he tells me. 'All of that happened to Rome which led to their collapse: it wasn't a shift from Republic to Empire that made it collapse, ultimately it was inflation and cultural change from nationalism and pride to be Roman to a more tribal mentality and focus on the needs of the individuals.' So he decided to educate his peers on Rome and to sign up to the marines 'to directly serve our country's efforts in resisting the push of a culture that wants to destroy the West'.

'What are your predictions on what will happen? What do you want to happen?' I ask Benjamin.

'The best thing I can do to thwart this decline of the West is to do what I've always dreamed of doing – having a big family and raise my children well and with the best values. I want at least four kids, but I'd like to have six. What about you? How many children do you want to have?' he asks.

Not six, that's for sure.

I know that Will wants to have at least four children too. I also know that Will is in his early twenties, owns a Jack Russell mixed with a Yorkshire Terrier and works in recruitment. And that he will be waiting for me in the corner of Côte Brasserie near the River Cam in Cambridge on a cold December morning.

My most conservative, innocent-looking outfit is soaked in rain from practising my French accent in an empty passageway close to the restaurant building (as well as the standard flight-attendant instructions). When I enter the brasserie, a young man, fairly handsome, in a black sweater on top of a white shirt is waving at me. He had insisted I send him a photo of myself before meeting. 'Ha it's just so I know who I'm seeing!:)' I chose a picture in low resolution to escape any facial recognition systems and removed all metadata before sending it to him.

'Good to finally meet you,' he says. His smile is timid but friendly. Apart from his politics he seems perfectly normal.

'So you're from near Cambridge?' I ask.

'Yes, it's a lovely little conservative town,' he replies. 'No immigrants there, but this might change. You can already see the changes creeping in on the countryside. In a few years it will look like London.' He despises London for its liberal mindset and its cultural diversity. 'At least in my area all of my friends are right-wing too.'

Will gets a chocolate croissant and we order some English breakfast tea. 'The perfect mix of French and English culture,' I say. Mixing those is okay to Will. He is proud to be European and tells me he wishes for Europe to remain European. 'You sound quite pro-Europe – how did you vote in the referendum?' I ask.

'Oh, um, I appreciate European culture but I'd still rather leave.'

He describes himself as a white nationalist and says he likes traditional values and dislikes degeneracy. 'White identity is very important to me. I guess I would hope to find someone who shares those morals and views.' Ideally, he wants to be in a marriage based on Christian values, although he admits to being agnostic. 'I love Christian values and would always look to apply them to my life and marriage, regardless of whether or not I have faith. Maybe one day I will find faith.'

'How did you end up on WASP Love?' I ask.

He tells me that he simply googled 'dating site for whites', as he was looking for a place to find like-minded potential partners, something the 'mainstream' dating apps don't necessarily offer. 'I'm sure it's gonna get much bigger,' he tells me. 'As more people start to realise that we're doomed, they will come to places like this.'

'Have you met anyone else yet over WASP Love?' I ask.

He looks down, a little embarrassed. 'Not in person, no. But it's good to connect with people from across the world there.'

We agree that Cambridge is a lovely place. 'Even with the rain, even with all the liberal students,' he says. He suggests we go for a walk after the tea but I tell him that I'm too cold and have to go back to the hotel. He puts on his Hollister jacket and we walk together towards his car. 'So when will you be back?' Never, at least not as Claire.

Others had more successful dates. 'I want to announce that I met my wonderful husband here on WASP.LOVE!' one user writes. 'I am thrilled and so very happy. Do not give up hope [...] Your other half is looking for you. God bless you all!'

WASP Love is only one of many alt-dating sites: for example, there are also White Date for European Singles and Trump Singles or Farmers Only for Americans. The motto of Trump Singles is 'Making Dating Great Again', while the promotion of White Date says: 'We follow classic roles where strong men take the lead and graceful women play the game.' White Date even asks you for your IQ and your personality type when you sign up. It lets you filter partners according to your hair-colour preferences, from Rapunzel to Venetian blonde – what a spectrum! You can also choose preferred ancestry markers – from Afrikaner, a South African ethnic group that descended from Dutch settlers, to Welsh and Cornish. Having said that, there are only a total of eight Welsh and Cornish men between the age eighteen and eighty on the app.

Generation Identity developed its own encrypted application that has been dubbed 'Tinder for Nazis'. But the app, called Patriot Peer, is about more than dating. It is about connecting white nationalists in romantic and non-romantic ways. 'No one knows what the person sitting next to you on the bus, in a café or at university is like,' writes an Identitarian on Telegram to promote the app. 'In a faceless crowd, patriots don't stick out.' The goal of the Identitarian tool is 'to motivate users to network and work together for a patriotic turning point'.[2] Taking part in patriotic events and connecting with fellow Identitarian sympathisers is rewarded with social credits; you can become the perfect patriot. 'This App will disrupt the firewall of fear. It features a radar for Patriots, and a gamification for activism.'[3] The AltRight.com website of American white nationalist Richard Spencer featured a special profile of Patriot Peer to promote the app internationally.[4]

Alt-dating is just one dimension of an emerging alternative online universe created by and for extremists. Harsher anti-hate-speech measures imposed by mainstream social media companies like Facebook and Twitter have provoked extremists to move to other platforms and establish substitute channels to network, coordinate and crowdsource their activities. Many controversial activists – on the right, the left and the religious extremist fringes – have moved to alternative platforms:

> I'd rather have Putin have my data than one of those SJW [Social Justice Warriors] in Silicon Valley
>
> Generation Identity leader Martin Sellner,
> spring 2018

Extremists who were kicked off popular social media due to their violent language have replaced Twitter with Gab, Facebook with VK or Minds, and Patreon with Hatreon. Gab, the alt-right's Twitter equivalent, gained over 400,000 users in just eighteen months. While on Metapedia the Holocaust only took place according to 'politically correct history', BitChute, DTube and PewTube offer 'censorship-free alternatives' to YouTube, attracting in particular conspiracy theorists and Holocaust deniers. 'I came to BitChute to escape JewTube,' one of the users writes after telling me that he believes 'YouTube is run by the Jews'.

There are three types of alt-tech platforms: 1) platforms created for extremists and used by extremists such as WASP Love and Hatreon; 2) ultra-libertarian platforms, platforms created by libertarians or commercially driven developers, which tend to operate in the name of free speech and tolerate extremist content such as Gab, Minds and 8chan; and 3) hijacked platforms, platforms created for entirely different purposes that have been hijacked by extremists but proactively work with the authorities to ban these from using their services such as Discord, Telegram and JustPasteIt.

In the wake of the Charlottesville rally in the summer of 2017, Twitter shut down hundreds of white supremacist accounts, the gaming app Discord closed several related channels and the world's most prominent neo-Nazi webpage Daily Stormer received twenty-four hours' notice before losing its domain. A #DailyStormerNeverDies campaign was sparked on Twitter and a mass exodus started. Permanently banned users and libertarian developers have formed alliances and started a coordinated attempt to build a parallel social media ecosystem to put an end to Silicon Valley's hegemony.

'This is war.[…] The Free Speech Tech revolution has begun,' announced the Alt-Tech Alliance in August 2017. The movement self-identifies as 'a passionate group of brave engineers, product managers, investors and others who are tired of the status quo in the technology industry'.[5] Its members frame themselves as the sole defenders of 'free speech, individual liberty, and truth'.[6] Their unique selling proposition is that – unlike Facebook and Twitter – they condone racist, inflammatory and even violence-inciting posts: an offer that has made them an appealing place of refuge for extremists whose accounts were removed from mainstream platforms, but also for freedom-of-speech warriors who are upset with the take-down measures of the big Silicon Valley companies.

In the weeks leading up to the creation of the Alt-Tech Alliance, it was not only Charlottesville's neo-Nazis who faced a crackdown by the social media companies. Figures with more appeal to mainstream audiences, such as the prominent British anti-feminist YouTuber Sargon of Akkad, were temporarily suspended from Twitter, causing outrage among libertarians and some conservative sympathisers. Tensions came to a head when Google engineer James Damore was fired after he drafted a memo entitled 'Google's Ideological Echo Chamber', which argued that the firm's diversity policies led to discrimination against white male conservatives. The libertarians of the Alt-Tech Alliance seized the moment to write:

If August 2017 has proven anything, it is that we are in a war to speak freely on the internet. The Free Speech Tech revolution has begun. There is no more dancing around this subject anymore. Silicon Valley companies are being propped up with billions of dollars from foreign interests. They are extraordinarily hostile to any form of conservatism, populism, and nationalism among other ideologies. Their employees, executives, and their users are all afraid to express themselves for fear of being fired or shamed by a dishonest and disgusting establishment media oligarchy.[7]

They have picked a strong opponent. Facebook counts 2 billion monthly users, has purchased more than fifty companies and holds over 70 per cent of the market share. Sounds like a monopoly? 'It certainly doesn't feel like that,' Facebook CEO Mark Zuckerberg told Senator Lindsey Graham during his 2018 US Senate hearing.[8] His response raised much laughter, although it wasn't entirely wrong: there is indeed a growing niche audience that is exploring alternative solutions.

As the big tech firms come increasingly under fire – whether in the US Senate, the EU, the British Home Office or the German Ministry for Justice – non-state actors ranging from radical libertarians to extremist users spot a unique chance to woo away unhappy clients. The Cambridge Analytica scandal sent Facebook's shares tumbling[9] and caused thousands of users to participate in a #Deletefacebook campaign, which was strongly encouraged on competing platforms that welcomed dissatisfied users with open arms.

Even the most extreme users found ways of keeping their online presence. The account of the British terrorist organisation National Action is blocked on Twitter in the UK but can be accessed via a virtual private network (VPN). Whitesingles.com redirects to the neo-Nazi forum Stormfront. And the Daily Stormer is still live, even after being banned from literally every country's domain including the Chinese '.wang' and the islandic '.is'. No doubt extremists have been skilful in using tech to circumvent laws: from VPNs and redirect mechanisms to Tor services on the Dark Net and private domains such as '.name'.

If you engage in extremist activities, keeping your information transfers independent and secure is worth nothing if your money transfers aren't. 'Fintech is the solution!' one user on the neo-Nazi platform Stormfront euphorically explains to me. He believes that cryptocurrencies 'are secure, instant and anonymous'.

Using the decentralised, unregulated currency to evade traditional financial services is more than a pragmatic solution to extremists. 'It's also a political statement,' says American cyber-security expert John Bambenek, who built a tool that tracks neo-Nazi bitcoin transactions. 'If you believe the banks are part of the Jewish world conspiracy nonsense, well, then there are only two ways to make financial transactions: it's either cash or it's bitcoin.' Against this background, it is unsurprising that American white nationalist Richard Spencer labelled bitcoin the 'currency of the alt-right' long before the bitcoin craze started.

After prominent alt-right figures were banned from mainstream crowdsourcing platforms such as Patreon and GoFundMe, and blocked by online payment providers such as PayPal, Apple Pay and Google Pay, some switched to Hatreon. The alternative crowdsourcing platform was used to fund anti-democratic projects such as the maintenance of the world's biggest neo-Nazi platforms Daily Stormer and Stormfront and hacking activities of the white supremacist Weev (see pp. 217–26). For example, Weev received $1.8 million cryptocurrency donations to his visible wallet address, which was tracked by Bambenek. He may have accumulated additional sums in his non-public wallets.[10]

Likewise, jihadists have attracted large sums through cryptocurrency donations. A pro-ISIS group was even able to generate enough money to reward its 'cyber-jihadists'. 'We have exchanged parts of our bitcoins to equip the brothers who helped in our last missions with computers,' one of the group's members wrote in their private chat group in December 2017. On Telegram and the Dark Net, terrorists have increasingly called on their sympathisers to donate in cryptocurrencies.[11] For example, the Al-Qaeda-linked organisation al-Sadaqa campaigned for bitcoin donations in November 2017, while Indonesian ISIS leader Bahrun Naim used the cryptocurrency to transfer money to his followers.[12]

Bitcoin transactions, however, can be tracked, and wallets are easily traced back to their owners due to the highly transparent blockchain technology this cryptocurrency is built on. As a result, many extremists have resorted to anonymous cryptocurrencies such as Monero, 'which best maintains our privacy', as neo-Nazi hacker Weev put it.

From alternative social media and news channels to extremist messaging apps and cryptocurrencies, the changes that new media ecosystems are undergoing resemble those that are under way in the political landscape. The loss of trust in the mainstream benefits the radical fringes: an increasing number of users turn their backs on established social media outlets. On the one hand, there are those that quit social media altogether to express their discontent or disillusionment with the platforms. On the other hand, there are those that migrate to other platforms in protest.

Due to the network effect, every new user significantly enhances the value of a network, and every lost user exponentially decreases its value. This means that platform migration dynamics set in motion by takedown policies could significantly change the social media landscape in years to come. At this point, it may be worth asking whether we will see a decline of the big tech platforms to the benefit of their ultra-libertarian rivals. Have we perhaps reached peak Silicon Valley?

The creation of this parallel alt-tech universe is a dynamic that might challenge the hegemony of the big social media firms. In the long run, it may also change existing power relations on the internet and revolutionise the way our societies connect and network. One of the risks the emerging safe havens entail is the carte blanche they offer to those seeking to promote counterfactual, anti-science and conspiratorial narratives. A powerful way to incentivise individuals to network and join forces is to give them common riddles to solve and challenges to tackle. The next chapter will explore the transnational communities of lunatic and paranoid conspiracy theorists who do that well. It will also illustrate why the alt-tech empire provides a fertile playground for such movements.

8

Follow Q: Inside the Bizarre World of Conspiracy Theorists

Why, sometimes I've believed as many as six
impossible things before breakfast.
LEWIS CARROLL, *Alice in Wonderland*

A rabbit, a red X and an alarm clock. Follow Q down
the rabbit hole into a collectively imagined world so
massive that it can claim to explain the past, present and
future. Enter QAnon. [1]

Painstakingly kept records of celebrity bloodlines,
carefully curated news pieces and a lexicon full of sci-fi
Hollywood movie references. This is where new tales
are born each day, and where all classic conspiracy theories come together: 9/11 and 7/7 were inside jobs,
the deaths of Diana, Kennedy and Osama bin Laden
all faked, staged or lied about, the origins of HIV and
the existence of aliens hushed up by scientists and the
media. [2]

I find myself surrounded by tens of thousands of
QAnon supporters who believe that Trump is secretly
working to expose a paedophile ring involving celebrities and political elites who have covertly been running
the country for decades. Department of Justice special

counsel Robert Mueller, they assure me, isn't really investigating Trump. Instead, Trump is working with him, the military and the US National Security Agency (NSA) to expose a massive conspiracy of the Deep State. The Great Awakening is seen as a kind of enlightenment period before Trump finally launches the Storm to lock up all political wrongdoers, including Barack Obama, Hillary Clinton and her campaign manager John Podesta, in Guantánamo.

Conspiracy theories are a phenomenon that has existed throughout history. They have a range of functions. People have always wanted to understand the origins of their misfortune, ensure their safety and improve their image.[3] But scientists have concluded that conspiracy theories are more often born in times of societal crisis than in times of peace and prosperity.[4] In 64 AD, a great fire destroyed the city of Rome and left hundreds of thousands of its inhabitants homeless. Faster even than the flames spread the rumour that Emperor Nero himself had set the city alight. Nero, in turn, accused the Christians of conspiring against Rome because they hated mankind and wanted the world to end.[5]

Across Europe, conspiracy theories have massively gained traction since the refugee crisis in 2015. In 2018, the largest cross-country study ever conducted on conspiracy theories found that a third of the British, German and French populations believe that their policymakers are 'hiding the truth' about immigration. In Hungary where Prime Minister Viktor Orbán has been accused of fuelling conspiracy theories about the Jewish billionaire philanthropist George Soros and 'the global establishment', the figure was close to half of the population. Sixty per cent of Britons believe in at least one conspiracy theory.[6]

Studies have found that the internet is not just conducive to the rapid spread of tales and hoaxes but also fuels conspiracy-theory logic and culture. First, it democratises knowledge, thereby empowering internet citizens to conduct their own research and open-source intelligence investigations – even if they have no knowledge of source-checking techniques. Second, the online information overload encourages cognitive filtering and pattern recognition processes that distort reality. The human mind likes to find patterns in chaos and to complete information gaps in imperfect stories and visuals – even if the outcome does not make any logical sense. Visual illusions are a good example of this.[7] Humans have a tendency to make arbitrary connections between unlinked things. Scientists even have a word for this: apophenia. The term was originally coined by the German neurologist and psychiatrist Klaus Conrad, who joined the Nazis' NSDAP in 1940. While apophenia can be a driving force for creativity in arts or poetry projects, it can also foster conspiracy theories and gambling addictions. Third, the internet provides an outlet for collaborative fiction creation, thereby boosting alternative explanations for real-world observations – from political dynamics to natural phenomena.[8]

'Ready for the Great Awakening?' one anon (as QAnon adherents call themselves) asks me. To him, terrorist incidents are false flags, plane crashes are planned and diseases are designed to kill. 'Then follow the White Rabbit.' A meme in the chat room shows Alice in Wonderland taking the red pill – mixing Lewis Carroll with the Wachowski siblings' *The Matrix*.

Like investigative journalists and intelligence officers, the anons are collecting alleged 'evidence' day and night. Their sources of information and inspiration are cryptic poems shared by Q, so-called 'breadcrumbs'. Q, who claims to be a US military intelligence official with access to classified information about the Deep State's agenda, attracts a weird blend of far-right activists, Trump-supporting evangelicals, climate-change deniers and bored teenagers. They self-identify as 'bakers' who collect Q's breadcrumbs to prepare the 'dough' – a synthesis of (mis)information. 'We are here to find truth,' one of them announces.

THE PAINFUL TRUTH
- THE GMOS IN YOUR FOOD IS KILLING YOU
- YOUR WATER IS BEING POISONED
- VACCINES HAVE TOXIC FILLERS
- BANKERS ARE ORCHESTRATING WARS
- THE MEDIA IS BRAINWASHING YOU
- THE GOVERNMENT IS A CORPORATION
- PEDOPHILIA IS REAL AMONGST POLITICIANS
- THEY ARE SPYING ON EVERYONE
- GOVERNMENT IS DESTROYING THE PLANET
- THEY KEEP YOU SICK TO PROFIT OFF YOU
- THEY FUND BOTH SIDES OF THE WAR
- THEY SPLIT THE LANDS AND CREATED CONFLICT
- TERRORIST GROUPS ARE ELITIST GROUPS
- THEY CREATE FAKE TERROR ATTACKS

– THE ONLY TERROR IS FROM THE ELITE THAT MOST PEOPLE IGNORE

Since Q started posting in October 2017, solving enigmas has taken over the life of many committed anons, sometimes consuming all of their spare time.[9] 'Do we know when we expect the Storm?' I ask one hyperactive user called Andrew.

'The Storm is upon us now – the Yellow Vests represent "We the People of a global higher consciousness",' he replies almost instantly in December 2018. The populist protest movement of the Yellow Vests (or Gilets Jaunes) was launched in France two months earlier by a coalition of ideologically diverse citizens in reaction to President Emmanuel Macron's announcement to increase the fuel tax.

Apocalyptic fantasies can be appealing, as they offer a bridge between fictional tales and real life.[10] As the British historian Norman Cohn showed in his famous book *The Pursuit of the Millennium*, millenarian expectations of profound societal transformation often went hand in hand with social unrest in the Middle Ages.[11] The term 'apocalypse' comes from the Greek word *apokalypsis*, which means 'uncovering, disclosure, revelation'.[12] But it's hard to deny that the predicted disclosure has been delayed multiple times by now.[13] 'Lol, 5453 threads, and still no storm', one commentator wrote mockingly on the image-board website 8chan, which is used widely among far-right and conspiracy-theory adherents. 'The entire country is laughing at you Q losers.'

As the predicted disclosure is constantly postponed, the clash between imagination and reality can create cognitive dissonance, a feeling of mental discomfort. The incentive to reinterpret facts and reframe experiences tends to grow the more time and money one invests in the failed apocalypse.[14] Just take the Doomsday preppers who spend $6,000 on freeze-dried and dehydrated food cans worth around 50,000 servings in order to survive 'the inevitable zombie apocalypse', which televangelists like Jim Bakker, host of the American *Survival Food* show, predict and postpone on a weekly basis.[15] (Next to these zombie apocalypse kits the fifteen-kilo Brexit emergency boxes of chicken tikka and beef and potato stew look fairly reasonable.)[16]

Conspiracy theories, however absurd and counterfactual, can inspire dangerous real-life action. The thirty-year-old Nevada resident Matthew P. Wright, who blocked off a highway close to the Hoover Dam in an armoured vehicle in June 2018, had subscribed to the QAnon motto: 'For where we go one, we go all'.[17] Two years earlier, Edgar Welsh, firefighter and father from South Carolina and firm believer in Pizzagate – the QAnon predecessor conspiracy theory which claimed that Democrats were running a massive child-abuse network from their alleged headquarters at Comet Ping Pong, a DC pizza restaurant – opened fire in the pizzeria to free nonexistent children.[18] In January 2019, a QAnon supporter killed his brother with a sword because he believed that he was a lizard.[19]

'Military, we need a plan and must expose evil to light,' Max writes in late 2018. 'Can me and my pals Raid MI6 DVD & GO2 Offices in London ourselves please?' another anon comments. Max claims that he had a top-secret clearance during the Vietnam War. He is convinced that 'the elites' use voice and facial recognition on all of us to classify and monitor everyone. 'I hope the hell I am just paranoid,' he says. 'I do not believe evil is so easily defeated or stupid, unless Satan's IQ has declined significantly in the last 2000 years.'

Q's motto, 'expand your thinking', and his enigmatic research instructions help to keep apocalyptic beliefs alive in defiance of reality. A random sample of breadcrumbs from Q looks like this:

November 22 2017 16:52:24
3 sides form what shape?
Expand your thinking.
Re-read crumbs
Q

November 23 2017 22:21:46
What news broke
American contractors where?
Hanging from feet
Re-read dumps.
Why is this relevant?
News unlocks map.
Expand your thinking.
Q

November 24 2017 01:14:46
Who knows 'where the bodies are buried'
The map is in front of you.
Re-read.
Expand your thinking.
Purpose of time being spent here.
Q

Conspiracy theories often have obscure origins – some even start as a joke or prank. The Book of Q, an early collection of Q's messages, suggested that QAnon might be 'the longest lasting LARP (Live Action Role Play, aka prank)' in the history of 4chan.[20] Several media outlets and Wikileaks have also speculated that QAnon started as a hoax that got out of hand.[21] BuzzFeed even ran an article with the headline 'It's looking extremely likely that QAnon is a leftist prank on Trump supporters'.[22] Anonymous blames ohour1, a troll who was excluded from the hacker collective.[23]

There are a few hints. In the mid-1990s, a group of left-libertarian cyber revolutionaries and underground artists from Bologna set up the so-called Luther Blissett Project, named after the famous striker who played for the England national football team in the 1980s.[24] Since then thousands of artists across Europe and America have adopted the name Luther Blissett to stage media pranks and cultural sabotage initiatives. QAnon uses several references to the plot and language of the novel Q, which was published under the pen name Luther Blissett in 1999.

I join the task forces 'Weaponised Weather', 'Organ Harvesting' and 'Pedogate' on Discord. 'Is there anything that doesn't link to Clinton?' one member asks. Investigations are under way in multiple languages and across different geographies – from the UK, Sweden and Macedonia to the US, Russia and Mexico.

'How can I help?' I ask one of the moderators.

'I would like you to make reports to add to this server to see more information coming, especially Q-related, current events and telling the hard truths, even those the status quo won't accept. Are there any specific areas you might feel you are strong in?' Max replies. He is also a member of QEurope, QNN (an abbreviation of QAnon), Operation Name and Shame, Meme Warfare, The Freedom Fighters and several others. 'Such people like you are useful for spreading the information. Here you can join my server.' I follow Max into the QOffice. He explains that the news channel's bot already provides news from five sources, including Naturalnews, Southfront, No Agenda, Zerohedge and SGT Report.

'How much time do I need to spend on this?' I ask.

'No requirements for roles. You've got your skills, therefore you are allowed to use those skills. I'm more of an archivist.'

The QAnon archiving system, I have to admit, is impressive. QAnon adherents might be better sorted than some government bureaucratic divisions. I scroll through archive after archive of fake news, nonsensical graphics and absurd allegations, all numbered serially and categorised into different sections. Most channels link to other, more specialised ones – one just for YouTube news feeds, one for selected Twitter accounts, one for meme warfare resources. And in the midst of all these data collections and endless lists of abbreviations they even have a rhythm bot that posts music suggestions: Elvis Presley, Pink Floyd and Bob Dylan are among their 'music favs'.

Everywhere I look I spot the red X mark, which is meant to say 'We are being censored'. The symbol was originally approved by the Unicode 6.0 emoji oversight board (yes, there is an emoji oversight board) to signal a negation or warning but has been adopted by the alt-right to denounce the anti-cyberhate campaigns launched by Facebook, Twitter, Google and others.[25] In the world of QAnon, the tech giants are all part of the massive conspiracy.

You can sense the excitement in the QAnon groups. Joe is a man in his fifties who claims to have been 'so awake' since he was a teen. 'I love you all and not sure where I fit in all of this but I'm warming up,' he writes. He says he has been researching all of this all the time. 'I just felt led to join because I truly was happy to finally have people I could talk with because truly no one around me at work and home wanted to wake up.'

In the category 'bloodlines', the anons investigate the ancestry of everyone they are suspicious of: the Chinese Li family, the Rockefellers, the Kennedys, the Clintons, the Disney and McDonald's families, the Royal Family. 'The British queen is a descendant of Prophet Mohammed,' one anon claims. 'She is his 43rd great-granddaughter.' They believe that three families control the world as the Global Cabal of the New World Order (NWO): the House of Saud, Rothschild and Soros. Over generations they have accumulated wealth and control pretty much any powerful government, public and private institution you can think of.

'A healthy subconscious is the only real defense against their deceptions,' Joe argues. 'We're under THEIR control.[…] They are distorting language, per-spective and Truth […] blinding us to our heritage. Keeping us unable to even imagine that we are capable of astounding physical and intellectual performance.'

The anons believe that six news companies are con-trolling the entire information space: GE, News Corp, Disney, Viacom, Time Warner and CBS. 'Stop con-suming poison. Media lies and distortions cloud reality.

Chemicals in food and water poison the body and mind,' warns Joe.

What is better for us? Kicking up the THEM? Or spending our slave chits on the tools we need to survive and good wholesome food for our families and selves?[...] Many are capable. Which Ones will? STAND. Be the Hero of your own story. Until next time. What's in a name, My'Anon? Be Worthy. Patriots.

Joe suggests starting the day at 4 a.m. Eastern time, which is when the broadcasting day starts in the US. 'We need to have collected everything we need (evidence, sources etc) and get it to all MSM before 4am.' They structure the daily routine work into four-hour cycles with the following steps: 1) legal notice, 2) news, 3) prayer, 4) moderation rules for the day including banned topics and 5) the 'Presenter' gives an overview of what happened in the four hours. To stay in the group you need to be assigned a role based on a skills assessment in response to detailed role descriptions. You can be a Presenter, a Producer, a Scheduler Mentor, a Reporter Mentor, a Research Mentor or a Moderator.

'New QMap freshly baked. What do you think?' Joe shares the most complicated flow chart I have ever seen – Tokyo's metro map is simple visualisation compared to this. Arrows connect seemingly random words: Obama and Clinton arrows point to the words 'handkerchief', 'pizza' and 'cooking parties', which link to 'secret code language' and 'weird art' to 'Satanism' and 'human trafficking'.

When I was young I loved playing association games. You could train your mind to picture one idea that would immediately provoke the next image in your head. The more exotic the connection and the less likely the chain of thoughts, the more hilarious the story would be. But you always knew this was an exercise in fantasy.

'Interesting!' I finally respond, still fascinated by the amount of detail and complexity in this 'Cartography of the Globally Organized Corruption Networks'. The anons have found a way to connect the CIA and MI6 to the Rothschilds, the Vatican, Facebook, Hollywood, the Nazis, the Illuminati and aliens to explain not just the world wars, climate change and terrorist attacks but also vaccinations, paedophilia and cannibalism. Why opt for the most straightforward explanation for today's political dynamics if you can go for the most complicated one?

Conspiracy theories don't have to follow any logic, and their adherents might even believe in entirely contradictory claims. Research shows, for example, that people who believe that Princess Diana faked her own death also have a higher tendency to think that she was murdered. The same study found that individuals who think that bin Laden was already dead when US special forces raided his Abbottabad compound in 2011 are also more likely to believe that he is still alive.[26] These individuals possess what psychologists call a 'conspiracy mentality': if you believe in one conspiracy theory, you are also more likely to believe in other conspiracy theories, even if they contradict one another.[27]

People with fewer years of education are more likely to believe in conspiracy theories. If you know very little about a subject, you are more likely to have high confidence in your knowledge and judgement. This is known as the Dunning–Kruger Effect, or 'Mount Stupid'.[28] (Il)logical deductions can of course go on and on and on, rendering conspiracy theories bottomless: there are even conspiracy theories about conspiracy theories. To the Swiss-German historian Daniele Ganser the term 'conspiracy theorist' is a 'political battle cry' invented by the CIA – an unlikely scenario considering that Austrian-born philosopher Karl Popper used the term in 1940, seven years before the CIA was created.[29]

On 8chan, users can post questions to Q, as if approaching an oracle:[30]

What is the big secret in Antarctica?
Will stock markets fail?
Is Boris Johnson trust-worthy? And May good or bad???
Is time travel possible?
Is Mueller working for us?
Is Michelle Obama a man?
One time, Q and I'll shut up. Is ZOG/MARX both going down?

Some anons also get annoyed by hived-off conspiracy theories:[31]

Just to shut the Flat Earthers up, Q. Is the earth flat?
No. Q.
Is JFK Jr alive?
No. Q.

The success of QAnon is baffling. QAnon mutated from conspiracy theory on the fringes of 4chan and 8chan into a mass movement that has conquered mainstream social media channels as well as pro-Trump rallies. In 2018 alone, ISD's social media monitors identified close to 30 million uses of the word 'QAnon' across Twitter, YouTube and other blogs and forums such as Reddit and 4chan. On YouTube, QAnon videos often attract hundreds of thousands of views, and self-described bakers are in the tens of thousands, with offshoots in almost every part of America and Europe. QAnon followers have a significant overlap with the Reddit board r/The_Donald, one of the alt-right's favourite mingling hotspots, according to data analysis from the influential twenty-first-century news website Vox. In August 2018, a photo of the leading QAnon conspiracy theorist Michael Lebron visiting Trump in the Oval Office appeared on social media and sparked controversy.[32]

Even celebrities, like the actress Roseanne Barr and former Red Sox pitcher Curt Schilling, jumped on the bandwagon and helped to popularise it.[33] At some point, QAnon videos would appear first when searching 'Tom Hanks' on YouTube.[34] When you enter the words 'the truth about' in the YouTube search box, you can delve into a virtual universe of lies in which Sweden is full of sharia zones, vaccines cause cancer and Jewish bankers plot to take over the world. For years, political agitators like Alex Jones have been using the platform to deliberately spread lies. The host of the world-famous conspiracy theory platform Infowars repeatedly told his 10 million monthly website visitors that the Sandy Hook school shooting in 2012 was a hoax, an 'inside job' that was completely 'staged'. In 2018, he was sued for defamation by Lenny Pozner and Veronique De La Rosa, the parents of six-year-old Noah, who was among the twenty children killed in the shooting. As a result of Jones's claims they had become the target of hate campaigns and had to move house seven times.[35]

I have to admit, there is something uncomfortably thrilling about being a member of a secret community that creates its own universe of wildly assembled 'evidence' to explain the source of all evil. It's an escape into a world where you can focus all your attention on putting together different pieces in an important puzzle like in a Dan Brown novel. Any scientific finding becomes negligible, probability is seen as a redundant variable. This makes everything possible and nothing verifiable.

The first step for most anons is to build out the global network of Q, to convince more people to 'follow the White Rabbit'. The whole alt-tech universe is used for mobilisation: Q leaves his breadcumbs on 8chan, then the anons do the 'baking' and planning across Gab, Reddit and Discord. But they also produce viral memes and videos for Instagram, Twitter, Facebook and YouTube.

'Can you share this graphic with your social media network, please?' asks Raven in the British offshoot of the movement, Q Britannia. The goal of Q Britannia, I learn, is to 'give the people of the UK somewhere to network, share information, archive, and find ways to take back our country'. The administrators explain:

> The focus should always be on uncovering information that can be used to show corruption, and wake

people up. Q will, no doubt, reach the UK in time. At which point there are going to be some shocking revelations and bitter pills for all of us.

There is a practical side to combining different conspiracy theories – you can unite conspiracy theorists from all corners of the internet and boost the overall reach of the movement. QAnons have demonstrated considerable ideological (and logical) flexibility in their attempts to tailor their tales to different audiences. They have co-opted the Yellow Vest demonstrations and boosted hardline Brexit campaigns and Tommy Robinson protests. By injecting their conspiratorial narratives into these movements, they can leverage already existing networks and impact their political direction.

Since its emergence in the UK, the anons have strongly campaigned for Brexit. Members of Q Britannia accused remainers such as Labour politician Lord (Andrew) Adonis of having links to Satanism and not wanting the EU border to be closed due to his involvement in human trafficking. In an investigation carried out with ITV, I found that campaigns like #BrexitBetrayal and #StandUp4Brexit were paired with the hashtags of QAnon and the Great Awakening.[36]

A survey showed that Brexit and Trump voters were much more likely to believe in conspiracy theories about immigration than those who voted for remain or Hillary Clinton. For example, 30 per cent of leave voters believed in the Great Replacement conspiracy theory as opposed to 6 per cent among remain voters.[37] Although there is no profile for conspiracy theorists, they tend to significantly overlap with individuals who feel negatively impacted by globalisation.[38]

In the 1960s, the American historian Richard Hofstadter wrote about the prevalence of a paranoid style in the rhetoric of 'pseudo-conservatives' as a combination of 'heated exaggeration, suspiciousness, and conspiratorial fantasy'.[39] But today conspiracy theories are more numerous and more widespread than in the pre-internet age.[40] Online alt-right activists have become the new 'pseudo-conservatives', sociologist Andrew Wilson of the University of Derby argues. They use conspiracy theories in combination with hashtag activism on social media to bring extremist viewpoints into the mainstream.[41]

Online tactics to spread conspiracy theories are getting ever more creative. 'Regarding red pilling everyone – getting True Lies QAnon message out,' Raven posts in the Discord group, 'I was just thinking how many random people from all over the world use the live streaming Periscope app. During major discussions like we are having right now, how about many of us open Periscope accounts and broadcast our discussions out there – kind of like a RAID from us – all over the world.'

Some anons have created business cards and merchandise with Q slogans and designs. 'We'll need a folder for Q business card templates,' Raven writes. 'These are similar to memes, but card format, and with a link back to True Lies QAnon on YT, or a website, or a hashtag that gets them connected to the anons. I want to take one or two best designs and get them processed through Vistaprint.'

QAnon has not come only to the UK. There are also offshoots in Germany, the Netherlands, France, Sweden, the Balkans and other countries. The founder of Dutch

Leaks, a platform that claims to expose cover-ups of the Dutch and European political institutions, thanks the community for having inspired his Dutch-language Discord channel modelled on True Lies QNN. 'We can share our information and make our network bigger in this way,' he says. 'We are doing a lot of building plus advertising on social platforms to attract more aware people.'

Never before have extreme actors and movements been more internationally networked than today. Global forums and meeting hubs on the internet – whether for romantic encounters or collective detective games – have allowed fringe groups to turn into significantly more sizeable online communities. Their unique selling proposition is that they foster ties between like-minded individuals from across the world. Connections may be made based on bizarre commonalities, such as the belief in conspiracy theories or the desire to prevent an assumed extinction of the white race. Such networked online communities can serve as both gateways and accelerators of radicalisation. But most importantly, they enable regional movements to lift their influence on to a transnational level.

These global networks can then be leveraged for real-world mobilisation.

PART FIVE

Mobilisation

Unite the Right: Watching the Alt-Right Plot Charlottesville

'White shirt, khaki pants. Clear shields, black gloves, black helmets.' This is the dress code the neo-Nazis finally agree on. 'Bring your MAGA hats, that way if Antifa [anti-fascists] attacks us, we look like average Trump supporters,' Jason Kessler recommends to us, writing under his username MadDimension. He is the organiser of the white nationalist rally scheduled for 11 and 12 August 2017 in Charlottesville to protest the removal of the statue of Confederate soldier Robert E. Lee. I joined his closed Discord group in June with my American-looking avatar when I noticed that the event was becoming a hot discussion topic in the white supremacist corners of the internet.

Jason Kessler's goal is to give the digital alt-right movement an attractive offline face by bringing together its various sub-communities and other useful allies. Speakers announced for the event include alt-right celebrities like Richard Spencer, president of the white supremacist National Policy Institute, and Mike Enoch, who is the host of the anti-Semitic podcast 'The Daily Shoah'. They are given VIP status in the Discord group and used to promote the event within neo-Nazi circles. 'We'll get Richard Spencer to sign a copy of *Mein Kampf* and offer it as a prize,' one member of the organising team writes.

Half disgusted, half fascinated, I observe the discussions within the organising team: they range from logistical questions about shuttle-service information and available carpools to demonstration tactics and a so-called 'Antifa watch'. Over several weeks in the run-up to the march, members of the Discord group debate the best strategies for appearing normal and legitimate. They all agree with the words of the Daily Stormer founder Andrew Anglin: 'We want to hit the average. We want normal people.'[1]

Bainbjorn is one of the most engaged proponents of the normalisation-through-fashion approach. In the private chat room he posts swastikas and a meme that shows a Jewish baby being tortured, accompanied by the words 'No gas chamber for you'. But in public he wants to make a good impression: 'Optics are very important and the Nordic resistance is doing this the right way. If everyone shows up with their own versions of things we look disorganized and like common rabble,' he argues.

The organisers even urge people whose outward appearance is not appealing enough to stay home. The official rules for Unite the Right include:

> Look good: Dress in a way that's flattering, not in a way that makes you look like a clown or a LARPer. Remember you are representing our movement. If your appearance is seriously lacking (morbidly obese, disfigured etc – be honest), please do not go to the rally and instead spend the time working on yourself.

Masks, KKK hats and Nazi symbols are forbidden. We are advised to wear sunglasses and hats instead of masks, to only show flagpoles, signpoles and shields instead of guns, knives and batons. 'I like the aesthetic of shields, in general,' Bainbjorn writes. 'Optics saying that we are about defense. All of this is in our own defense. Until we're pushed too far.' The argument is that bringing a gun puts the whole movement and its cause at risk, that now is not the time for war, not yet. 'Whatever violent ideas we entertain on the Radical Agenda are not to be carried out here,' warns the Daily Stormer. '[…] If you try to start a revolution this weekend, it will not be the revolution you bargained for, I promise. If you want to prove yourself a warrior, show some discipline first.'[2]

Looking hip, proud and innocent has top priority in alt-right circles, since disguising and rebranding old ideologies by adopting modern symbols and styles is at the core of their strategy. Some call them crypto-fascists for precisely this reason. A recent study found that extreme-right groups strongly adapt their visual communication on Facebook to contemporary youth cultures. Since the 1980s, the far right has seen a huge aesthetic shift.[3] Images of women are no longer reflecting old gender-role stereotypes, like the trad-itionally dressed mothers of National Socialism, but rather 'idealised girlfriends' of modern-day youth cul-ture: they may wear anything from sexy miniskirts to oversized hoodies and skater caps, and usually have an ambitious workout schedule and an active Instagram account.[4]

The far right's obsession with aesthetics stems from the desire to look legitimate and appealing to more mainstream audiences. Fashion and lifestyle serve extremist movements as a gateway to their political ideologies.[5] This heavy focus on aesthetics is not exclusive to the far right. Like the alt-right, ISIS has modelled itself as a cool counter-culture and lifestyle brand that resists mainstream thinking while still adhering to the latest cultural touchstones.[6] Powerful brands capture the public imagination and build a community of believers around them. Story, creed, icons, ritual and lexicon are all key elements a brand needs to create emotional attachment to it.[7]

Combining all of these components, the Unite the Right organisers are skilfully building a 'we versus them' brand. 'We are not afraid. You will not divide us,' says their official Facebook event page. The obvious question is: how the hell did pro-Zionist counter-jihadists and anti-Semitic white supremacists end up joining forces? And why have palaeo-conservatives and ultra-libertarians teamed up now? The answer is: leverage. These ideologically contradictory sub-communities of the alt-right already know each other from pro-Trump campaigns. Yet this is the first time they bring their activism to the real world. 'A historic moment', as some alt-right figures called it.[8]

'It goes without saying that many of these groups have their differences,' the alt-right activist Hunter Wallace writes. But he explains why Southern heritage activists, the alt-right, white nationalists, anti-communists, cultural nativists, trolls and patriots should unite. By joining forces against their common enemies online and offline, he says, they can be stronger. 'The Right can push the Left aside in the streets and break the spell of political correctness in mass social media spectacles. We can summon the culture war from online spaces into the streets and win that fight.'[9] The Daily Stormer echoed this idea: 'We need to do everything we can to get as many people to attend this rally as possible. Whatever differences we have with whoever will be there is irrelevant. This is about making a statement.'[10]

Despite the organisers' efforts to create a convincing 'united right' brand, ideological differences between the different far-right communities resurface regularly. 'Separate is beautiful,' writes one white separatist in the group and posts a rainbow flag that says 'every race deserves a safe space'. 'WTF? No!' a white supremacist complains. 'We accept the rainbow flag because the colours are separate,' the other one replies. Meanwhile some cultural nativists and ultra-libertarians, like the Vice Media co-founder turned far-right vlogger Gavin McInnes, try to convince the organisers to reframe the rally around freedom of speech instead of white identity.

To reach the various sub-cultures, the event organisers prepare campaigns that tailor their messaging to different target audiences across the ideological spectrum. They heavily promote the event across Facebook, Twitter, 4chan and Reddit and on far-right websites and forums, but the tone and narratives of the propaganda changes depending on the platform. More mainstream audiences are targeted with messages around issues of identity, heritage and free speech; on the more extreme side of the spectrum, advertising materials focus on white replacement narratives and anti-Semitic conspiracy theories.[11]

Nearly a third of the people tweeting in support of the march express grievances around racial issues, in particular perceived 'anti-white politics' and a 'white genocide'. An almost equally large share reveal grievances against the political left, most importantly anti-fascists (Antifa).[12] Antifa movements date back to the 1920s and 1930s when their members fought European fascists. Since the 1980s, Antifa groups such as Anti-Racist Action have confronted far-right activists, sometimes using militant means. With the recent renaissance of white supremacist movements, Antifa has stepped up its counter-action over the past few years.[13] Other frustrations voiced by Charlottesville online supporters are tied to freedom-of-speech infringements, the loss of Southern heritage and anti-establishment resentment.[14]

But this is just the tip of the iceberg. The real issue tends to lie somewhere else.

'Convo, how long has it been since the last time you went on a date?' Nikephoros asks.

'Four years,' Convo replies.

'No way. You're kidding me right?'

Convo got bullied and lost his friends for defending his girlfriend in high school. In his freshman year at college he then found she had been cheating on him the whole time 'with a 30 year old furry'. 'So five years no friends. Then four years no dates,' he concludes.

He is twenty-one, in his senior year of college in California. He plans on leaving California and getting a PhD. 'After that I'll have nothing to lose out on by being a nazi,' he says.

'Eh. Most of us in these groups have our careers on the line,' Pathos from New York writes. 'PhD is no different, I don't think.'

Convo's last date was not satisfying either. 'A 4/10 Asian girl who wouldn't stop talking about her relationship with her mother,' he writes. 'I saw her about two months ago and she really wanted to talk with me more but I said haha listen I'll call you. But I don't know her number. Kill me!'

'Don't wanna just bang tinder whores for a few years?' Pathos suggests.

But Convo responds that he doesn't like sex very much. 'It's not really a huge motivational factor for me.' He adds that he has a good memory, 'so I'll be depressed for months after slamming some slag'. After several of his online friends try to convince Convo to join social groups instead, like Ultimate Frisbee or men's bonding groups, he flips. 'I'm not a retard. If I wanted to meet people, I could.'

When feelings of loneliness and insecurity are blamed on external circumstances like political, cultural and societal trends, the real trouble starts. Personal struggles turn into collective ones, and collective conflicts become personal. Often the identity of individuals starts to fuse with that of the group when they share grievances or traumatising experiences with each other.[15] A perceived oneness with the group can then lead to a higher willingness to commit acts of self-sacrifice for the group's ideology, vision and honour.[16] This is how suicide terrorists are born – whether in the form of ISIS martyrs or neo-Nazi shooters.

As the date of the rally draws closer, I contemplate flying to the US to attend the march. But after a number of members inform us of the types of guns and rifles they are planning to take with them I decide against it. Not everyone seems to plan on following the shields-only policy. 'If you have a legal permit to concealed carry this should be fine. Check the local laws but Virginia is very friendly on this issue,' Jason Kessler reassures the gun enthusiasts.

White supremacists and far-right sympathisers from across North America announce their participation. Some even fly in from Canada or the US West Coast. Everyone who can't make it to the rally is urged to donate money.[17] The Daily Stormer proudly claims to have raised US$150,000 from over 2,000 contributors across the world.

On the evening of 11 August 2017, hundreds of neo-fascists gather on the University of Virginia campus. The mood on Discord is celebratory. The carefully orchestrated march yielded exactly the results the organisers were aiming for: newspapers across the globe showing the proud faces of white nationalists marching in the tiki-torches twilight, the hashtags and pictures of Charlottesville trending on social media. Indeed, the spectacle generated so much publicity that the tiki-torch producer felt the need to distance itself from the white nationalists to avoid losing its core business at family barbecues, pool parties and Hawaiian-themed restaurants.[18]

The next morning, around 500 protesters arrive at Lee Park, now called 'Emancipation Park'. Many are carrying Nazi symbols and semi-automatic rifles. The Traditionalist Worker Party, the National Socialist Movement, Vanguard America, Identity Evropa, the Fraternal Order of Alt-Knights, the Ku Klux Klan and right-wing militia groups – all of these concentrated in one place is a rare sight. Not all protesters are explicitly anti-Semitic, some are crypto-Nazis, others even pro-Israel. For example, counter-jihadist commentators like Faith Goldy, who was sent by Rebel Media, and Lucian Wintrich, the former White House correspondent of the influential American far-right website Gateway

Pundit join the protests. On social media, European Identitarians and British far-right influencers promote and cheer the #UniteTheRight campaigns.[19]

The official rally is set to start at 12 p.m. but at 11 a.m. the Virginia State Police declare the assembly unlawful and start clearing the park. The Mayor of Charlottesville announces a state of emergency due to an 'imminent threat of civil disturbance, unrest, potential injury to persons, and destruction of public and personal property'.

Online and offline you can sense that the atmosphere is getting increasingly tense. On the Alt-Right Discord server some outraged attendees and watchers urge the protesters to launch a counterattack on the police and counter-protesters. 'We move out, regroup, and come up with a more effective counter strike,' one protester writes. 'This is a minor setback at its worst. Make no mistake that this is concrete evidence that the Jew is terrified of us and they know that we are a real threat to them. We will never tire. We will never slacken. Hail victory! Hail our people!'

I log into the livestream of Tim Gionet (aka Baked Alaska), a white supremacist social media influencer. A few months earlier, the neo-Nazi activist had called on his tens of thousands of supporters to boycott Netflix as punishment for the release of the comedy-drama series *Dear White People*.

Shortly after I join the livestream, Baked Alaska gets maced in the face by a counter-protester on his way to the rally. I watch as his online audience is growing more aggressive with every minute that passes. Like in most other livestream chats that I'm monitoring, an increasing number of watchers are begging for violence now. Some are calling the protesters weak for not fighting the police and counter-protesters. Here is a sample:

FUCK COPS ANTIFA NIGGERS AND KIKES!
KILL YOURSELF SHITSKIN
These thugs need to be stopped
BURN ALL NIGGERS
hang em again
THIS IS WAR
DEATH TO ANTIFA
SMASH ENEMY TRANSPoRT
THE COMMIES AND NIGGERS WANT WAR, THEN LET'S GET SERIOUS AND GIVE IT TO THEM
HANG THE NIGGER FOLLOWING YOU
This is weak
NIGGERS ARE WINNING, LETS BE HONEST
i think it's time you stop being nice and start a fucking riot you pussies
your a fucktard
This is Cucksville
SOMETIMES VIOLENCE HAS TO BE MET WITH VIOLENCE! FUCK EM UP!
DEATH TO THE NIGGERS
ITS TIME TO KILL THE ENEMIES OF THE WHITE RACE IF THATS NOT OBVIOUS
need the Blues Brothers to come run these cunts over
KILL ANTIFA!

Shortly afterwards, at around 1.45 p.m., protester James Alex Fields accelerates and drives his car into a crowd of counter-protesters. A 32-year-old woman named

Heather Heyer is killed and nineteen other people are left injured. 'If you're not outraged, you're not paying attention,' read Heather Heyer's last public Facebook post.[20]

While this was the most tragic incident during the protests, it was not the only violent escalation. DeAndre Harris, a twenty-year-old black man, suffered head and spine injuries after being attacked by white supremacists. He was beaten up in a Charlottesville parking garage by six men with a metal pipe and wooden boards.[21] These incidents illustrated how quickly online hatred and incitement to violence can translate into real-world action.

After the news of the car attack breaks, I go back on the AltRight Discord server, where a controversial debate has kicked off among its members. 'Do not be blackpilled by today's events,' one urges. He promises that they will 'hit back harder and repeatedly until the enemy is completely defeated'. Some joke about the incident, sharing pictures of cars with distasteful comments like 'Do you like my new car?' Others even glorify the attack. 'Whoever he is, he is a hero. I salute him,' one writes.[22]

The aftermath of the Charlottesville rally weakened the global alt-right. The attack caused major damage to their image and reduced the movement's ability to reach the average American. In the weeks that followed, most alt-right social media accounts and Discord servers were closed down. At the same time, the rifts between the ideologically disparate sub-groups widened. Mainstream far-right influencers blamed the more extreme voices of the alt-right for the backlash against the entire movement.

Despite this, Charlottesville set a precedent for online far-right mobilisation. Its organisers and participants bridged ideological and geographic differences for the sake of impact around common rallying points. Attempts to unite all corners of the right-wing spectrum have since continued, including across Europe. The Right Wing United (RWU) server is one example.

RWU numbers 400 people when I join in 2018. The international group that was founded a couple of months after Charlottesville claims to be 'dedicated to bringing together conservative, traditionalist, and counter-leftist groups and directing them towards safe, sane, and effective activism'.

Its protocol outlines the group's guiding principles:

> We all agree with the legalization of firearms. We believe that we need to stand up to the loud and obnoxious minorities that oppose democracy. Social groups such as 'Social Justice Warriors', Communists and 'Antifa' are here to dismantle our nations from the inside. Western traditionalism has been forgotten. Moral values have been left behind, with modern youth culture promoting short-sighted primitive behaviour. With your help, we can start to re-install the values that made the western world great. Libertarians and nationalists, Atheists and Christians, all united alike. It is time to stand up as one big family, and say no to the left.

To find out more about the political opinions and aims of RWU members I enter the polls room:

> Should women be allowed to vote?
> 8 yes, 23 no.

Should men marry women younger than them?
28 yes, 5 no.
Are heterogeneous societies doomed to fail?
39 yes, 6 no.
Is it okay for people to be proud of their racial heritage?
67 yes, 2 no.

RWU is traditionalist in every sense: it is anti-abortion, anti-LGBT rights, anti-Islam, anti-socialism, pro-gun, anti-diversity. In the UK, most members voice support for the BNP. 'UKIP is good, but not harsh enough,' one writes. He goes on to argue that the current Tories don't even deserve to be called 'Tories' or 'Conservatives'. 'They are anything but that. At least on social issues and immigration.'

In the US, RWU policy is to keep backing Trump but not rely too heavily on him to push through the agenda of the movement. 'Trump is not going to save us. Only we can save ourselves. However, we should not demonise Trump if he fucks up or is unable to complete a goal.' Their estimate is that contemporary conservatism and nationalist thought is too much entangled with Trump. 'As such we should be doing everything we can to support Trump's public image and chance of winning in 2020.'

If Trump loses or is disgraced, they believe, nationalism and conservatism will have lost the battle for the hearts and minds of the public. For this reason, they plan to unmarry nationalism and traditionalism from Trump. Even if all goes well, Trump will only have six more years in the White House. 'We need institutions that will last longer than this, and that will not fail if

Trump fails or is taken out by external actors. In short, our movement is bigger than Trump, we can use Trump to accomplish some of what we want but the mindset of Trump making or breaking us is wrong.'

The model of society RWU is aiming for may be traditionalist but the tactics it is prepared to use are futurist.

Should we genetically alter humans?
12 yes, 9 no.
Should the internet be decentralized?
37 yes, 3 no.
Which social media platforms do you use?
Facebook: 27
Minds: 16
Twitter: 34
Gab: 24
Instagram: 35
Comvo: 2
Reddit: 22

The internet, social media and technological inventions are seen as a major boon to their efforts. By building meme archives, creating bot accounts and using the whole array of social media – from Facebook and YouTube to Minds, Reddit, Gab, Telegram and Twitch – the online movement is gearing up to launch campaigns and organise street protests.

The RWU political calendar features both far-right events and leftist events they want to counter. For January 2019 alone, they list the Political Meeting at St Kilda Beach in Melbourne, which escalated in violent clashes between protesters and counter-protesters, the March for Life and the Women's March, both in Washington DC.[23] The Conservative Political Action Conference in the US and the Finnish, Lithuanian, Belgian and Portuguese elections as well as the European Parliament elections are also on their radar.

Many elements in RWU's guide to attending rallies resembles that of the Unite the Right organisers:

> Remember that the way you present yourself does not only reflect on you, but on the people around you. If you show up at a rally looking or acting like shit, that reflects poorly on everyone else who showed up on your side, and even reflects poorly on your own values. Your appearance and behavior matter.[24]

Back in the RWU poll rooms:

> Is it possible for a political group or person to rebuild their reputation after their optics are ruined?
> 3 yes, 18 no.

Since Charlottesville, many extreme-right groups refrain from using Nazi symbols and fascist language in the publicly accessible channels. 'Some white nationalists carefully avoid the term supremacy.'[25] Facebook's training slides now teach its moderators to spot the linguistic nuances of extremists. This mirrors Islamist attempts to avoid detection through trigger words that feature on jihadist watch lists such as 'Khilafah' (caliphate), 'Kufr' (unbeliever) and 'Dar al-Harb' (the house of war).

The European Parliament elections of May 2019 rank particularly high on the RWU agenda. In early 2019, they start preparing materials for their influence campaigns.

> We decide to make meme contest on topic of Euroscepticism and nationalism. This May we have European elections in Europe and we need as much Eurosceptic memes as possible to share around. Best OC [Original Content] will be rewarded with money prize, how much depends how many memes will enter the competition and what's the quality of them. If you have any questions DM me, post memes in #activism instead of #shitposting-and-memes and ping my name so I save and rate it. I'll give you 1 month to come up with the best you have. GOD SPEED.

Each member of RWU is assigned a rank – from administrator and moderator to senior associate and associate. The community prides itself on being 'a fraternal organization, an extended family of sorts'. All of its members are required to join the battle and demonstrate loyalty to avoid being punished with downranking or exclusion. 'If your brother or sister is in true need of something you must give of yourself for their benefit.' To enable the army of campaigners to produce appealing marketing materials, the administrators share polls on favourite colours by gender and age group as well as psychological tips on the use of layout and fonts.

Political and economic turmoil raging across Europe is seen as a major window of opportunity by malicious campaigners. Far-right actors across the world have begun to co-opt mainstream protest movements against the status quo in an attempt to transform widespread anger into their own rebellion. RWU members view the Yellow Vests as a first step towards launching a so-called European Spring. The movement that originally started as a series of demonstrations in France against President Macron's fuel-tax increases in November 2017 saw both the political right and left descending into the streets, authoritarians and anarchists rubbing shoulders. This unlikely alliance was brought together by a sense of economic grievance and hatred of the political establishment.[26]

Even in its early days, the Yellow Vest protests attracted Islamophobic, homophobic and anti-Semitic crowds.[27] In December 2018, Yellow Vest posters and graffiti labelled Macron 'the Jews' bitch' and 'Jewish trash' and an opinion poll found that the most popular party among protesters was Marine Le Pen's Front National.[28] Online far-right groups such as RWU, European National and QAnon have been leading the expansion of the movement into other geographies. In the UK, spin-off revolts saw demonstrators blocking bridges in central London and harassing MPs outside Parliament in January 2019.[29] Some of them were wearing badges of the anti-Muslim groups English Defence League and Wolves of Odin. In Canada and across Europe, QAnon activists have added a pinch of conspiracy theory, with protesters decorating their vests with Qs. 'If they want a war we'll give them a war, let's give them a fucking war,' one protester shouted at a rally in London, while a woman was seen performing the Hitler salute at a protest in Leeds. Alt-right trolls on Reddit then turned footage and pictures of the Yellow Vest protests into memes to spread the message on mainstream channels.

Large-scale mobilisation can now be achieved within a matter of hours. It was early on a Sunday morning in August 2018 when the German-Cuban Daniel H. was stabbed to death at a festival that celebrated the founding of Chemnitz, a city in the German state of Saxony. Just a few hours later, after it had emerged that the arrested suspects were refugees from Iraq and Syria, 6,000 people from across the country took to the streets to protest against migration in the old town of Chemnitz. The demonstrations quickly morphed into violent riots. Far-right activists chased and physically assaulted migrants, and ten protesters were charged with giving the Hitler salute.[30] Protests continued in the following days and weeks, and violence against migrants spread to other parts of Germany. A few days after the initial protest, three men whipped a Syrian migrant in north-eastern Germany with an iron chain, seriously injuring the twenty-year-old man.[31]

Like the Charlottesville rally, the Chemnitz protests united different parts of the far right. Supporters of the far-right populist parties Pro Chemnitz and AfD marched alongside militant neo-Nazis and hooligans. Even members of the right-wing terrorist organisation Revolution Chemnitz, which planned attacks against politicians, journalists and left-wing activists, joined.[32]

But, unlike Charlottesville, Chemnitz was not planned months in advance. The protests happened as an ad hoc reaction to a news story. Even in the hours leading up to it there were few coordinated protest announcements or explicit calls to take the streets. Instead, mobilisation was largely content-driven: far-right influencers spread misinformed views while the investigations into the stabbing were still under way, inciting anger and indignation among their sympathisers. Many encrypted far-right groups on WhatsApp, Telegram and Discord wrongly claimed that two men had been killed and that the victims had been trying to protect women from harassment. Far-right YouTubers livestreamed speculative rants, using these pieces of disinformation. The Identitarian rapper Chris Ares was the number-one trend on German YouTube for fourteen hours.[33]

The smartphone era has given rise to new forms of large-scale mobilisation through livestreams and instant messaging apps. Social media, and Dark Social in particular, allows radical actors to turn trigger events into focal points for instant mobilisation. The German anti-fascist Amadeu Antonio Foundation called this 'management of indignation'.[34] The opportunities offered by livestream rebellion can take positive shape, such as the solidarity marches of #jesuischarlies and #noussommesunis in the aftermath of the *Charlie Hebdo* and Bataclan terrorist attacks in Paris. the#FridaysForFuture movement led by 16-year-old Swedish climate activist Greta Thunberg is another example of such positive online mobilisation. But they can also lead to hateful and potentially violent riots against perceived enemies.

The global far right's ultimate goal is to galvanise young people online into joining their 'resistance' against globalism and liberalism. To do so they build armies of tech-savvy and social-media-savvy agents of change who might set the scene for a dramatic tipping point in redesigning the political systems and power relations in both Europe and the US. Loose networks of radical activists use the whole spectrum of social media and online advertising tools to stage large-scale protests – both meticulously organised ones, as in Charlottesville, and spontaneously improvised ones, as in Chemnitz.

10

Schild & Schwert: Attending a Neo-Nazi Music Festival

East Germany. 9°C, rainfall. I'm standing in the queue for Europe's biggest biannual neo-Nazi rock festival in the small town of Ostritz at the German–Polish border. This is the second time Schild & Schwert has taken place. Earlier in the year, over 1,000 white supremacists from across Europe showed up to join the first neo-Nazi networking event here. It was held on Hitler's birthday, 20 April. The name means 'shield and sword'.

On the agenda for this November weekend are political talks, MMA (mixed martial arts) and rock – all Nazi-themed. I wonder which will be worse: the speeches by political activists such as Thorsten Heise, the militant neo-Nazi who is the vice president of the National Democratic Party of Germany (NPD), the show fights and martial arts lessons with Kampf der Nibelungen, who train for the final race war, or the performances of National Socialist (NS) bands such as Burning Hate, Painful Life and Terrorsphära with lyrics about the survival of the Aryan people.

'Yeah, we've been waiting for an hour now,' a short woman next to me suddenly says. Her green eyes are framed by black kajal on her waterlines, her ear holes as big as €2 coins. She introduces herself as Jane. 'I hope we don't miss Terrorsphära! It's so slow.' The tip of her right shoe is impatiently scratching at the surface of the pavement. Her trainers feature a prominent 'N', as do the shoes of the person in front of her and the person in front of that person. I look around to spot dozens of Ns in the queue.

New Balance shoes have become the favourite shoe brand for neo-Nazis, not just in the US. The Boston-based company is the only American athletic shoe brand that has not outsourced its production to firms abroad. After the brand's vice president of public affairs, Matthew LeBretton, told the *Wall Street Journal* that with Trump 'we feel things are going to move in the right direction', videos of New Balance customers setting their shoes on fire in a symbolic anti-Trump act appeared on social media. In the meantime, white supremacist movements seized the opportunity to hijack the brand, with Andrew Anglin declaring the shoes 'the Official Shoes of White People'.

My black Adidas skate shoes are the only item that make me stick out from the crowd. Otherwise I can easily blend in with my black leather jacket on top of a black full-body jumpsuit.

A man at the front of the queue is escorted away by the police. They seem to be taking everyone separately to a large parking lot on the opposite side of the road. 'What are they doing over there that takes so long?' I ask Jane.

'They are interrogating you and checking for weapons and stuff,' her friend Oli replies. He has more beard than head hair and is wearing dark blue jeans and a windbreaker.

'Weapons?' I ask.

Oli's bright blue eyes turn to me. 'Oh yeah. Well, some stupid kids brought knives here.'

'How silly,' I say.

'Yeah, as if we needed them inside, where we'll just be among ourselves. No outsiders can come in, no Antifa, not even journalists. We're among friends.'

'Well, the Romanians and Polish aren't used to that,' Jane comments. German NS rock festivals count as the largest international networking events for white supremacist groups. Even militants of forbidden movements such as Blood & Honour and its violent wing Combat 18, which instructed its members to keep death lists, operate in small cells and use nail bombs against migrants, were present at the previous event in April.[1]

'Do you get many international participants here?' I ask.

'Lots,' Jane tells me. 'The two in front of us are definitely not German, I think they might be English.' I hear them converse in a language that sounds more like Polish but refrain from correcting Jane.

'Oh look. Thorsten!' Oli cries, pointing at a tall, middle-aged man who is now led away from the queue, two policemen holding on tightly to his arms. 'I just hope the police won't have received my arrest warrant yet,' he adds in a tone that sounds half concerned, half thrilled by the idea that they might know who he is.

'Ah, I wouldn't worry, these police tracking systems are slow; it takes several weeks for them to update,' Jane says. 'Did you not run fast enough?' she jokes, giving him a wink. 'I usually run away when they try to get me. A few weeks ago, they tried to interrogate me.

I didn't even do anything, was just drunk and kicked a container on the street. So I just started running, wasn't too drunk after all.'

'Not this time: the police caught me, arrested me, questioned me and everything,' Oli says.

'What for?' I want to know.

'Bodily harm,' Oli responds, with a proud grin.

'I mean, what happened?' I ask him.

'Well, you know, bodily harm,' he repeats as if that says it all. For lack of words, I simply nod. Jane's wild laugh allows me to take a deep breath. As I watch her hands move around in big gestures to accompany her next police anecdote, I spot the pairs of hearts and diamonds that feature beneath two 9s on her knuckles: a 'German virgin' in Texas hold 'em poker. At least no '88', the standard neo-Nazi number combination that stands for the initials of 'Heil Hitler'.

More police cars arrive on the street in front of us; they bear number plates from all across the country. Some armoured police trucks and special units are on the ground too. At least I do feel safe, kind of. The German police are known for their ties to extreme-right movements. In 2011, it was revealed that many officers of the police force and secret services had been involved in the support networks of the terror organisation National Socialist Underground. Between 2000 and 2007, the group had murdered nine migrants and one female police officer and plotted a total of over forty assaults, including explosives attacks.[2]

'This is so annoying, I don't want to miss the start of the concerts. I took a day off for this,' Jane says. She works on the assembly line at a major German car producer. As a temporary worker it isn't that easy to get a day off when you wish to, she tells me. 'But I did it. Now we just have to make it into the festival!'

Behind us stands a pretty woman in her twenties with long blonde hair, wearing jeans and a black trench coat. The only thing that is special about her appearance are her bloodshot eyes. I find it difficult to watch the profound sadness these eyes are expressing and am anxious for her, until she is joined by a tall, handsome man whose looks are equally inconspicuous.

'Are you by yourself?' Jane suddenly asks, as if she hadn't noticed until now.

'No. My boyfriend is already inside. He didn't know they would stop letting people in.'

She nods, turning to her friend. 'Shall we go in as a pair?' I'm relieved that she doesn't suggest the two of us go in together, as I know that I will have to tell the police my real name.

'Follow me, please,' a firm voice tells me just at that moment. A policeman leads me to the parking lot where dozens of other policemen are standing and watching the scene. 'Any weapons or dangerous objects on you?'

I shake my head.

'Pardon?'

'No, I don't have any.'

'Do you have an ID with you?' I hand it over to him. 'What's your date of birth?' he asks.

'1991,' I reply. 'I mean 24 July in 1991.'

'Okay, I'll have to keep this for a bit,' he tells me, and when he notices that I'm shaking he adds, 'Sorry for making you wait in the cold but our internet is quite bad here.' Jane was right – the police systems aren't the fastest.

'Are you googling me?' I ask him, slightly alarmed. 'No, we just check if there are any arrest warrants against you.' I nod. 'Is this your first time at a festival like this?' I nod again. He grins. 'I can tell.'

I enter the festival grounds. The police presence is significantly less visible. I see only a few officers patrolling some outside areas. As Jane's friend said, 'we'll just be among ourselves' in there.

'Where do I find the main concert hall?' I ask two middle-aged men sitting at the bar of a little beer tent.

'You sound Bavarian,' one of them says, ignoring my question. 'We are from Munich.'

'I'm Austrian,' I tell them.

'Why don't you join us?' the man asks. 'This is the southern German corner here.'

'Which you are part of too,' the other one adds. They burst out laughing. I decide that this is not the moment to start an argument about the Anschluss of Austria by the Nazis eighty years ago. I'm more interested in their opinions of 2018 than 1938.

'So what made you come up all the way from Munich?' I ask them.

'Terrorsphära.' This will be the highlight of tonight; they start at 1 a.m. The hardcore band from Tirol was founded in 2013 and in five years has collected over 8,000 likes on Facebook. Its official music videos on YouTube attract tens of thousands of views.[3] Terrorsphära itself calls its music genre 'Non-conformist Brutal Beatdown Death'.

After listening to the two south Germans' stories about traffic jams and late trains, I turn to the girl next to us, who joined the men a few minutes ago. 'How did you meet?' I ask her after learning that she'd just arrived from Hamburg.

'At a concert last year. Since then I've been joining them for these events.' She pauses to take a bite from her burger before asking 'What's your name?'

'Anna,' I reply promptly.

'Hannah?!' she cries. A few people in the tent stare at us. Hannah is a Hebrew-given name, while Anna is usually the Christian version.

'No, Anna,' I reply, trying to stay calm.

'Good joke,' she says, now laughing. 'Nice name. It would have been such a shame if you were called Hannah.'

Roughly 250 neo-Nazis are now within the closed-off grounds. After talking to a dozen people or so I understand that some had come for the politics and others for the music or the martial arts, but they all share a sense of community. Apart from the fact that everyone is white, the participants are from mixed backgrounds: some are old, others look like they have barely turned eighteen. Some come from socially deprived backgrounds and work in low-paid manual jobs, others wear expensive brands and appear well educated. About 20 per cent are female, the rest are men.

Some of the people around me look like typical skinheads with shaved heads and fascist symbols proudly inscribed on their skin or printed on their T-shirts. Others appear so normal that you might come across them on the Tube without even taking note of them. A few of them look as if they could have key roles in politics or business: nattily dressed with fancy watches and neatly parted hair. These tend to be leading members of the extreme-right parties NPD or Die Rechte, both of which have sent speakers and flyers to the festival.

As I pass by the merchandise shops to take a closer look at their collections of NS-themed T-shirts, a vendor takes something off the shelf that looks like a model battleship. 'How about this German warship?' The price tag says €120.

'Ah, no thank you.'

He tells me that they've run out of all M and L size T-shirts. 'We had too many people wanting to buy the MMA shirts this summer – it was absolutely crazy,' he says.

I walk past the other shops with 'I love HTLR', 'Reconquista' and '88 Crew' T-shirts piled up on the shelves. There are even pillows and bedlinen with NS symbols.

'So have you made up your mind?' I turn around. A man in his thirties with neatly combed blond hair stands by the shelves. 'I can recommend this hoodie to replace your cheap leather jacket.' He looks and sounds like the kind of person who could have sat next to me in the business administration courses during my bachelor's degree. But Patrick Schröder is a well-known neo-Nazi in Germany who was convicted of performing the Hitler salute in 2015.[4] He is a regional leader of NPD and CEO of the extreme-right fashion label Ansgar Aryan, which he founded in 2008. By 2016, his online clothes shop had already grossed €460,000.[5] His T-shirts are even worn by AfD campaigners.[6]

'I think I'll—' I start.

'Oh, don't say you're coming back tomorrow. There might not be a tomorrow.' He walks over to me and hands me one of the catalogues. 'Here you go. Come on, the ladies' shirts are down here,' he points at a lower side table. 'The altitude of the table reflects my attitude towards gender equality,' he adds. Intuitively, I wait for the punchline but quickly realise that there is none. I walk over to the 'girls' section' of the stand.

Patrick Schröder seems to have left his 'nice Nazi' attitude at home today. Within neo-Nazi circles he is known as an image consultant and gives workshops to fellow travellers on how to be a 'nice neo-Nazi'. 'One has to train people so that they have a better appearance, not just the clothing but also how they come across.'[7] Partick Schröder himself tries hard to not be the stereotypical white supremacist. His label Ansgar Aryan falls into the 'nipster' category.

Extreme-right fashion brands live from doing their business in the legal greyzones. To circumvent the legislation that bans NS symbols in Germany, labels like Ansgar Aryan use slightly modified versions and invent new symbols that look similar but aren't covered by the laws. For this reason, neo-Nazi businessmen like Schröder love using code words, abbreviations and jokes to avoid prosecution. One of Ansgar Aryan's most popular T-shirts says 'HKN KRZ', which stands for *Hakenkreuz* (meaning swastika in German). 'You go beyond what's acceptable,' Schröder told Spiegel TV in an interview to justify the T-shirts. 'That's what rappers do, what labels do, what the left does as well. Anyone who wants to provoke does it. And that's the whole point of it: to "trigger" young people.'[8]

The word 'trigger', the use of satire and transgression to make extreme ideologies appear harmless: all of this sounds a lot like the alt-right. Indeed, one of Schröder's sources of inspiration is Richard Spencer, who regularly features on his online radio station FSN TV (FSN stands for 'Free, Social and National'). The background of Schröder's Twitter profile features a banner of the 'Unite the Right' campaign.[9] 'Our goal is the soft, painless and entertaining introduction to our political attitude,' he said in one of his Sunday livestreams. The primary target group for his influence campaigns are young people, so his key tool is youth culture: music and fashion.[10] 'If you want to reach young people then there's no point in speaking about World War II, so I'd rather speak about the last *Simpsons* episode or something. That's a lot more effective,' he told Spiegel TV.[11]

'How about this one?' He points to a female top that says *Keine Gnade* ('no mercy').

'No, thanks.'

Visibly disappointed by my reply, Schröder walks a few steps away. He shakes hands with a man in a 'Defend Europe' shirt before turning back to me. 'So, give me a hint. Where are you from?' When he learns that I am Austrian, he says: 'Oh nice, you have Martin Sellner there. He is great.'

'Do you know him?' I ask.

'Oh, we've crossed paths, yes. I've had a few beers with him.' I stare at him. 'Yeah, I know I shouldn't be saying this out loud here. People don't agree with Generation Identity. But I like their methods. I think they do exactly the right thing to have a real impact.'

Behind us, a group of well-dressed men are sipping their beers. 'I also campaigned for the AfD,' I hear one of them say.

'Good,' another one comments. 'It's not even worth voting for the NPD, not worth it. They will never make it. The AfD, however, stands a real chance.'

When I enter the main indoor concert hall, the MMA show fights are already fully under way. Two bald men in black clothes are groaning on stage, while dozens of people are watching and cheering. After every round, when the fighters return to their corners, the announcer takes the floor, urging everyone to join boxing clubs and learn how to fight. 'As Germans it's important to be able-bodied, to know how to handle weapons,' he says. 'We can also support you in this. Just get in touch – and we have really good contacts all across Germany – if you want to equip a room or something similar.'

As he says this, the moderator looks around the crowded room. Not everyone gives the impression of spending all their spare time in gyms and MMA training sessions. 'You need to get up off your arses and get fit. If you can't join a boxing club, then just rent your own indoor facilities or, even better, train on the streets.' He sees the war of cultures as inevitable and imminent. 'The earlier you get prepared, the better,' he declares. 'We won't have any other option in the end than to fight, so you should really start now.'

The MMA movement Kampf der Nibelungen also hints at the need to fight the prevailing system and liberal democracy. Its mission statement reads:

> While in most 'fight nights' across the country participation of the athlete depends on his declared belief in the liberal democratic basic order, Kampf der Nibelungen doesn't view this discipline as part of a foul political system but wants to establish it as a fundamental element of an alternative and mainstream it.[12]

Kampf der Nibelungen don't just have good contacts within far-right political circles and the football hooligan scene in Germany, they also have strong support networks abroad. The Russian hooligan Denis 'Nikitin' Kapustin, who speaks fluent German and once kept a framed photograph of Joseph Goebbels in his bedroom,[13] is sponsoring them with his extreme-right label White Rex.[14] He is based in Moscow and originally started hosting events in Russian cities like Voronezh, Lipetsk and Novorossiysk, but since 2013 he has been building a Europe-wide network of National Socialist hooligan combatants, sponsoring tournaments and weapons-training camps in Italy, France, Hungary, Germany and Greece.

Nikitin also attended the previous Schild & Schwert festival and I start wondering if he is also here today. '2yt4u' ('too white for you') is the motto of his brand, which also sells axes and knives in addition to T-shirts. His online shops and MMA events are heavily promoted on social media, where he proactively reaches out to football fans who want to get trained for combat, including in the UK and continental Europe. From instruction videos on YouTube[15] to event announcements on Facebook, this content is tailored to appeal to the tribalist mindsets and martial spirits of hooligan communities.[16]

Not everyone who has come here tonight is a hooligan-turned-MMA fighter. Later that evening, I find myself chatting to a tattoo artist from Romania. 'So if you want a tattoo, you'll have to come back tomorrow. We're done for tonight.' His friend from Russia just stands next to us, glaring at me. The Romanian tells me that it's his second time. 'I came here in April,' he says. 'But to be honest, this is not for me.' He seems to avoid my eyes.

'Why are you here then?' I ask him, feeling that I've met the first person that isn't completely mad.

'Work.'

'There she is!' a tall man shouts just at that moment, walking towards me. I cringe, about to start running, just when something brushes my back.

'Oh Michael!' a female voice shouts in my ear from behind me. I turn around to see the blonde woman with the sad eyes from earlier in the queue. 'I thought I had lost you to the police out there,' she says as he approaches. I sigh in relief.

When I walk back into the main hall, Fehér Törvény are playing. The extreme-right hardcore band from Budapest have been around since 1995. I can't make out a single word in the lyrics or any tone in the melody but the crowd seems to enjoy the aggressive yelling that even makes the heavy drums appear measured. A couple next to me are dancing wildly; she is wearing a police cap and rubbing her bum against his Ansgar Aryan jeans. I don't know how to dance to NS rock, so just stand there looking around.

'You look lost. Are you alone?' a man with a beefy neck and heavily tattooed shoulders screams in my ear. He looks like he's been doing a lot of MMA. Even his eyes reflect some sort of hunger for combat.

'Ah no, I came here with my boyfriend,' I tell him. 'But we had a fight. He left me standing outside for an hour.'

After some small talk he tells me that he is an NPD member but votes for the AfD. 'Strategically the only valid option, as the NPD doesn't have a realistic chance of getting in power.' Not an uncommon way of thinking among neo-Nazis, as I start to realise. 'We are all fucked anyways. It's too late now for politics to change any of this,' he says, grabbing my arm. He is wearing a White Rex shirt.

'What do you mean? What do you think will happen?' I want to know.

He is now not more than a few millimetres away from my face. 'We'll become a mixed race.'

'I see.' I say. 'How long do we have?'

He looks at me as if he hadn't expected to give a clear timeline for his apocalyptic idea of the future. 'Five years, ten maximum,' he finally replies. 'But it's been planned for a long time.'

I wonder how far I can go with my bogus naivety. 'Who planned this?'

I underestimated how quickly his paternalism could turn into aggressive impatience. 'Why are you asking all those silly questions?' His eyes have turned into thin slots. 'You behave as if you didn't know the answers to these obvious questions.'

I look down, a little scared now. 'I'm new to this … er … scene,' I mumble.

He calms himself, now pausing between every word as if he is explaining simple calculus to a schoolkid: 'We. All. Know. Who. Don't you? Kohl and Gorbachev.' In July 1990, the West German Chancellor Helmut Kohl travelled to Moscow to meet with Soviet leader Mikhail Gorbachev and seal off one of the most important deals in the history of the twentieth century: the reunification of Germany.

'How old are you?' he asks after staring at me a few seconds.

'Twenty-three,' I reply without hesitation.

'Well, you will see it all then. I'm forty-five and even I will still have to live through this.' He pulls me closer to his face so that I can smell the scent of beer. His arm around my shoulders tightens. 'Don't ever go outside on the streets by yourself, do you understand?' I can feel his breath against my ear. 'Women aren't safe any more out there.' How ironic, I think to myself, I don't feel safe in here.

I've had enough. 'I'm coming out,' I text my friend who is waiting in a car outside the closed-off festival grounds and leave without a word. My heart is still racing. If I found the Trad Wives easy to be enticed by, I have never found it more difficult to pretend to belong to a group of people than in the festival grounds of Ostritz. Meeting neo-Nazis in real life did not bring me any closer to their reality. Laughing at anti-Semitic jokes and dancing to white-power rock is simply not my thing. I find it hard to connect with them on a human level, to look past their ignorance towards their own history or to have even the slightest understanding of their ways of perceiving the world.

The only thing I do see more clearly now is how much the online space has revolutionised their modalities of mobilisation. It is so easy for a core group of radical actors to organise, fund and advertise large-scale protests and events. They sell neo-Nazi fan merchandise and hipster clothes online and crowdsource in cryptocurrencies to fund their protests. Their aggressive outreach campaigns tap into the internet's different sub-cultures – from the rechtsrock and synthwave music scenes to the mixed martial arts community. While their event livestreams, field reports and tailored ads reach the mainstream; the logistical preparations usually happen in the hidden corners of encrypted chat rooms.

In many cases this is also where attacks against perceived enemies are planned.

PART SIX

Attack

11

Black Hats: Trained by ISIS and Neo-Nazi Hackers

Like most people, I had no idea what to expect from a black-hat hacking course – learning to hack for illegal and malign purposes simply hadn't featured high on my list of priorities in life. It was hence with very little experience that I first joined the pro-ISIS hacking group MuslimTec in the autumn of 2017.

Bayyi and Mahed make it easy for newcomers. They start by teaching us the very basics. 'Your first goal is to learn how to find vulnerabilities in digital systems,' Bayyi explains in a Hacking 101 session. Most of the instructions are in English, but sometimes the administrators and certain members switch to German, French or Italian. I get the impression that Bayyi and Mahed are German, but they are good at keeping their identity concealed, even to their roughly one hundred students in the secret Telegram chat group. Most of the members seem to be based in Europe but use VPNs, proxies and Tor to erase any digital footprint.

The level of knowledge and competence in the group varies widely: from highly tech-savvy kids to complete amateurs like myself. 'Salam aleykum,' an instant welcome message from IslamTec says whenever a new member joins the group. 'Aleykum assalam ya akhi,' responds the latest novice with a friendly smiley. 'Do you speak Arabic?' he wants to know. 'Akhi, IslamicTec is a bot! It will not respond to your message,' another user responds drily, prompting virtual laughter.

At the top of our reading list is 'Searching Shodan for Fun and Profit', a guide written by Indian security consultant Sajal Verma to train cyber-security experts. Shodan is known as the 'Google for hackers' and can be used to find anything connected to the internet – from routers, websites and printers to security cameras, traffic lights and even petrol stations, power grids and nuclear power plants. Its geolocation filters allow users to search for items in specific geographic locations. For example, you can look for webcams in New York, wind farms in rural France or bitcoin servers in Iceland. In February 2018 it was revealed that hackers had made US$3 million in less than two years by exploiting Jenkins servers[1] and mining massive amounts of the cryptocurrency Monero.[2]

'Then look at these.' Bayyi continues the hacking lesson and shares a database of default passwords. 'You will need to practise. Go ahead and give it a try.' The username 'Admin' and the password '1234', I shall soon find out, are *much* more common than I would have guessed. Whether we talk about personal devices or public applications, far too many people keep their username and password in the default settings.

Mahed likes to test us. 'Let us see if you did listen. Can you become admin on this site?' He shares a link to a website of a property management firm in California. 'And one more contest! How would you become admin here?' A popular holiday resort in Matheran, India. I contemplate trying it myself but decide that hacking a website based on ISIS instructions for the sake of research would be a step too far.

'What do you want to learn about next?' Mahed runs a short poll, giving us options ranging from hacking devices to obfuscating your online identity. Some members have, well, very specific questions. 'I wanna hack some local porn website in Lahore, Pakistan,' one writes. 'Can anyone help me?'

It may sound surprising but internet pornography played a significant role in the successes of jihadist movements. After the birth of the World Wide Web in 1995, Al-Qaeda recruiters offered thousands of young men guidance and redemption for their sexual sins. Watching free porn, they would argue, was just one example of how their lives were being corrupted by toxic Western values. 'For every one hundred young boys watching Pornhub.com, there would be one or two who could be recruited into their ranks,' write former CIA agent Malcolm Nance and cyber-security expert Chris Sampson in *Hacking ISIS*.[3] Cyber literacy was a welcome by-product that these young members would bring to jihadist organisations, and ironically it often came from their obsession with internet porn and online gaming.[4]

'Okay, some of you wanted to know more about device-hacking techniques,' Mahed writes. SQL injections, he explains, are among the most commonly used hacking techniques. By injecting a code into a system, it allows you to take control of a database server. It can be used to steal and edit data or to destroy a database. Our teachers share a screenshot of a database, explaining that you could make the system spit out the following personal and financial details of its users:

- Full name
- Address
- Email address
- Payment-card number (PAN)
- Expiration date
- Card security code (CVV)

A few days later, a frosty Monday in November 2017, I spill hot coffee over the keyboard of my laptop when opening the *International Business Times* to check the latest news. 'Pro-Isis hackers hijack 800 US schools' sites with Saddam Hussein photo, "I love Islamic State" message', says one of the headlines. School websites in Tucson, Arizona; Newtown, Connecticut; Gloucester County, Virginia; and Bloomfield, New Jersey were affected. A pro-ISIS group operating under the name Team System DZ has claimed responsibility for the cyberattacks. 'The FBI is trying to determine who was behind the hack,' according to the article.[5]

In a public statement the host of the compromised websites, SchoolDesk, speculated that the attack might have been an SQL injection.

> Our technical staff discovered that a small file had been injected into the root of one of the SchoolDesk websites, redirecting approximately 800 school and district websites to an iFramed YouTube page containing an audible Arabic message, unknown writing and a picture of Saddam Hussein.

A few days later, the Prince Albert Police website is hacked as well, by the same group. Anyone visiting the police website that morning would find a page showing an ISIS flag and a message reading: 'Hacked by Team System DZ. I love Islamic State.'[6]

Back in the MuslimTec group, Bayyi has in the meantime shared pictures of the hacked websites in the Bloomsfield school district, which displayed ISIS recruitment videos for several hours. 'More hacked sites to come ☺ ☺,' he writes. 'What if next is not a school but a power plant?' Mahed adds. 'Darkness across the lands of dar al-kufr.' He shares the SSL certificate of Stadtwerke Borken, an electrical power company in Germany.

Just watching and studying the group is no longer an option. I contact the FBI and send a memo outlining my observations on MuslimTec. The school hacks were an example of so-called 'capture the flag' operations, nothing too sophisticated but bad enough to disrupt operations in public institutions, create significant financial burdens for private companies, generate worldwide attention and, most of all, terrorise thousands of families. Sending your child to a school that has just been hacked by ISIS gives you a queasy feeling.

'The Islamic State is the first extremist group that has a credible offensive cyber capability,' F-Secure chief research officer Mikko Hyppönen warned in 2015.[7] Al-Qaeda had attempted to recruit Arab members of the Anonymous collective, a loose community of hackers and trolls, but failed to develop a sophisticated skill set. Most serious hackers would describe groups like the AQ Electronic Jihad Organisation (Tanzim Al Qaedat al-Jihad al-Electroniya) and the Holy War

Hackers Team (Team Al-Hackers Al-Mujahidin) as amateurs who were at best engaged in 'cyber graffiti'.[8]

In 2018, the cyber desk of the Herzliya International Institute for Counter-Terrorism (ICT) warned that Islamist cyber terrorists have been developing capabilities and hiring hackers. The reorganised United Cyber Caliphate (UCC) hacker group also trained a group of female hackers. The group first focused on social network accounts before turning to cyberattacks against educational institutions and critical infrastructure.[9]

The problem is that terrorism isn't just about real skills, it's about perceived capabilities and about the ability to instil fear. 'Operation "False Flag" or how we trolled the Media!' Mahed announces in December 2018. 'We decided to take revenge on the stupid kuffar [non-believer] media by photoshopping a well-known tool named "SuperScan" into a magic dangerous Jihadist Cyberweapon. And just like we did expect the usual stupid trolls did buy our story.'

The combination of hacking and trolling isn't unique to ISIS. In March 2016, printers across US college campuses suddenly started printing flyers with swastikas. From the University of California to Princeton, students found pieces of paper saying:

WHITE MAN ARE YOU SICK AND TIRED OF THE JEWS DESTROYING YOUR COUNTRY THROUGH MASS IMMIGRATION AND DEGENERACY? JOIN US IN THE STRUGGLE FOR GLOBAL WHITE SUPREMACY AT THE DAILY STORMER.

'I cannot believe what just came out of the printer. Clearly, we need to further isolate it from the internet.

#racist #garbage,' tweeted Ed Wiebe, a researcher at the University of Victoria in Canada.

The man behind the hack, Andrew Auernheimer, who goes by the handle Weev, describes himself as a 'hacker and troll of fair international notoriety'. He used Shodan to find unprotected devices on US college campuses, a bit like the ISIS hackers. 'Capture the flags' and DOS (denial of service) operations are not just popular with jihadists, they are also one of the alt-right's favourite tactics. Most of these hacking activities were pioneered and championed by the Anonymous collective, whose motto was simple: no rules exist and the goal is to outthink, outwit and outhack your opponent. As an increasing number of Anonymous members became politicised, polarised and radicalised, some went on to become jihadists, while others turned to white nationalism.

Weev's blog piece 'Why hackers must become nationalists' calls on the hacking community to form alliances with right-wing activists. His video and pod-cast series iProphet attracted tens of thousands of weekly viewers for a period. In his first episode 'On Dead Celebrities', released in July 2009, he celebrates the deaths of Ed McMahon, Farrah Fawcett and Michael Jackson. 'God is destroying the celebrities, the prized celebrities of the media Jews, to express his dissatisfaction,' he claims. But celebrities aren't the only ones he wants to 'eradicate'. 'I want everyone off the Internet,' Weev was quoted saying. 'Bloggers are filth. They need to be destroyed. Blogging gives the illusion of participation to a bunch of retards [...] We need to put these people in the oven!'

In 2009, Weev hacked Amazon and temporarily deleted all gay and lesbian romance novels from the online shop, causing a billion-dollar fall in the company's stock price. The black-hat hacker said he wrote a script that helped him to find all gay- and lesbian-themed books. He then used invisible iFrames, which are normally used to insert advertisements into websites, to exploit the complaint feature on the Amazon website. This 'caused huge numbers of visitors to report gay and lesbian items as inappropriate without their knowledge', according to Weev. On Twitter an #amazonfail campaign was kicked off shortly after the incident and sparked calls for a boycott.[10]

One year later, he and his company Goatse Security were involved in an even more severe hack: he exploited a security loophole in the AT&T servers, obtaining the personal details of hundreds of thousands of iPad owners. Weev handed over the email addresses of numerous high-profile managers and public officials, including those of New York Mayor Michael Bloomberg and former White House Chief of Staff Rahm Emanuel, to a journalist at the American blog Gawker.[11] This time he got into serious trouble: the FBI issued a search warrant against him and soon afterwards arrested him in his home in Arkansas, where they also found cocaine, LSD, ecstasy and schedule 2 and 3 pharmaceuticals.

Eventually Weev was found guilty and sentenced to three and a half years in prison for identity theft and hacking.[12] On the day before his sentencing in 2013, he posted on Reddit: 'My regret is being nice enough to give AT&T a chance to patch before dropping the dataset to Gawker. I won't nearly be as nice next time.'[13] When he was released a year later after the appeal court overturned the conviction, Weev became the chief technology officer of the Daily Stormer. His first article, entitled 'What I learned from my time in prison', showed his bare chest with a swastika tattoo.[14]

Weev ended up moving to Transnistria, a Russia-backed breakaway region in Moldova, bordering Ukraine. He himself would give the story a different twist:

> The FBI framed me for terrorism and I was driven out of my job forever. I, however, did not maintain my silence and continued poking at ZOG, so in June of 2011 in retaliation for my lawful political speech I was kidnapped to a foreign jurisdiction and falsely charged with computer crimes. After I got out of prison on a costly appeal that left my life in shambles, I fled the United States as a political refugee and became a crowdfunded blogger dedicated to racial issues.[15]

Then the shutoffs started, as he would say.[16] In 2014 his became the first account ever to be suspended from the crowdsourcing platform Patreon. Soon afterwards his Gratipay was also shut down. He claims he lost his bank accounts as well as his PayPal and dozens of brokerages. 'They did their best to keep me away from any source of income,' he would say.[17] In one of his livestream AMAs (Ask Me Anything) that I joined, he told us that he was 'the world's most censored man'.

Wherever the hacker was, he kept finding new ways to continue his stunts and to receive funds. For a while Weev fundraised on the alt-right crowdsourcing site Hatreon, advertising his activities as 'fascist polemic, trolls, hacks, poetry reading, lulz'. By 2018, forty-nine patrons were supporting him financially with an average of US$532. This means that he made around US$25,000 just through this platform.[18] When the Daily Stormer lost its .com domain in late 2017, the hacker went on a podcast hosted by the Charlottesville organiser Christopher Cantwell, blaming 'the Jews' for the lethal escalations in Charlottesville. 'If you don't let us dissent peacefully, then our only option is to murder you. To kill your children. To kill your whole families.' He even planned to send Nazis to the funeral of victim Heather Heyer and posted:

> All I want is to see [Jews] screaming in a pit of suffering on the soil of my homeland before I die [...] I don't want wealth. I don't want power. I just want their daughters tortured to death in front of them and to laugh and spit in their faces while they scream.

But Weev seems like an incredibly broken and lonely person. In January 2018 he wrote that he missed America every day. He claimed that he could pay his bills and pick up women, but he doesn't speak any conversational Russian and misses having real discussions. 'My life is fucking hard,' he says. 'I pretend on video that it doesn't get to me because I have an obligation to appear strong and not falter for the youth, because video soundbites are what most of the public sees and I don't want kids thinking that my life in exile is total despair and I'm miserable, but it is and I am. I'm fucking lonely and I hate it.'[19]

I want to find out more about Weev, his motivations and sources of inspiration. After finding his email address in the depths of the internet in September 2018, I start typing up a message: 'Hi Weev,' then I pause, feeling a little ridiculous. How do you address a neo-Nazi hacker? And what do you write to him to not sound like a journalist? As so often with my avatars, I settle for a half-truth – as in roughly every second word in this message is true:

I'm a patriotic activist from the south of France writing a book on counter-cultures, transgression and free speech. I've been following your blog and would like to interview you, would you be free to chat over voice on Discord or Viber?

Name-dropping tends to work well, so I add:

I have been in touch with the YouTuber Nikolai Alexander because I've been trying to set up something similar to Reconquista Germanica in France (in case you've heard of them).

Weev has got used to people trying to trick him into giving away his whereabouts – journalists, intelligence officers and anti-racist activists. He is naturally afraid that I might want to track him down. I have to say, I'm not keen on the outlook of him geolocating me either, so I am glad when he writes back: 'I am happy to have communication with you but unfortunately there is no good way to have an anonymous voice conversation and I can hardly give someone from the internet a potentially exploitable rail onto a voip application.' VoIP (Voice over Internet Protocol) apps are technologies used for voice or multimedia communications over the internet. I wonder if he considered that risk when leaving a voicemail for a Jewish woman in Montana in 2016, calling her a 'fucking kike whore' and telling her 'this is Trump's America now'.[20] Weev's email concludes: 'If you have any questions I am happy to answer them.'

First, I want to find out more about his views on trolling and hacking. Does he think of those tactics as powerful political tools or is he just doing his tricks out of fun or boredom? To my surprise, he tells me that he doesn't care about metapolitics and counter-culture movements. He cannot find himself worrying about whether what he is doing is working or not, he says, 'though clearly, by any quantifiable standards, what me and my crew are doing is working – I don't know about you'. He just has 'a lot of fun pissing off kikes and making nigger jokes on the Internet. That's what matters to me,' he adds. Even if there wasn't any political impact? 'I would still do this if it were a fruitless endeavor,' he writes.

But he recommends getting in touch with his friend Andrew Anglin, who 'is big on reading Alinsky' and 'personally has achieved an enormous amount of success'. Saul Alinsky, the American father of community organisation and author of *Rules for Radicals*, inspired the campaigns of Obama and Hillary Clinton, who wrote her senior thesis about him. The left-leaning twentieth-century ideologue was long hated by the political right but alt-right campaigners have started to employ his tactics, perhaps more effectively than the contemporary political left.[21]

Weev tells me that he doesn't make speculative predictions on events he can't control, but speculating on the election victory and continuing success of Donald J. Trump was a good decision: 'It has earned me a literal fortune in bitcoin.' He explains that he does most of his business in bitcoin and some in Monero, which, according to him, is better from a technical standpoint. In contrast to bitcoin, it is non-transparent and transactions cannot be traced back. 'Less people are using it right now but I expect that this will change in the future,' he writes.

Weev continues to explain that he does not get his inspiration from previous counter-cultural movements and that he is not trying to build a counter-culture. 'I am trying to change the mainstream culture.' He tells me that he believes 'studying how previous dictators came to power is the most important thing as well as studying quantitative techniques from the marketing and advertising industries such as multivariate testing and choice modeling'.

Movements that greatly influenced him, he claims, are all from the hacking world: the early Anonymous 'pre-SJW/CIA subversion', the Phrack High Council, GOBBLES, GNAA, b4b0 and Bantown are probably big influences. He warns that to understand these you need to be a highly technical person and capable of understanding memory corruption exploits – hacks that allow you to modify the contents of a software memory. Then he adds: 'I'd also say Internet polemics from the late 80s and early 90s are highly relevant to me, but I don't really think they should be studied, as modern polemics are far more instructive and sophisticated.'

I tell him that I'm interested in learning how to hack and whether he has any tips. I'm not the first person to ask that, apparently. He explains to me that there is no way to garner deep insight into 1990s hacking culture, the heyday of hacking and the free software movement, as none of these communities exist any more. Most of the records surrounding them are technical in nature, he says. Becoming a legitimate hacker, according to Weev, is a difficult pursuit that takes most people over a decade of commitment. 'Not something you will find easy to do on a whim.'

In his How To, he lists the skills hackers should acquire first:

- Learn C.[22]
- Learn just a little bit of x86 assembler.[23] You don't have to be great at this at first, but you need to sort of kind of know what the fuck is going on.
- Work through *Hacking: The Art of Exploitation* by Erickson.[24]
- Learn JavaScript.
- Go through the big exploit archives. Start in the 1990s. Look through exploits. Figure out how they worked. Turn the clock forward to the modern era, so you slowly accustom yourself to newer exploitation techniques.
- Get really good at x86 assembler, and learn IDA Pro and OllyDbg.

Apart from learning these technical skills, he also recommends a range of infiltration and forgery techniques to get around security boundaries that cannot be solved with hacks alone:

- Get jobs that fill roles that you might find useful to compromise people working within in the future.

This means sysadmin stuff, helpdesk stuff, etc. Also, you can usually get into everything at a company just by being hired as a sysad. If you can talk your way into a systems role repeatedly, you don't need zero-days,[25] you can get given the keys to everything.

- Getting a job as a skiptracer[26] in the collections industry will give you access to datasets that will turbocharge your ability to dox individuals.
- Become a more competent programmer by submitting git pull[27] requests for fixes on outstanding bugs and desired features on well used open source products. Get a dev job.
- Try to talk your way into random restricted areas, and call up random support lines and talk them into giving you sensitive customer information. This is a hugely useful skill.
- Learn to pick locks and break into buildings that you have permission to be in (riskless if you get caught but lets you actually field test barging through locked doors and evading security).
- Practice credential forgery very often, just takes photoshop and a print shop.
- Read poetry, particularly 19th century stuff and really old epics, eddur, and sagas. Sounds weird but it gives you huge insight into manipulating people with language.
- For the same reasons, getting copyediting positions in advertising where multivariate testing is done is also a useful thing. Same with learning hypnosis, cold call sales, all sorts of things.

While the technical skills can be learned and practised individually, the second set of recommended techniques are impossible to carry out without a hacker crew who can divide up responsibilities, and share techniques and successes with one another. Some hacking attacks, such as sophisticated memory-corruption exploits, require multiple people, according to Weev. In this scenario, attackers would exploit bugs in the memory space of a computer to alter programs or even take full control over them. 'That's why it's important to form bonds with others and form a hacker crew,' Weev concludes. 'You need a wide variety of people working in concert to really get cool shit done. Like, if only one dude gets a job as a skiptracer in your crew then suddenly your whole crew has access to sick ass databases like Accurint that are limited to law enforcement and the financial industry.'

GenKnoxx has known the world of hacking since the early 2000s. The first time I saw her was in the back of a Thai restaurant in Washington DC in January 2017. Rarely have I been made more aware of my own gender bias than when I found myself staring in disbelief at a woman with short brown hair awaiting me with a cocktail at the hidden downtown bar. So she was the one who had briefed me on hacking and cyber security and sent me ISIS Telegram links for over a year? 'Whatever you do, don't link my real to my virtual identity,' was among the first things she told me. Her day job in the US government doing counterfeit investigations was anything but boring, but her night job was even more exciting.

'ISIS would want to kill me if they knew who I was,' she explains six months later when we meet in a small pub close to Victoria Station in London. She has just come back from her fifth DefCon, the world's biggest hacking conference, which takes place in Las Vegas every year. She wears a white hoodie and black nails; a little gorilla is dangling from her violet bag. In August 2018, the Cyber Caliphate vowed to kill Anonymous Hackers behind a campaign that took down several ISIS propaganda sites and social media channels. The internet jihadists photoshopped Anonymous masks on to orange jumpsuits, the standard ISIS prisoner clothes that make reference to the Guantánamo uniforms.[28]

A few hours later, I'm in the Black Heart, a crowded pub in Camden, with GenKnoxx and a bunch of DefCon participants. 'This weekend I'll figure out a way to "qwn" the Daily Stormer,' one of them shouts over the loud after-work chatter as we wait for the live rock gig to start. In gaming lingo, 'qwning' means to defeat or humiliate someone. For reasons I start to understand, all of them address each other using pseudonyms.

Like trolling, hacking isn't inherently bad. Hacking can simply mean to make 'unusual or improvised alternations to equipment or processes'.[29] For example, white-hat hackers of the French hacking community Le Loop or the San Francisco-based HackerOne security network test systems and perform 'ethical hacks'. Hacking isn't just an action, it's an attitude: to question every object around us. 'Anything can be hacked and everything should be hacked because everything can be improved,' Mitch Altman, the famous San Francisco-based hacker and inventor said, 'not just tech but food and art and craft, music, photography, video, software, science, ourselves, and we can hack society, we can hack the planet, the planet surely needs some improving.'[30]

'The international hacking community is a small world,' GenKnoxx tells me. According to her, there aren't more than 200 competent hackers worldwide with the capabilities you need to hack into critical infrastructure. 'I would say of these, only two dozen are horrifically dangerous ... in a way that no one can defend,' she goes on. 'They code faster than you can read. We are talking about kids that have been in front of computers since the age of six.' GenKnoxx pauses to take a sip from her pint and unlock her phone. When the screen lights up, she continues: 'They just see it. They can pull up any website, program or anything and they can scroll down ... fast ... and you watch their eyes go around, they spot a loophole and all of a sudden it's done.'

The South Koreans train top hackers, she says; so do the North Koreans, but they are not as good. The Chinese are highly sophisticated and the Russians try hard but don't quite get to the same level. The Israelis are much better at defence. They have some of the most resilient systems and cutting-edge protection mechanisms. But even the best defence mechanisms don't offer complete protection from hacking. 'People often imagine that you can simply build a wall around critical infrastructure,' GenKnoxx says. She compares cyber-security measures to rocks rather than a wall: there always remain gaps in between. To walk around the rocks and get to the valuable thing in the middle, you need the right equipment and you have to know the path, but in theory anybody can get in. 'You can never have one hundred per cent cyber and information security.' Even the Israelis admit that.

When I enter the headquarters of Cyberbit, one of the world's leading cyber-security firms, on the outskirts of the Israeli city Ra'anana, their vice president for Europe, the Middle East and North Africa explains: 'The mean time to identify a cyberattack is 206 days. It then takes an average of 69 days and US$3.8m to contain an attack.' Before joining Cyberbit, Yochai Corem was an officer in the Israeli Intelligence military unit. 'Robust infrastructure is the single most important factor, if you want to protect yourself from cyberattacks,' he tells me.

'State actors are much more dangerous than non-state actors like terrorists,' he says. 'Unless of course non-state actors are supported by state actors.' And state-supported non-state hackers become ever more creative. In July 2018, Hamas created a fake dating app to target hundreds of Israel Defense Forces (IDF) troops with malicious software hiding behind the stolen profiles of young women. In its so-called Broken Heart operation, Israeli intelligence forces prevented the honey trap from succeeding, but the app's mere existence exposed the new dangers posed by identity theft and hacking.[31]

Over the past few years, a range of fairly low-skill but high-impact hacks demonstrated how easy it is to exploit the vulnerabilities of infrastructure. The mass hack of the German Bundestag in 2015[32] was followed by the email hacks of Hillary Clinton's campaign manager John Podesta in the run-up to the 2016 election[33] and the Macron data leaks ahead of the 2017 French presidential election.[34] In 2017, the WannaCry phishing incident affected over 230,000 computers across the world using a relatively simple malware cryptoworm. High-profile targets ranged from national public services like the British National Health Service (NHS) and the German railway operator Deutsche Bahn to Russian government ministries and major international corporations such as the French car manufacturer Renault and the American logistics firm FedEx.[35] Ironically, twenty-two-year-old

Marcus Hutchins, who stopped the WannaCry epidemic (by simply registering its web domain), was arrested on his plane back from the DefCon conference a few months later for creating the Kronos banking Trojan, another mass hacking.[36] In April 2019, he plead guilty to creating and distributing the malware, which could mean to up to ten years in prison.[37]

Across the spectrum of cyber warfare, security experts are most concerned about chemical sites and other industrial infrastructure that process, store or transport large quantities of hazardous materials.[38] 'But even if you take down dozens of websites at the same time, that is a big deal,' GenKnoxx says. The next step is to intercept communications and extract data, to hack CCTV cameras or voting systems – something even teenagers can do nowadays. Emmett Brewer was eleven years old when he hacked into a replica Florida voting site in under ten minutes at DefCon. In August 2018, he was one out of fifty kids between eight and sixteen who managed to hack into an imitation of US election websites.[39]

Politically motivated hacks are becoming more frequent. On 4 January 2019, the director of the German National Cyber Defence Centre rings me in the office. 'Hi, do you have more information on the hacks?' he asks. I forward him more screenshots and messages from the Discord channels that the hackers frequented. The ongoing investigations into the hackers' identities are running at high speed, as the pressure to arrest the perpetrators is mounting. Within the next few hours, the hack scandal makes international headlines. 'Hackers Dump Data on Merkel, Politicians in Giant German Leak', Bloomberg writes;[40] 'German politicians targeted in mass data attack', reads the BBC headline.[41] It's a Friday afternoon and I sense that I'll have to drop my weekend plans.

In November 2018, Eva von Angern took a call from a colleague who informed her about strange emails he was receiving from her. Soon afterwards, she started receiving push notifications that her passwords on Facebook, Instagram, Snapchat and Pinterest had been changed. But von Angern, the local MP of Die Linke in Saxony-Anhalt, was just about to start a panel discussion about violence against women. When the panel was done, she couldn't log into any of her social media accounts any more. On Facebook, her account started posting anti-migrant messages to her followers and her Amazon account completed several purchases: an anti-fascist handbook, a drug test and a plastic penis, using her credit card details.

Von Angern wasn't the first victim of the hacker, Johannes S., who turned out to be from the far-right hacking and trolling communities that I was monitoring. Over the course of the year, the accounts of several German social media influencers were compromised – what they had in common was that they had voiced support for refugees or criticism of far-right internet culture. But the hacker had saved his most spectacular social media coup for December. In the design of an Advent calendar, he started leaking the personal details of one of his political opponents each day. As Christmas drew closer, the persons concerned became increasingly high-profile. While the earliest doors contained the private details and documents of left-leaning YouTubers, activists and journalists, the last few doors were reserved for prominent politicians, including Merkel and

President of Germany Frank-Walter Steinmeier. Some MPs learned that their accounts had been hacked only when reading the news. In total, at least 993 former and current politicians, 8,000 emails and 35,000 visuals had been affected by the leaks.

The hacks were a wake-up call to the German authorities and political actors: some were baffled that a twenty-year-old was able to carry out a high-impact cyberattack against the country's leading decision makers and journalists. It did not even require highly sophisticated technical skills. In most cases, all the hacker had to do was exploit security loopholes such as weak passwords. Whenever his target's protection was too strong, he resorted to hacking the accounts of their relatives or friends to access private chats. For example, the messages of the federal chairman of the Green Party Robert Habeck got leaked after his wife's Facebook account had been hacked. The hacker even managed to crack accounts with activated two-factor authentication by calling up the customer services of Twitter and phone companies to deactivate or obtain the two-factor codes.

Both political decision makers who neglected to install better cyber-protection mechanisms and the security agencies who failed to foresee such an attack share responsibility. After the Bundestag was hacked in May 2015 by the Russian cyber-intelligence unit APT28, also known as 'Fancy Bear', it became clear how vulnerable the parliament's IT system was. Back then, a simple UN link that contained a Trojan horse allowed the hackers to access the hard drives and mail boxes, with all their classified documents, of sixteen parliamentarians.[42]

This time the stolen data was less politically sensitive but highly personal. To the victims, losing control over credit card statements, private chats and pictures of family members was a humiliating and frightening experience. But beyond the personal damage the hacks caused, they were also an attack on democracy itself. Germany's Minister of Justice Katarina Barley called the incident a 'serious attack' designed to undermine confidence in the country's democracy and institutions. It illustrated the disproportionate power a single student – with limited funds and followers – can exercise over his opponents from his bedroom. Cyber weapons have allowed fringe players, even those that lack financial or human resources, to paralyse and disrupt political processes and business operations, and to terrorise entire countries.

Anonymity has made it possible for everyone to troll anyone, and easy for a few minds to terrorise many. To exercise that power, you don't need to be wealthy, influential or well educated, you just need to be connected to the internet. As the lines between trolling and terror get blurred, Russians and counter-jihadists can pose as ISIS, and ISIS can fake hacks. Regardless of the severity of the actual hack, sustained damage might be caused. Even smaller ideologically inspired pranks can affect the collective psychology. It is not the infrastructure that is most vulnerable to improvised alterations, but our heads.

There is little doubt that the new technologies that have benefited our daily lives the most are also those that put us at the greatest risk. Our own dependence on the interconnectedness of critical infrastructure has rendered us most vulnerable to cyberattacks. A world where our streets are not lit and trains are not running, where we can no longer rely on ATMs to reliably issue money or computers to safely store data, is not as far away as it seems.

In the past, the damage jihadist and far-right hackers have caused was limited to material and monetary losses. Most recently, hacks of political institutions have gone beyond this: they have entailed not just financial losses, but, more worryingly, a loss of trust – in democratic processes as well as in political representatives. And while past hacks may have led to millions of dollars or files being lost, future hacks could lead to millions of lives being lost. If terrorists continue upgrading their cyber skills, there is a real risk of more sophisticated hacks targeting power plants or self-driving cars.

At this point in time, though, it is the hybrid threats we should be worried about: the mix of cyber and real-world terrorism.

12

Gamified Terrorism: Within the Sub-cultures behind the New Zealand Attack

My heart is racing and I feel sick as I leave the office. I can still see the men and women collapsing one by one as they are hit by the rain of bullets, and I can hear those gunshots fired with the semi-automatic rifle.

I should not have watched the livestream of the mosque attacks in Christchurch, New Zealand.

'It's the birthrates. It's the birthrates. It's the birthrates,' reads the beginning of the 28-year-old attacker's so-called manifesto 'The Great Replacement'. His words are too familiar. I've seen them a thousand times over: from the Identitarians in Europe to the alt-right in the US, from the boards of 8chan to the private chat rooms on Discord. My undercover contacts with Generation Identity, the most vocal proponents of the Great Replacement conspiracy theory, weigh on my conscience now.

Over the coming days it emerges that the terrorist had donated to Generation Identity's Martin Sellner, as well as to the French Identitarians, prompting the security services to launch an investigation into his links to the Identitarian Movement.[1] Martin Sellner and the Identitarians had repeatedly told me they do not endorse violence. Yet I can't help asking myself if it hadn't just been a matter of time before the Great Replacement conspiracy theory would provoke violence like this.

The Great Replacement theory combines all four features of a violence-inciting ideology, so-called 'crisis narratives': conspiracy, dystopia, impurity and existential threat.[2] The idea is that Europeans are being replaced with racially and culturally distinct migrants (impurity) by a cabal of the global elites and complicit actors in governments, tech firms and media outlets (conspiracy), leading to the gradual decay of society (dystopia) and the eventual extinction of whites (existential threat).

As I start gathering all open-source information I can find on the internet to look into Brenton Tarrant's radicalisation pathway, I feel a mixture of sadness, frustration and guilt. Could the attack have been prevented? A few days before, Tarrant had tweeted pictures of the guns he would use. They featured the names of his role models, including the most lethal far-right terrorists of the twenty-first century, such as the Norwegian Anders Behring Breivik, who killed seventy-seven people in 2011, and the Canadian Alexandre Bissonnette, who carried out the Quebec City mosque shooting in 2017. Twitter did not detect the materials, and neither did any security services, as the visuals-only post escaped all existing text-based detection mechanisms.

When Tarrant announced the attack on 8chan, many users – including some of his online friends – did not know whether he was being serious. Even as his Facebook livestream began, commentators on 8chan appeared unable to grasp whether the attack was a prank or a real event. 'This is a LARP isn't it?' one asked. 'Not LARP, actually happening,' another replied. At the beginning of the livestream Tarrant says, 'Subscribe to PewDiePie,' the Swedish gamer-commentator and second most popular YouTuber. He then turns on the tune 'Remove Kebab', the Serbian anti-Muslim propaganda song from the Yugoslav wars that has turned into a white supremacist meme.

The Christchurch attack blurred the lines between trolling and terrorism. From the beginning to the end the terror spectacle was orchestrated to entertain a specific audience: the 8chan shitposters. Tarrant's so-called manifesto was dotted with jokes, language and ideologies that I have encountered numerous times in my research into online extremist networks. 'Well lads, it's time to stop shitposting and time to make a real life effort post,' he announced on 8chan. 'I will carry out an attack against the invaders, and will even live stream the attack via Facebook.'

His livestreamed shooting was an attempt to draw on the camaraderie within the far-right trolling community in the hope of receiving their applause, praise and respect. There is a sense of brotherhood and friendship in the attacker's last message: 'It's been a long ride and despite all your rampant faggotry, fecklessness and degeneracy, you are all top blokes and the best bunch of cobbers a man could ask for.' He then called on his viewers to spread his so-called manifesto and livestream, and to produce memes and shitposting content. 'If I don't survive the attack, goodbye, godbless and I will see you all in Valhalla!'

Christchurch happened as I was putting the finishing touches to this book. Usually when something significant and disruptive to your subject happens in the end stages of writing a book, you have to rethink, possibly even rewrite, major parts of the work. However, the attack in New Zealand felt like the culmination of all the observations I had committed to paper over the past couple of years. It was the logical continuation of the incitement to violence across the new alt-tech ecosystem, the real-world manifestation of the toxic online cultures described in previous chapters.

There is, of course, nothing new in the potential of extreme-right ideologies to provoke attacks. From Breivik to Bissonnette, we have seen similar ideas drive terrorism in the past decades. Yet policymakers and security forces have systematically underestimated this threat, investing their resources almost exclusively in the prevention of jihadist attacks. Today's statistics speak for themselves: in 2018, roughly as many far-right extremists as Islamist extremists received support from the UK government's prevention programme 'Channel'.[3] Germany now counts as many as 12,700 potentially violent far-right extremists, according to the latest report of the Interior Ministry.[4] And in the US, every single extremism-related murder of 2018 was linked to at least one right-wing extremist movement.[5]

What was new in Christchurch, however, was the escalation of gamification: the appropriation of gaming elements for terror, the use of violence at the intersection of fun and fear. Gamification – adding game elements to products, services or activities that have nothing to do with games – is a fairly novel concept. When Kellogg's first started putting little games as prizes into its breakfast-cereal boxes in 1910, the idea became an instant hit. By the 1950s, gamification as an employee motivator was born. The sociologist Donald F. Roy demonstrated how a daily routine game in which factory workers steal bananas leads to higher job satisfaction and productivity. A hundred years after Kellogg's gamification of cereal purchases, few employers, marketing agencies and political organisations are not using gamification to attract and keep recruits, customers or voters. Almost everything is gamified today, and that includes terrorism.[6] ISIS were among the first militant groups to gamify their propaganda: they photoshopped jihadi soldiers on to Call of Duty game ads and produced their own video games for recruitment. And it has escalated from there.

The Christchurch livestream quickly went viral. Facebook had to remove 1.5 million uploaded videos within the first twenty-four hours of the attack.[7] Glorifying memes, some calling the terrorist 'Saint Tarrant', others 'Invader Crusader', hit the extremist online echo chambers. Endorsements came in from far-right gamers, YouTubers and random sympathisers who referred to his attack as a 'Victory Royale'. Some gamers even turned his livestream video into a shooter game, displaying the scores and ammunition every time he shot another person.

On the Encyclopedia Dramatica I find an entry about Brenton Tarrant, starting with the words: 'INVADERS MUST DIE. Just when everyone thought the year would be shit and lacklustre, a new challenger appears.'[8] The article describes Tarrant as 'Master Chief Brenton Harrison Tarrant卐, a.k.a the Kiwi Kebab Killer', 'a heroic IRL JC Denton Aussie troll who took it upon himself to remove the Mooslem filth from a country whose existence was questionable at best'.

And then I stumble across a video featuring so-called 'Brentonettes', underage girls expressing their admiration for Brenton Tarrant. Some tell the camera that they want to marry him. I have seen many attempts to satirise violence and terror but this was just beyond comprehension. I honestly didn't know what to make of it.

Extremists and ultra-libertarians, who regard memetic antagonism and political transgression as forms of cultural expression, loathe the idea that the internet should be a serious place. They mock the suggestion that anonymous and pseudonymous websites need to be regulated like real-world market places. To them, the internet has been and will always remain a place of fun.

But after Christchurch some members of far-right platforms seem to realise that the racist memes were more than just transgressive jokes to many. In the days following the attack, I observe in real time how the dividing lines between those who were in for the trolling and those who were serious about the race war become sharper. While some react by encouraging copycat acts, others blame the toxic environment of their online communities for the attack.

Christchurch was a wake-up call for those who still believed in so-called 'digital dualism', the idea that the online and offline worlds are separate realities. The term was coined in 2011 by Nathan Jurgenson, the founder of the Cyborgology blog, and quickly entered the jargon of social media researchers. But attacks inspired by socio-technological dynamics in online radicalisation hotbeds increasingly prove that digital dualism is a dangerous fallacy.

Bridging the gap between the on- and the offline via features like geotagging, facial recognition and open-source intelligence (OSINT) gathering has been useful to any government, private company or digital citizen. But phenomena like doxxing and livestreamed terrorism expose the dangers that come with this new synthesis. Christchurch clearly challenged the idea that the internet is a separate place from the real world. It turned the virtual world not into an augmented reality but rather a degraded one.

As I enter the extreme-right group JFG World on Discord, a woman called Maria announces that she'll leave 'due to the fact that it's fucking up with my mental health'. Another user begins to share his thoughts: 'I don't even know where the fuck to begin [...] Why do people like you find dead bodies something to joke about?' He goes on: 'You think because you get to sit in your warm homes on a computer that you can just joke about horrible things like this? You are such disgusting bullies. Isn't it bad enough that people go through hardships of their loved ones? Seriously what do you guys really find funny?'

The first time I briefed counter-extremism units of the British Home Office about the dangers of shitposting, I felt a bit ridiculous. Warning government officials about some meme-posting trolls on the internet seemed rather silly, even in 2017 after their effects on the Trump election had become commonly known. But when I sat in the New Zealand High Commission in London to brief security officers, intelligence analysts and diplomats from Canada, the UK and Australia two years later, the threat felt chillingly real.

Everyone in the room was concerned about copycat attacks. Tarrant's so-called manifesto was designed to game the media and achieve maximum public attention. To journalists it reads almost like a ready-to-publish interview. But to his fellow far-right sympathisers, it is a mix of instruction manual and dark stand-up comedy script. His goal was to turn into the hero whose name would soon feature across some other terrorist's gun: 'inspirational terrorism'. A *New York Times* analysis revealed that at least a third of extreme-right terrorist attacks that had occurred since 2011 were inspired by similar attacks.[9]

In the days after the attack, I had seen far-right activists sharing translations of Tarrant's so-called manifesto on Telegram and the chan boards. One anonymous post on 8chan says: 'We have 3 languages already: French, Bulgarian and Russian. And we have German and Dutch translations on the way. Please, spread these everywhere you can. The entire world needs the fire of Brenton Tarrant ignited inside of them.'[10]

A few weeks later, in April 2019, a nineteen-year-old American named John Earnest opened fire in a synagogue in Poway, a city in Southern California. He killed one woman and injured three other worshippers. Christchurch was 'a catalyst for me', he wrote in the open letter he had left behind on 8chan along with links to a livestream. Once the post had appeared on the fringe image board, it was a race against time for the intelligence agencies. The FBI learned five minutes before the attack that a shooting was about to take place in Southern California. They had hints, but not enough to identify the man in time.[11]

The Poway synagogue shooter was obsessed with his European ancestry, quoting his genetic heritage in detail, like the members of MAtR and the singles of WASP Love. He emanated from the image-board trolling culture and was an active proponent of 'meme magic', like the members of Reconquista Germanica and QAnon. 'I've only been lurking for a year and a half, yet what I've learned here is priceless,' he wrote, thanking his fellow 8chan shitposters and praising the infographic redpill threads on 8chan. He believed that the 'global Jewish elites' are conspiring to replace the white race, as the protesters in Charlottesville and the neo-Nazis in Ostritz believed.

Earnest's posting history also reminded me of far-right terrorist Robert Bowers, who killed eleven worshippers during the Shabbat morning service at Pittsburgh synagogue in October 2018.

Before launching his attack, Bowers shared posts such as:

> Another kike who pretends to be white only when it suits their need to push genocide against Whites. Jews are such heathenish creatures. Their extermination cannot come soon enough. And it will come as more and more sheep wake up to their true intentions and who (((they))) really are. The synagogue of satan [sic] and his slimy offspring will soon cease to exist.

A few months after the Poway attack, 21-year-old Patrick Crusius carried out a shooting in a Walmart store in El Paso, Texas, killing twenty-two people. Shortly before the assault happened, the terrorist's post appeared on 8chan denouncing the 'Hispanic invasion of Texas' and calling for racial separation.[12] Then, in autumn 2019, a 27-year-old far-right extremist called Stephan Balliet carried out another shooting in the German city of Halle, which followed the exact same pattern: he livestreamed his attack, used 8chan insider-vocabulary and made reference to the Great Replacement theory. Similar to the wave of jihadist attacks that followed the calls for lone-wolf terrorism against Western targets by ISIS spokesman Abu Muhammad al-Adnani in 2016–17, the years 2018–19 saw a form of copycat terrorism taking shape on the far right: in the two weeks after the El Paso shooting alone, more than two dozen people were arrested under suspicion of planning to carry out similar mass shootings.[13]

Modern day far-right terrorists – from Robert Bowers and Brenton Tarrant to John Earnest, Patrick Crusius and Stephan Balliet – all frequented the same online communities, where conspiracy theories such as the 'white genocide' and violence-inciting language such as calls for 'slaughter' are pervasive.[14] Research found that belief in anti-Semitic conspiracy theories is a strong predictor for real-word hostility towards Jews.[15]

An analysis of 100 million comments on alt-tech platforms carried out jointly by the Network Contagion Research Institute and the Anti-Defamation League shows that anti-Semitic slurs have doubled since Trump's election on platforms like Gab and 4chan's /pol/ board. The n-word has also been used much more frequently since 2016.[16]

The document John Earnest left behind reveals that he believed in an impeding revolution, like Tarrant, like so many other far-right extremists I have introduced in this book. 'We are in the early stages of revolution. We need martyrs. If you don't want to get caught because you have children who depend on you, you can simply attack a target and then slip back into normal life. Every anon reading this needs to carry out attacks. They won't find us. They won't catch us. There are too many of us, and we are smarter than them,' he wrote.

Bowers, Tarrant, Earnest, Crusius and Balliet all subscribed to the idea that the 'inevitable race war' needs to be accelerated by staging terror attacks and mass shootings. To spark a civil war, they believe, you need to escalate existing divisions within society and encourage others to do the same. Tarrant wrote that he wants 'to add momentum to the pendulum swings of history, further destabilizing and polarizing Western society'. This idea is known as Accelerationism or as Siege-posting.[17] The book *Siege,* a collection of writings by the American neo-Nazi James Mason, has inspired many white supremacists to endorse violence. The US alt-right terror group Atomwaffen (meaning 'nuclear weapons' in German), founded in 2015, is one of the groups that used the book as their bible.

I take a look at my Telegram. There are dozens of groups that endorse this idea. For example, the administrator of the Right Wing Terror Center, a closed Telegram group that counts over 1,200 members, writes about the Christchurch shooter:

> This guy is a sign of things to come. In 2015 Dylann Roof got fed up with all the malice and abuse of Whites and decided to lash out in uncontrolled anger, killing a few blacks. Roof's actions are like the groaning of someone who is being woken up early in the morning. It's primitive and visceral. Tarrant's actions, by comparison, are fully conscious and on a whole different level.

He goes on:

> We are now at the beginning of the endtimes which
> last 10–15 years. The great crescendo to the ultimate
> collapse has begun, and we are hopeless to stop this
> avalanche. There is one peaceful solution, which is
> immediate remigration, but we all know that the elites
> won't have that. So here we go.[…] The warriors are
> being called to action and some are heeding the call at
> long last. As a White looking on to these events, I can
> only say that I feel relieved that they have happened.
> I have been reminded of the mortality of our enemies,
> and this is a great weight off our chests. Finally there
> is retribution and vengeance for the raped White girls
> in England, or the dead in France, the crushed in
> Sweden and Germany. A tiny modicum of justice has
> been done for the Whites lost.

It is surprisingly easy to find how-to instructions for
terror attacks. Anonymous accounts shared a manual on
8chan in 2018 that collated 'sanitised' excerpts from the
Al-Qaeda Training Manual and the *Mini-Manual of the
Urban Guerrilla* by Carlos Marighella, the twentieth-
century Marxist-Leninist activist who fought against
the Brazilian military dictatorship. The manual includes
a 'bomb-making intro', with an introduction to 'applied
chemistry' and 'bomb fuels'. I also find instructions for
terrorism, armed propaganda, liberation of prisoners,
execution, kidnapping and other forms of urban guerrilla warfare.

The explicitly violent far right continues to stay on
the fringes of the internet. But the ideologies and language that underpin their calls to action have long ago

reached the mainstream. Extremism expert J. M. Berger estimates that there are at least 100,000 Twitter accounts that support the American alt-right.[18] At ISD, we ran a 2019 Generation Identity Europe census and identified a total of around 70,000 followers of official GI accounts on Twitter, 11,000 members on Facebook, 30,000 members on Telegram and 140,000 subscribers on YouTube.[19] The volume of tweets around far-right extremist concepts such as the Great Replacement and remigration has greatly increased in the past seven years.[20]

Researchers who have monitored emerging trends in extremism are in shock after Christchurch, yet no one is truly surprised. The attack combined all the elements we warned of: alt-tech platforms turning into hotbeds for radicalisation on a global level. Identitarian conspiracy theories fuelling hatred and violence against ethnic and cultural minorities. Livestream functions on social media serving as a means for making terror go viral. Gamification and internet culture coupled with 'do-it-yourself' terrorism. And politicians mainstreaming the ideas that drive terrorists.

As I scroll down the news feeds of European election candidates, it becomes clear to me that we can no longer ignore the political dimension of the threat. In an attempt to pander to the young and online, far-right populist politicians have increasingly flirted with online sub-culture concepts, using references to their conspiracy theories, memes and insider jokes.[21] Our analysis at ISD found that Donald Trump was among the top ten most influential figures in English-language Twitter conversations surrounding the Great Replacement theory.

Far-right populists who sit in parliaments or head governments have played a crucial role in normalising, legitimising and amplifying the ideologies that drove the Christchurch and Poway attackers. In 2019 alone, we saw leading far-right populist politicians across Europe referencing the Great Replacement concept, either implicitly or explicitly. Many have adopted related language and conspiracy theories in their campaigns, such as the idea that Muslims are invading Europe to 'Islamise' and 'Arabise' the continent and turn it into a so-called 'Eurabia'.[22]

In April 2019, former Austrian Vice Chancellor H. C. Strache vowed to 'continue the battle against the Great Replacement'.[23] Dries Van Langenhove, the 26-year-old European elections frontrunner from the Belgian far-right populist party Vlaams Belang repeatedly wrote on social media that 'we are being replaced'.[24] Both politicians managed to win a seat in the 2019 European Parliament elections – H. C. Strache for the Austrian Freedom Party, despite a major scandal that involved him offering to sell the country's most widely read newspaper *Kronen Zeitung* to Russian oligarchs in return for campaign support; Van Langenhove despite revelations about an overtly racist and anti-Semitic chat group that his group supposedly ran on Discord.[25] Meanwhile, the French intellectual father of the Great Replacement conspiracy theory, Renaud Camus, withdrew his candidacy from the European elections following photos that emerged of one of his supporters posing with a swastika.[26]

On the day after the Christchurch attack, Donald Trump equated migrants with 'invaders', as Tarrant had done.[27] Hungary's far-right Prime Minister Viktor Orbán speaks of refugees as 'Muslim invaders' and former Italian Deputy Prime Minister Matteo Salvini claims that he 'halted the migrant invasion'. In Spain, the President of the far-right Vox party in Andalucía, Francisco Serrano, tweeted that 'along with the refugees are Islamic radicals who have been planning the invasion of Europe for years'.[28] The AfD in Berlin even featured the conspiracy theory on its campaign posters that said 'Learning from Europe's history [...] so that Europe will not become Eurabia'.[29]

The normalisation of violence-inciting ideologies poses new questions for extremism prevention. Should Twitter, for example, take down hateful or conspiratorial propaganda, even if it comes from democratically elected politicians? What if such content is posted from the official accounts of the President of the United States or the Deputy Prime Minister of Italy?

We have entered a new era of extremism. What was once fringe is now mainstream. Slogans of the extreme right have made their way into official campaign posters and election manifestos. Apolitical internet subcultures have turned political, while the political space has adopted the bizarre cultural elements of online communities. Fun and evil join forces, making it more difficult to distinguish between harmless prank and prosecutable crime. Where do you draw the line between freedom of speech and hate crime? Between citizen journalism and information warfare? Between trolling and terrorism? These are not just legal questions. They are questions that touch the very heart of democratic identity. How libertarian or authoritarian do we want to be? And how far can we afford to go – financially, morally, politically? What happens if we over-censor? How detrimental would the backlash against the entire political system be?

But equally, what is the cost of inaction?

PART SEVEN

Is the Future Dark?

13

It All Started So Well

As I wander down Webster Street in the small Northern Californian town of Palo Alto, I pass Victorian-style brick houses with generous balconies and creatively shaped duplex units with sculptural staircases and exotic trees. You can sense in the architecture that creativity and money know few limits in the heart of Silicon Valley. Palo Alto, which hosts the prestigious Stanford University, is home to the founding fathers of today's new media and modern communication technologies. The former house of Apple founder Steve Jobs is situated a few hundred metres from the homes of Google co-founder Larry Page and Facebook CEO Mark Zuckerberg.

Menlo Park, Facebook's international headquarters, is just a five-minute drive away. I enter the closed-off campus, immediately paralysed by the sensory overload. Are you hungry? Choose between authentic Thai curries, American burgers and exotic ice creams. Bored? Drop by at the computer game arcade to play Crash Bandicoot. Feel tense? Get a massage, join a yoga session or let an ergotherapist explain to you what you are doing wrong. Ran out of petrol? No need to drive to a service station; at Facebook the mobile fuel tank comes to you. The list of perks for the company's employees seems unending. There are few incentives to leave the campus, to eat out or to make new friends outside the Facebook bubble.

On Menlo Avenue, where accents and friendly looking faces from across the world meet in cheerful chats over ice cream, it is hard to imagine that this company hosts anything other than photos of happy families, yummy food and picturesque landscapes. The thought of extremists using its infrastructure to brainwash users, spread dehumanising ideas and call for violence seems surreal. But, increasingly, tech giants like Facebook have begun to realise that their platforms have been systematically used to hack people's minds.

Facebook failed to protect its users from personal data breaches and targeted manipulation, Twitter ignored the disinformation campaigns launched by fake profiles and bot nets on its platform and YouTube was reluctant to combat extremist and violence-inciting content. The Cambridge Analytica scandal and social-media-inspired terrorist attacks were among the many virtual earthquakes that have shaken the democratic pillars of the real world.

Cyber innovations have given rise to global networks of extremists who increasingly cooperate across borders to radicalise new generations of digital natives. If you asked Abu Musab al-Suri in 2005 what the jihad of 2020 would look like, he would have given you a surprisingly accurate answer: 'Leaderless' – 'no organisations, just principles' and 'by secret means, especially over the Internet' were the words the Al-Qaeda-linked veteran used in his 1,600-page manual on jihadist strategy.[1] Fifteen years and ten iPhone generations later, the internet ties together loose networks of extremists whose sole connection may be their shared enemies.

These extremist networks operate like rogue start-ups. In the vast market of ideologies, they occupy tiny market niches and the number of loyal supporters is negligibly small. Their goal is to expand into new geographies and reach traditionally impenetrable audiences. As early adopters of technology, they exploit new windows of opportunity provided by social media, big data, 'black box' algorithms, fintech and artificial intelligence. Their novel methods of radicalising sympathisers, influencing the mainstream and intimidating opponents change the nature of radicalisation and terrorism. They may also redefine our power structures, information ecosystems and democratic processes.

Today, no internet user is safe from radicalisation campaigns, and no election immune to foreign interference. An American schoolkid playing Fortnite in his bedroom may unwittingly become an agent for Russian propaganda, a Malaysian teenager can be recruited as a regional correspondent for ISIS fighters in Iraq and a German Facebook user commenting on a *Süddeutsche* article might turn into the target of a large-scale trolling storm. As much as the internet has speeded up daily annoyances like buying groceries, paying bills or sending out party invites, it has also accelerated criminal activities: you can steal personal data, spread disinformation or blackmail other users in a matter of minutes.

In coming years, newly released AI tools – so-called 'deep fakes' – could further enhance the professionalism of extremist online campaigns. AI can write newspaper articles and books,[2] generate pictures of people that don't exist[3] and manipulate faces in real time.[4] Such technologies could be used to produce hoax articles, create social bots, change footage and edit speeches. In early 2019, the NGO OpenAI decided against the release of its 'deep fakes for text tool' because its researchers feared misuse.[5]

Even without such sophisticated AI tools, we are already seeing the effects of the tech-savvy extremist campaigns. They have exacerbated political and societal fragmentation and accelerated the populist surge across Europe and the US. In pursuit of their envisioned models of society, culture and governance, extremists have opened a Pandora's Box of paradoxes: they sell a return to traditional power relations as female empowerment, build transnational networks to advance nationalist agendas and demand absolute techno-liberalism to spread anti-liberal views. Indeed, their visions are rife with contradictions or what their favourite author, George Orwell, called 'DoubleThink':

They prepare for race wars to preserve peace.

They collect disinformation to find truth.

They use women's rights to promote misogyny.

They exploit free speech to silence opponents.

They build global communities to spread anti-globalist ideas.

They invest in social bonds to encourage antisocial behavior.

They use modern tech to achieve anti-modern goals. Ultimately, going back to a distant past where your race, sex and religion determine your rights and privileges, where some lives matter more than others, would mean reversing the biggest gift the generations of the twentieth century have bestowed upon the children of the twenty-first. Beyond jeopardising the civil rights achievements of the past century, a combination of traditionalist ideologies and cutting-edge technologies could give rise to entirely new forms of autocratic regimes: from psychological manipulation to social monitoring and genetic testing. The emergence of such a toxic hybrid could pave the path for a truly dystopian society.

But as is usually the case with dystopias, it all started with utopian thinking.

Facebook set out to 'connect people' in 2004. It opened up new ways for bonding and belonging. But in doing so, it also divided people. Its architecture reinforces tribal thinking among users. It fosters 'us versus them' framings that pit groups against each other. It creates artificial connections and encourages the exclusion, discrimination, denunciation or even punishment of those who don't belong. 'Insanity in individuals is something rare – but in groups, parties, people, and ages, it is the rule,' Friedrich Nietzsche noted in *Beyond Good and Evil*.[6]

Tribalism is deeply human. Its dynamics have no political colour or ideological direction. However, splits tend to occur along ethnic, sexual, cultural or religious lines – the deepest layers of our identities.[7] And social media has given fringe groups seeking to sharpen these lines the weapons to artificially boost their tribes. The result is disturbing but not surprising. 'Tribalism in America propelled Trump to the White House,' as the US-based tribalism expert Amy Chua puts it: the urban coastal elites versus the rural working class.[8] 'Values tribes' were responsible for the Brexit vote, as the British editor and journalist David Goodhart argues: the cosmopolitan, socially liberal 'nowheres' versus the locally rooted, socially conservative 'somewheres'.[9] Whether we call it 'values tribalism' or 'identity politics', the digital age has significantly exacerbated this phenomenon.

Somewhat counter-intuitively, having many social media friends from ideologically diverse backgrounds does not protect you from online tribalism. In fact, quite the opposite is true. One of the biggest paradoxes of Facebook is that the more friends you have, the less diverse becomes the content you see. This is because its filters have more information to work with and will learn the nuances of your ideological leanings, topic preferences and sense of humour based on whose posts you like and engage with.

The tech firms are fully aware of these polarisation dynamics on their platforms. For years the entrepreneurs of Silicon Valley have been trying to appease the policymakers of DC, London and Paris instead of fixing the problem. Google, YouTube's parent firm, spent around US$18 million – more than any other company – on lobbying operations in 2017.[10] Facebook's numbers don't look very different from that; the firm increased its investments in lobbying by 32 per cent in the same year. Despite these remarkable persuasion efforts, a number of European governments have started to introduce stricter regulations for cyberspace, sometimes in an attempt to remove responsibility from their own ranks.

May, Merkel and Macron committed to closer cooperation to counter online extremism. While British and French regulation attempts are still in their infancy, Germany in 2017 became the first country to penalise extremist content in the virtual world. This controversial 'NetzDG' legislation requires websites with over 2 million active users to take down terror propaganda and hate-speech content within twenty-four hours.[11] While some hailed it as a promising model for cleaning up the internet, others denounced it as 'a dangerous example for other countries'.[12] The concern is that less democratic countries like China and Turkey might use anti-hate-speech laws to justify the censorship of political opponents.

In response to mounting political pressure, Facebook, Microsoft, Google and Twitter have developed artificial intelligence mechanisms for machine-led removal of harmful content. For example, they created a database that collects the hashes – the digital fingerprint of videos and images – of terrorist materials. When an account shares a piece of content that has been flagged in the database, it will be removed before users can see it.[13]

AI-led technologies have helped social media companies to automatically remove content that is classified as child pornography, adult nudity and ISIS-related terrorism propaganda. But the mechanisms are far from perfect. Hate speech and extremism tend to be too context-specific to be reliably identified by AI. Machines wouldn't have a clue, for example, if harmful content is shared by a BBC reporter to report on it, by an activist to counter it or by a satirist to make fun of it. In some cases, an insult or threat might also be self-referential rather than targeting others.

High penalty fees imposed on companies that host extremist materials can create incentives for taking down content when in doubt.[14] This prompts the question whether public policies that seek to control online content go hand in hand with over-censorship. The UK-based free-speech organisation Article 19 warned of vague legal concepts and disproportionate sanctions that could lead to abuse and excessive censorship.[15]

Another problem is that extremists are surprisingly resilient in response to rigid legislation. They tend to find loopholes in the infrastructure and ways to circumvent laws. Some groups avoid detection by changing the pixels of visual content, which distorts their hashes. Others have used code words to escape keyword-based removal policies. And those who want to continue with overtly extreme or violence-inciting statements move to the alt-tech space. Policies that only regulate the big platforms while neglecting the small extremist safe havens will therefore be insufficient. They ignore the reality that we are dealing with a cross-platform threat.

'We are only seeing part of the puzzle,' Erin Saltman, Facebook's counter-terrorism and counter-extremism manager for Europe, the Middle East and Africa, tells me in the Facebook London office. 'Facebook is used as a secondary platform – often the campaigns are coordinated elsewhere. There are over a hundred different platforms that extremists might use before launching a campaign on Facebook. Telegram is just one of them.' Saltman has herself infiltrated Hungarian far-right groups and worked for several years at the forefront of counter-extremism programmes. She knows what Facebook is up against. 'We change our policies; bad actors change their tactics,' she tells me.

Tens of thousands of Facebook employees are involved in this cat-and-mouse game. They cover everything from bullying, offensive humour and extremism to violent groups, identity theft and hacking. Over 300 staff members focus on terrorist content only. Sophisticated photo- and video-matching technology flags potentially illegal and harmful visuals that are then assessed by human review teams. But there are millions of such pieces of content that would need attention and it's not always straightforward. The moment you enter the greyzones, it gets trickier. 'For example, it isn't illegal to tell a lie,' Saltman notes. 'Just to deliberately defame someone is. But if you believe your own lies or conspiracy theories, you don't break the law.' Hateful content is equally hard to assess; the boundaries between what is illegal and what isn't tend to be blurry: it often takes Facebook half a dozen lawyers to judge whether something should be classified legally as hate speech or defamation, or whether it breaches the company's community standards.

All this exposes the limits that governments and companies face when trying to maintain control and power over the digital space. It also raises questions about the ownership and governance of the internet and brings back the target conflict between the security and the liberty of internet citizens. What's the difference between legitimate and illegitimate means of political influence? How do we deal with tactics that manipulate opinions but are part of what the platforms were designed for? How should we respond to incidents that don't meet the traditional security threshold but have an impact on our democratic system? And how can we make sure we are not always lagging one step behind extremists?

In the end, all removal policies treat the symptoms rather than the sources of the extremism problem. This is not a war against content or people. It is a struggle against the dark sides of human nature that technology brings to light. 'Our phones and computers have become reflections of our personalities, our interests, and our identities,' FBI director James Comey said in 2014.[16]

Facebook and YouTube's profit formulas are based on harvesting and selling human attention. Their algorithms are programmed to appeal to the human psyche, and are thus nothing else than a mirror of our deepest desires and fascinations. The truth is we are no different from the people who took pleasure in watching gladiators finishing off their opponents in Ancient Rome or those who enjoyed viewing traitors being hung, drawn and quartered in medieval England. 'If it bleeds, it leads' is as true today as it was 2,000 years ago. The scenes that move, intrigue and fascinate us still tend to be extreme and often violent.

Our subconscious preference for radical content means that few policymakers and even fewer private businesses have a genuine interest in combating extremism or hate speech. Politicians respond to the demands of their voters, prioritising the politically useful over the strategically valuable. Meanwhile the tech firms are slaves to their own business models, which rely heavily on income from advertisements and are therefore ruled by our consumption behaviour.

If one of your key performance indicators is the number of monthly users on your platform, you have little incentive to remove bots and fake accounts – especially if you know that they might make up a significant proportion of your active users. If another of your key performance indicators is measured in the time these users spend on your platform, then taking down extreme content that captures the attention of its users – regardless of how extreme or distasteful it is – makes little sense from a sheer business perspective. The fact that recommendation algorithms are trained by the people who spend most time on their platforms means that extremely committed users (such as addicts, conspiracy theorists and extremists) have a disproportional influence on what other users see.

Many of today's socio-technological problems are vicious circles. Peaking levels of loneliness, addiction and tribalism are both a source and a consequence of new tech. The world of social media bubbles, gamified dating, selfie competitions and immersive video games nurtures and is nurtured by these factors. As connections become increasingly virtual, interactions increasingly gamified and communications increasingly artificial, people become ever more lonely, addicted and tribal. In turn, they spend more time on social media, dating apps or video games.

Extremist groups are not just early adopters of tech. They are also early exploiters of the weaknesses tech creates in society. From live-action roleplays to livestreamed mobilisation and gamified terrorism, virtual extremist communities offer their members new modes of entertainment, distraction, instant self-gratification and evanescent ego boosts. They use tech to give individuals what tech has taken from them: belonging, self-confidence and identity. Or illusions of that.

Ultimately, this intertwined nature of technology and society means that tackling one in isolation from the other will likely fail. Technological progress does not occur in a societal vacuum; neither do societal developments happen without technological consequences. If we are to counter the rise of high-tech, hyper-social extremist movements, it won't be enough to blame either society or technology alone. It won't suffice to look for society-focused or tech-centred solutions alone. Instead, we need to understand and leverage the interplay between the two: what do the latest technological innovations do with us as society, and how do they reflect our zeitgeist, weaknesses and desires?

14

Ten Predictions for 2025

To prevent extremists from staying one step ahead of the curve, we need to become better at predicting future trends in a rapidly changing environment. The goal should be to plan for all possible future scenarios instead of having to resort to ad hoc defence and damage-mitigation strategies. We need to ask questions such as: how will the challenges evolve in the coming years? What will the next threats in terrorism and extremism look like? Against the backdrop of overlapping dynamics of political developments, societal changes and technological advances, trend predictions become ever more difficult. I consulted ten worldleading counter-extremism experts to help me find answers. I asked them all the same question – 'What do you think the next big extremism threat will be in the next five years?' and received a (perhaps unsurprisingly) diverse set of answers. Here is what they told me.

Non-Traditional Mobilisation

Daniel Köhler, expert on far-right terrorism and director of the German Institute on Radicalization and

De-Radicalization Studies (GIRDS), argues that we will see an 'increased dissolution of traditional boundaries between groups and ideologies'. New means of online communication and issue-based mobilisation have allowed extremists to organise themselves in more flexible ways without the need to formally establish a group. He also warns of 'neighbouring threats like organised crime through various new mobilisation themes such as environmentalism and the integration of recruits from non-traditional backgrounds in violent milieus'.

'Do It Yourself' Terrorism

US-based cyber-terrorism expert and co-author of *Hacking ISIS* Chris Sampson views the use of chat sites and apps to promote lone-wolf actions like 'do-it-yourself' terrorism and copycat attacks as the next big threat. This could take the form of increased remote training, similar to the ways in which ISIS shared video instructions and PDF manuals on bomb making via encrypted channels. 'By teaching remotely, they'll be able to grow their forces without worrying about limitations by distance.' He also estimates that the merging of livestreamed attacks and flash-mob calls could be devastating.

The Exploitation of Grievances and Extremism Itself

Nigel Inkster, director of Transnational Threats and Political Risk at the International Institute for Strategic Studies and former head of operations of the British

Secret Intelligence Service cautions that 'existing grievances that have generated significant violence are unlikely to go away' but says it is hard to say how they will manifest themselves. Dense and badly designed and managed urban environments might be breeding grounds for extremism, according to him. He also said that 'we can expect to see nation states increasingly exploiting extremist causes as a way of exercising asymmetric power'. This might lead to a vicious circle between extremism and counter-extremism responses.

State-Led Terrorism

This aligns with the predictions made by Mia Bloom, professor of communications at Georgia State University, who specialises in suicide terrorism and female extremists. The Canadian academic believes that the greatest threat of terrorism in 2025 will come from states that employ the most repressive measures against their own citizens based on their religion, identity, ethnicity, sexual orientation and political affiliation. As states find themselves unable to eliminate certain subversive ideologies, they might resort to brutal responses, in her view. This trend can already be observed in places like China, where the government has placed Uyghurs in so-called re-education camps under the banner of counter-terrorism.

Mainstreamed and State-Backed Terrorism

Michael Weiss, an American journalist and co-author of the *New York Times* bestseller *ISIS: Inside the Army of*

Terror, is increasingly worried about far-right nationalist movements turning violent. While he warns against underestimating the continuous threat posed by Islamist extremism, which is likely to endure, he believes the far right could evolve into a more powerful force – especially in Europe. Although death tolls from lone-wolf attacks tend to be higher in the US owing to the ready availability of assault rifles, he estimates that the situation is worse in Europe because far-right movements are often aligned with political parties that have been elected to government. 'At what point do gangs or militias loyal to the men in charge become exponents of the state?' he asks. For example, Estonia's fascist party EKRE, now in command of the Interior Ministry, has a youth wing that very much resembles the Hitler Youth, he explains. 'If these "populist" parties continue to win at the ballot box, then it's not difficult to see how the sorts of racist violence we lament when we see it on the nightly news become standard practice throughout Europe, carried out with impunity.'

Global Far-Right Resurgence

The psychology professor and author of *The Psychology of Terrorism* John Horgan warns that the next big threat by 2025 could be a reflection of the global resurgence of far-right extremism. 'This is likely to have profound implications for the functioning of what we think of as liberal democracies, and will give rise to multiple new kinds of terrorism.' Studies have found that mainstreamed far-right extremism can be an amplifier of both jihadist and far-right-inspired terrorism.

It can lend credibility to Islamist extremist narratives of an ongoing war between Muslims and non-Muslims while also emboldening violent racist and xenophobic movements.

Diversified Threat Landscape

J. M. Berger, American author of books such as *Jihad Joe* and *Extremism* and research fellow at VOX-Pol, predicts that 'we're going to see a continued increase in all types of extremism both in the US and globally. The landscape is probably going to be a lot more diverse by 2025.' As social media offers proponents of fringe ideologies the opportunity to form international networks with like-minded users, it is likely that we will see a much more fractured extremism landscape. A range of new extremist sub-cultures with niche audiences has already emerged and established a global presence.

Environmental Terrorism and Drones

Peter Neumann, professor of security studies at King's College London and founder of the International Centre for the Study of Radicalisation (ICSR), contends that the two major extremism threats will be jihadist and far-right extremist in nature. 'They reflect the two big fault lines in our societies, and will continue to produce violent actors for some time.' But he adds that 'radicalisation of the environmental movement' might grow, 'especially if climate change progresses and policymakers and societies find no adequate way of addressing the problem'. A variety of innovations could also revolutionise the tactics employed by extremist actors; in particular 'the use of drones to deliver explosive devices would create huge challenges for protecting potential targets'.

Migration and Misogyny as Fuels

Joe Mulhall, senior researcher at the British anti-racism organisation Hope Not Hate, believes that the far-reaching effects of global warming will have a serious effect on political extremism in the years to come. 'Be it increasing migration from the global south or increased resource scarcity, there will be those who seek answers in parochial, nationalistic and xenophobic solutions. Sadly, I fear that far-right extremism might rise along with our sea levels.' He predicts that another, more immediate threat is the growth of politicised violent misogyny. 'Anti-feminism and anti-women politics is a growing sub-section of right-wing extremism more generally, although primarily online,' he says. 'We have already seen numerous deadly terrorist attacks emanating from this movement and I am afraid we might see a growth in this come the next decade.'

Deep Fakes and Cyber-Warfare Techniques

Jacob Davey, researcher at the Institute for Strategic Dialogue and expert on the international far right's online playbook, argues that we have seen a range of activities associated with internet culture entering the mainstream in recent years. Shitposting, trolling and memes are no longer the domain of the 4chan brigade. 'They are now key tactics for PR firms, advertisers and even the President of the United States. Extremists have been at the forefront of this mainstreaming.' According to him, extremists will seek more effective tools to confuse, disrupt and broadcast as these techniques become ever more mainstreamed. 'We're already starting to see this with the spread of deep fakes, but to really understand what will become the new vogue for extremist digital strategy we need to understand that it is the transgressive which drives fringe communities.' He concludes that possible options could include the use of cyber-warfare techniques, and more effective spoofing technology to confuse matters.

15

Ten Solutions for 2020

Whether these predictions prove true or not, any one-dimensional solution would not do justice to the various overlapping challenges and the ever more complicated extremism landscape. Responses to the evolving threat cannot rely on enhanced platform monitoring or content removal alone. Fear of government surveillance measures that target minority communities has driven many alienated Muslims into the hands of jihadists, while anger over perceived freedom-of-speech infringements has made more people vulnerable to the rhetoric of the extreme right.

Instead we need a holistic, longer-term approach based on an alliance across different sectors and political parties. Politicians, tech firms, social workers and civil society all have an indispensable role to play in the battle against online extremism, distortion and intimidation. They can work together to deal with violence-inciting materials and enhance societal resilience to radicalising and manipulative messaging that fall within the legal greyzones. Here are ten of the most promising cutting-edge initiatives; some are as creative and controversial as it gets – from AI-led take-downs to satirical counter-trolling.

Tech Against Terrorism

The ecosystem in which extremists operate is no longer linear or limited to a few platforms: instead, the emerging alt-tech empire has transformed the threat into one that crosses various platforms. These evolutions in the digital space mean sharing knowledge, databases and technologies is necessary in order to succeed in the ever more complex online battlefield. The UN-mandated initiative Tech Against Terrorism has brought to life the world's first major counter-extremism cooperation between bigger and smaller tech firms. By collecting best practices – from hash-sharing databases to powerful AI systems – the initiative helps to optimise the identification and removal of terrorist content across different platforms. Most importantly, it provides smaller online platforms with limited budgets and human resources with the proactive tech tools they need to protect themselves from terrorist exploitation of their services. The use of synergies and collective learning strategies across the tech industry is badly needed. But the danger of false positives remains significant even when the world's leading tech experts join forces to optimise their technological tools and mechanisms.[1]

Policy Against Polarisation

Often social media users are targeted by political propaganda without being aware of it. How often are you shown content in your social media feeds without knowing why? If users are to have even a remote chance of understanding when their content is being amplified, recommended or filtered, higher levels of algorithmic transparency and accountability will be needed. Reducing the opaqueness of black-box algorithms will therefore be required as a first step to raise awareness about online manipulation, micro-marketing and hyper-targeted propaganda. With the ongoing migration of extremists to smaller, often more extreme alt-tech platforms, anti-hate-speech laws will need to go below the 2-million-users minimum of the current NetzDG legislation. Beyond algorithmic transparency and hate-speech laws, the hosts of social media discussion forums and commentary sections should be encouraged to moderate hateful debates, debunk disinformation and remove harmful materials. Better moderation strategies will ensure that materials and messages that fall within the legal boundaries but can nevertheless harm the online discussion culture or fuel polarisation dynamics do not remain unchallenged.

Help Against Hate

What can be done to immunise activists against extremist intimidation? Sometimes hate speech and harassment fall into the legal greyzones and leave internet users vulnerable to anonymous campaigns by malicious actors who will never have to fear legal consequences for their action. HateAid is an initiative that Fearless Democracy founder Gerald Hensel launched to prevent extremists from reaching their goal of silencing their opponents. By providing self-help guides on topics such as doxxing and cyber harassment and by offering a platform for connecting and supporting victims of online hate, HateAid helps to build resilience among journalists, activists and other at-risk audiences that are likely targets of extremist intimidation campaigns.[2]

Counter Conversations

How can we use the latest technologies to our advantage to identify online users at risk of radicalisation and help them escape the toxic narratives of extremist recruiters? In 2017, the Institute for Strategic Dialogue (ISD) piloted the world's first deradicalisation project to employ social media network analyses to identify members of violent extremist movements and use social media messaging services to reach out to them. The project was carried out in cooperation with experienced deradicalisation-intervention providers, including former extremists, survivors of terrorist attacks and psychologists. Once radicalised individuals had been identified through their online engagement with extremist groups, intervention providers initiated a conversation via Facebook Messenger. One in ten sustained conversations had a tangible positive impact in that it led to significant attitude or behaviour changes. This experimental approach of direct online engagement with radicalised audiences illustrates the potential to further explore the use of social media analysis and messaging in deradicalisation programmes.[3]

Elves Versus Trolls

Sharing pieces of disinformation or propaganda is not illegal but it doesn't need to go unchallenged. The

Baltics, where media manipulation by the Kremlin propaganda machine is a major concern, are currently leading the way in countering disinformation. The so-called Baltic Elves are made up of thousands of voluntary activists who spend their spare time dismantling the disinformation campaigns of Russian trolls – from exposing biased news pieces and misleading statistics to debunking fabricated stories and half-truths. Currently, Lithuania counts around 3,000 elves, Latvia has around 150 and Estonia two dozen. Taking inspiration from the approach of the Baltic Elves, stronger coalitions of fact finders and social media campaigners could be formed across Europe and the US to effectively debunk and counter online media manipulation and disinformation.[4]

Trolling the Trolls

Who says you can't troll the trolls? In April 2018 the German satirist Jan Böhmermann founded his own counter-troll army called Reconquista Internet. Within a matter of hours, the Reconquista Internet server counted three times as many members as Reconquista Germanica – around 20,000. Although it started as a prank, the initiative quickly turned into the first counter-trolling army of this size. This accidental birth of a civil rights movement demonstrates how a broad church of digital citizens from across the political spectrum can make a change by organising credible anti-hate-speech campaigns. The potential of peer-to-peer trolling remains unexplored but should be treated with caution: imitating the tactics of extremists may quickly slip into similarly troubling social dynamics and can exacerbate polarisation dynamics by encouraging black-and-white thinking.

Hacking the Hackers

Why don't we beat the hackers with their own weapons? Several anti-extremism activists have developed strategies to hack and embarrass ISIS jihadists. For example, Anonymous has hacked and spammed multiple ISIS accounts with pornographic images.[5] By confronting them with their worst enemies – nudity, promiscuity and homosexuality – they damaged the jihadists' morale and diminished their credibility among their followers and potential recruits. There also is a simple time factor: if you keep terrorists busy dealing with their reputation management, they will have less time to spread propaganda, recruit new members and plan attacks. Eventually, these repeated annoyances led many of the jihadists to shut down their social media accounts.[6]

While some researchers and activists make a convincing argument about the successes of creative projects that try to outsmart and outwit extremist hackers,[7] the effectiveness of such efforts is hard – if not impossible – to measure. Even if effective, this kind of tit-for-tat activism raises a range of legal and ethical questions: is hacking for good a legitimate tactic? Might these trolling campaigns negatively impact extremists' willingness to engage with other counter-extremism offers such as deradicalisation initiatives for fear of being mocked?

Arts Against Anger

How can the creative industries help to transcend trad-itional counter-extremism measures? Artists are in a unique position of power over the human mind: they can provoke changes in the attitudes and behaviours of their audiences by taking them to unexplored territory, offering entirely new perspectives and breaking taboos. They can gain access to the human unconscious by engaging with fear, anger and other deep-lying emotions. Art installations, literature, music and performing arts can make a vast contribution to stimulating empathy and decreasing anger towards out-groups by blurring black-and-white narratives. The creative industries have perhaps the biggest underestimated potential to engage new audiences and explore sensitive questions around identity, race and religion. To name just one example, the Hate Library is an installation developed by author Nick Thurston and historian Matthew Feldman that presents toxic discussions from social media to shed light on the language and tactics of far-right groups across Europe.[8]

Mobilising the Middle

Is it possible to prevent organised troll armies from launching hate campaigns and taking over the comments sections on social media pages? The initia-tive #ichbinhier has proved that lending a megaphone to the moderates in the middle can work as an effective counter-strategy. #ichbinhier is a community on Facebook that is committed to preventing the spread of toxic discussion cultures on social media. Whenever they identify a large-scale hate campaign they launch a counter-campaign in which all #ichbinhier members like each other's posts. By accumulating likes, their comments are prioritised by the algorithm and show up higher than those of the extremists. When users visit the discussion forums, they no longer see hateful comments first but instead are shown the constructive and positive posts by #ichbinhier members.[9]

Education Against Extremism

Digital literacy programmes are needed both in traditional education settings and outside of schools and universities. Younger generations, the digital natives, as well as older audiences, who are increasingly using new media spaces to inform themselves, should be provided with the resources they need to enhance their critical thinking, media literacy and digital citizenship and brace themselves for extremist grooming and manipulation strategies. Digital education initiatives should encourage everyone connected to the internet to engage with questions such as: how has social media changed the information ecosystem? How do algorithms work and how are they exploited by extremists online? How can credible media sources be distinguished from biased, unreliable or distortive information providers? By enabling internet citizens, whether old or young, to identify deception and manipulation, extremist strategies can be deprived of their allure.

These experimental approaches can render the online strategies of extremists inefficient by reclaiming their biggest comparative advantage: socio-technological innovation. We need strategies that bridge the gaps and conflicts of interests between different industries and political structures. The growing rifts between governments and tech firms, as well as between (and within) moderate political parties, have been detrimental to counter-extremism efforts.

After joining a dozen different extremist groups, I am convinced that any response that focuses purely on technology-led intervention and on regulating the digital sphere will not work. It is true that the way a platform is designed can stimulate, manipulate and escalate our attitudes and behaviour. But compassion and empathy are not predetermined by algorithms. Even if the digital DNA of some platforms carries a dangerous potential to handicap our emotional and social intelligence, we need to move away from the idea that it robs us of our ability to love, hate or fear.

If technology is no more than an extension and multiplier of human flaws and qualities, we need to return to a more human-centred approach. Questions around identity, trust and friendship in the online world must be raised if we want to break through the 'us and them' thinking that all extremist movements have in common. Only an open-minded approach that puts people at its heart will allow us to take back the digital sphere and avoid going *forward to the past*.

A Note from the Author

The most challenging part of writing a book is hardly ever the writing. Access is what matters. Access to (good) data, (interesting) interviewees or (relevant) meetings. Every researcher, regardless of their subject or method, knows the hassle. Some might even have nightmares about the tedious and often fruitless process of dealing with incomplete or (worse!) incompatible datasets, bureaucratic institutions that make Josef K.'s anguish look innocuous, or the unfriendly PAs of even unfriendlier interviewees.

This book is about deception and manipulation: it exposes extremist strategies in the cyberspace to radicalise, influence and intimidate different target audiences. To gain insights into these techniques, I first had to get access to some of the most exclusivist and secretive groups out there. But the book was produced at a time when access to extremist content was becoming increasingly restricted: tech firms like Facebook closed their APIs for data analysis, while extremist groups introduced rigorous vetting processes. In fact, the book is partly about this loss of access, of both oversight and insight, that security services, researchers and journalists are faced with when conversations go underground.

To enter the closed-off worlds of extremists, I was therefore often left with no option but to use deceptive tactics myself. I adopted a Muslim-sounding name to be recruited into ISIS channels, wore a blonde wig to match the profile picture of my white nationalist avatar account and imitated a Bavarian accent to be accepted by an extreme-right trolling army. Does that make me a hypocrite? Possibly. But I am convinced that to counter extremist networks online, we need to understand their drivers, expose their tactics and predict their next steps.

Getting insights into the plans and plots of extremists does come at a certain expense: not least for my own safety and that of my family, friends and colleagues. But not knowing what extremists are up to could be even more disastrous, for all of us. Sometimes it is necessary to go beyond asking what the cost of action is and also ask what the cost of inaction would be. It was based on this conviction that I adopted fake identities for this research. However, I do apologise to anyone I had to deceive or mislead in the course of researching for this book.

After having been victim myself to various attempts of doxxing – the leaking of personal data – I took privacy concerns very seriously. Throughout all of the stages of the research and writing I did my very best to protect everyone quoted in this book. I used pseudonyms for all non-public individuals mentioned in the book or used the names of their anonymous online accounts. Whenever I saw explicit calls for violence, concrete and targeted threats or plots for criminal acts, I reported them to the responsible authorities.

A few comments and conversations were shortened and lightly edited for reader-friendliness; likewise some abbreviations and jargon terms were removed to make the book accessible to a non-expert audience.

Glossary

Accelerationism: A theory that argues that technological and social advance should be speeded up to increase instability and result in revolutionary change.

Alt-right: A loose collection of extreme-right and white nationalist groups originating in America. The movement is known for its online mobilisation and use of internet culture in its communications.

Black hat: Black hats are hackers who engage in illegal hacking activities for personal financial gain or ideological reasons.

Daily Stormer: A popular neo-Nazi hate-site and a key area for the dissemination of alt-right propaganda. Following a call to action by its founder Andrew Anglin, the page became a platform from which activists launched information operations.

Dark Social: A term used in marketing to describe material shared in ways that are difficult to track, such as emails, short message service (SMS) systems and encrypted chat.

Doxxing: To dox means to research and publish an individual's personal data, including, for example, their address, phone number, pictures and other private documents. Doxxing has been adopted as a harassment and intimidation tactic by extremists and politicised internet trolls.

Eurabia: A conspiracy theory coined in the early 2000s by Bat Ye'or (aka Gisèle Littman), who argued that Western countries are slowly being brought under Islamic rule.

Extreme right: Groups and individuals that exhibit at least three of the following five features: nationalism, racism, xenophobia, anti-democracy and strong state advocacy.

Far right: The political manifestation of the extreme right.

Gab: Gab.ai is a social media platform that functions in a similar fashion to Twitter. It was designed to promote freedom of speech and has loose terms of use. It has recently been heavily adopted by the extreme right globally.

Identitarianism: A pan-European ethno-nationalist movement, which focuses on the preservation of European ethno-cultural identity and is inspired by the French intellectual right-wing movement the New Right.

Live action role play (LARP): An improvised role-play game where participants physically play characters in a fictional setting.

Meme: Coined by Richard Dawkins in 1976, a meme refers to a unit of transfer for cultural ideas. Today the term is used to refer to user-generated content – often humorous visuals that spread rapidly throughout social media channels.

New Right: A school of thought that emerged in France in the late 1960s as Nouvelle Droite and has inspired a range of extremist groups, most notably the Generation Identity movement.

Reddit: A popular content-sharing and discussion site, divided into interest-based boards called 'subreddits'.

Red pill: A piece of information that facilitates an individual's awakening to the 'truth' of extreme-right-wing ideology, enabling radicalisation. The term is commonly used by the extreme right, twisting its original meaning, taken from the movie *The Matrix*.

Remigration: The call for forced deportation of migrant communities, with the intent of creating an ethnically or culturally homogeneous society; essentially a non-violent form of ethnic cleansing.

White hat: Contrary to black hats, white hats are hackers who hack for ethical reasons, for example to test the security of information systems.

White genocide: A conspiracy theory popularised by white supremacist David Lane, who argued that white populations are being replaced through immigration, integration, abortion and violence against white people.

ZOG: An acronym often used by neo-Nazis; it stands for Zionist Occupation Government and refers to the anti-Semitic conspiracy theory that governments in America and Europe are controlled by Jews.

Acknowledgements

First of all, I would like to thank all interviewees – the experts and researchers as well as the extremist activists and ideologues. Despite being terrified by what I saw and heard during my undercover experiences, I am also grateful for their trust, insights and openness.

A special thanks to my fantastic editor at Bloomsbury, Angelique Tran Van Sang, whose feedback was invaluable and who has made this book so much more readable and engaging. I would also like to thank my truly brilliant literary agent Luke Ingram of the Wylie Agency, who had so much confidence in this project, at times more than I did. Without his support and feedback this book would not exist in its current form.

I would furthermore like to thank Jacob Davey, Frederick Ladbury and Joe Mulhall for their inspiration and friendship. Long conversations about the frightening developments in the world have inspired major parts of this book. My friends Lena Schmidtkunz, Alessa Lux, Eva Vögerl and Jade Zhao have come to my rescue whenever I felt like drowning in the dark worlds of extremism. Thank you.

I would also like to thank the incredible team at ISD, especially Jacob Davey, Rashad Ali, Jakob Guhl, Chloe

Colliver, Jonathan Birdwell, Henry Tuck, Iris Boyer, Cécile Guerin, Cooper Gatewood and Christopher Stewart, who have been constant sources of inspiration. I additionally want to thank Nicola Bruce, a former intern at ISD, for her outstanding research on women within the Manosphere. And lastly, I am deeply grateful to Sasha Havlicek, for being the coolest boss as well as a great role model.

I want to extend my gratitude to Andreas for being the best protector at the Schild & Schwert Festival and for waiting for me in the rain, and to Joe for his tips and protection during my undercover time with Generation Identity. I am also deeply indebted to Raphael Gluck, Chris Sampson, GenKnoxx and Amarnath Amarasingam and Peter Apps for their intelligence sharing and their help navigating the darker corners of the internet.

Finally, I would like to thank my entire family for everything. You gave me the security, stability and support in a world that can sometimes seem scarier, lonelier and more lunatic than it actually is. There have been so many challenging moments throughout the research for this book – from a series of death threats to massive trolling campaigns. I would not have been able to continue studying this subject had I not been in the company of so many cool-minded, light-spirited and warm-hearted friends, colleagues and family members.

Notes

I: WHITES ONLY

1 For analysis see Elisabetta Cassini Wolff, 'Evola's interpretation of fascism and moral responsibility', *Patterns of Prejudice* 50(4–5), 2016, pp. 478–94.

2 Stanley G. Payne, *A History of Fascism: 1914–1945* (Madison: University of Wisconsin Press, 1995).

3 Richard Drake, *The Revolutionary Mystique and Terrorism in Contemporary Italy* (Bloomington: Indiana University Press, 1989).

4 Jason Horowitz, 'Steve Bannon Cited Italian Thinker Who Inspired Facsists', *New York Times*, 10 Febuary 2017. Available at https://www.nytimes.com/2017/02/10/world/europe/bannon-vatican-julius-evola-fascism.html.

5 Ibid.

6 Antonio Regalado, '2017 was the year consumer DNA testing blew up', *MIT Review*, February 2018. Available at https://www.technologyreview.com/s/610233/2017-was-the-year-consumer-dna-testing-blew-up/.

7 Aaron Panofsky and Joan M. Donovan, 'When Genetics Challenges a Racist's Identity: Genetic Ancestry Testing among White Nationalists', American Sociological Association, 2017.

8 American Sociological Association, 'White Supremacists use a decision tree to affirm or discount the results of DNA tests', August 2017. Available at https://phys.org/

news/2017-08-white-supremacists-decision-tree-affirm. html.

9   Cf. Panofsky and Donovan, 'When Genetics Challenges a Racist's Identity: Genetic Ancestry Testing among White Nationalists'.

10 Christophe Busch et al., *Das Höcker Album: Auschwitz durch die Linse des SS* (Darmstadt: Verlag Philipp von Zabern, 2016), and Alec Wilkinson, 'Picturing Auschwitz', *New Yorker*, 17 March 2008.

11 Roger Griffin, 'The role of heroic doubling in ideologically motivated state and terrorist violence', *Internal Review of Psychiatry* 29(4), 2017, pp. 355–361.

12 George Hawley, *Making Sense of the Alt-Right* (New York: Columbia University Press, 2017), and Angela Nagle, *Kill All Normies: Online Culture Wars from 4chan and Tumblr to Trump and the Alt-Right* (London: Zero Books, 2017).

13 The full text of the NAR constitution is available at http://northwestfront.org/about/nar-constitution/.

14 The website of the Northwest Front is available at http://northwestfront.org.

15 Sven Svenhed, 'North West Front: The North West Volunteer Army', uploaded to YouTube in September 2012. Available in the US at https://www.youtube.com/watch?v=W14DdNUDL7g.

16 Dylann Roof's full manifesto can be found at https://assets.documentcloud.org/documents/3237779/Dylann-Roof-manifesto.pdf.

17 Matthew Francey, 'This guy wants to start his own Aryan country', Vice, February 2013. Available at https://www.vice.com/en_us/article/4wqe33/this-guy-wants-to-start-his-own-aryan-country.

18 Jacob Davey and Julia Ebner, 'The Fringe Insurgency: Connectivity, Convergence and Mainstreaming of the Extreme Right', Institute for Strategic Dialogue (ISD), October 2017. Available at https://www.isdglobal.org/wp-content/uploads/2017/10/The-Fringe-Insurgency-221017.pdf.

19   Kevin C. Thompson, 'WATCHING THE STORM-FRONT: White Nationalists and the Building of Community in Cyberspace', *Social Analysis:The International Journal of Social and Cultural Practice* 45(1), 2001, pp. 32–52. Available at www.jstor.org/stable/23169989.

20   Christopher Clarey, 'World Cup '98; Hooligans Leave Officer in a Coma', *New York Times*, Archives 1998. Available at https://www.nytimes.com/1998/06/22/sports/world-cup-98-hooligans-leave-officer-in-a-coma.html.

21   A more detailed description can be found at http://northwestfront.org/northwest-novels/author-on-the-nw-novels/.

2: REDPILLING FOR BEGINNERS

1   Author's translation of the original tweet: 'Wenn man länger lebt, als man nützlich ist, und dabei vor lauter Feminismus das Stricken verlernt hat.'

2   Eva Thöne, 'Dialog unmöglich', Spiegel Online, 15 October 2017. Available at http://www.spiegel.de/kultur/literatur/frankfurter-buchmesse-die-auseinandersetzung-mit-den-rechten-a-1172953.html.

3   National Bolshevism is an ideological hybrid of fascism and Bolshevism.

4   Julian Bruns, Kathrin Glösel and Natascha Strobl, *Die Identitären: Handbuch zur Jugendbewegung der Neuen Rechten in Europa* (Münster: Unrast Verlag, 2017).

5   Natasha Strobl, *Die Identitären: Handbuch zur Jugendbewegung der Neuen Rechten* (Münster: Unrast Verlag, 2014).

6   Bruns, Glösel and Strobl, *Die Identitären: Handbuch zur Jugendbewegung der Neuen Rechten in Europa*, and 'A New Threat: Generation Identity United Kingdom and Ireland' (Hope not Hate, 2018). Available at https://www.hopenothate.org.uk/2018/04/13/a-new-threat/.

7   Guillaume Faye's 2015 speech at the National Policy Institute is available at https://www.youtube.com/watch?v=Ss-QNSiN2oY.

8   Max Roser, 'Fertility Rate', Our World in Data, December 2017. Available at https://ourworldindata.org/fertility-rate.

9   For all features see https://patriot-peer.com/de/home/.

10 Jacob Davey and Julia Ebner, 'The Fringe Insurgency: Connectivity, Convergence and Mainstreaming of the Extreme Right', ISD, October 2017. Available at https://www.isdglobal.org/wp-content/uploads/2017/10/The-Fringe-Insurgency-221017.pdf.

11 Matthew Karnitschnig, 'Austria heads for right-leaning coalition', Politico, 15 October 2017. Available at https://www.politico.eu/article/austria-heads-for-right-leaning-coalition-early-projections/.

12 Ronald Beiler, *Dangerous Minds: Nietzsche, Heidegger, and the Return of the Far Right* (Philadelphia: University of Pennsylvania Press, 2018), and Casey Michel, 'Meet the favorite philosophers of young white supremacists', ThinkProgress, 22 June 2018. Available at https://thinkprogress.org/this-philosophers-of-young-white-supremacists-33605ba538c0/.

13 Sue Prideaux, *I am Dynamite!: A Life of Friedrich Nietzsche* (London: Faber & Faber, 2018).

14 https://www.youtube.com/watch?v=Lb5zUG9UzFE.

15 Martin Sellner, *Identitär: Geschichte eines Aufbruchs* (Schnellroda: Verlag Antaios, 2017), p. 117.

16 Mark Townsend, 'Senior member of European far-right group quits over neo-Nazi link', *Observer*, 11 August 2018. Available at https://www.awin1.com/awclick.php?mid=5795&id=201309&p=https://www.theguardian.com/world/2018/aug/11/generation-identity-leader-quits-neo-nazi-links.

17 Joe Mulhall, 'Failed Defend Europe Mission Comes to an End', Hope not Hate, 17 August 2017. Available at https://www.hopenothate.org.uk/2017/08/17/failed-defend-europe-mission-comes-end/.

18 Markus Willinger, *Generation Identity: A Declaration of War Against the '68ers* (Arktos Media, 2013).

19 'Premier League clubs warned over "far-right" Football Lads Alliance', *The Times*, 30 March 2018. Available at https://www.thetimes.co.uk/article/premier-league-clubs-warned-over-far-right-football-lads-alliance-omgq2lppv.

20 Hannibal Bateman, 'Generation Alt-Right', *Radix Journal*, 14 April 2016. Available at https://www.radixjournal.com/2016/04/2016-4-14-generation-alt-right/.

21 Ibid.

22 James Poniewozik, 'Andrew Breitbart, 1969–2012', *Time*, 1 March 2012. Available at http://entertainment.time.com/2012/03/01/andrew-breitbart-1969-2012/.

23 The concept of the 'Overton Window' describes the window of politically viable views and was developed by Joseph P. Overton.

24 Whitney Phillips, 'The Oxygen of Amplification: Better Practices for Reporting on Extremists, Antagonists, and Manipulators Online', Data & Society Research Foundation, 2018. Retrieved from https://datasociety.net/output/oxygen-of-amplification/.

25 Lizzie Dearden, 'Generation Identity: Far-right group sending UK recruits to military-style training camps in Europe', *Independent*, 9 November 2017. Available at https://www.independent.co.uk/news/uk/home-news/generation-identity-far-right-group-training-camps-europe-uk-recruits-military-white-nationalist-a8046641.html.

26 Andrew Gilligan, 'The "hipster fascists" who anti-racism campaigners say are breathing new life into the far right', *Sunday Times*, 20 May 2018. Available at https://www.thetimes.co.uk/article/the-hipster-fascists-breathing-new-life-into-the-british-far-right-6hvtmq63k.

3: TRAD WIVES

1 MGTOW Wiki, 'Sex Market Value'. Available at http://mgtow.wikia.com/wiki/Sex_Market_Value.

2   R. F. Baumeister and K. D. Vohs, 'Sexual economics: sex as a female resource for social exchange in heterosexual interactions', *Personality and Social Psychology Review* 8(4), 2004. Available at https://www.ncbi.nlm.nih.gov/pubmed/15582858.

3   MGTOW Wiki, 'Sex Market Value'.

4   'The Republican Lawmaker Who Secretly Created Reddit's Women-Hating Red Pill', *Daily Beast*, 25 April 2017. Available at https://www.thedailybeast.com/the-republican-lawmaker-who-secretly-created-reddits-women-hating-red-pill.

5   Anti-Defamation League, 'When Women are the Enemy: the Intersection of Misogyny and White Supremacy', July 2018. Available at https://www.adl.org/resources/reports/when-women-are-the-enemy-the-intersection-of-misogyny-and-white-supremacy.

6   'Male Supremacy', SPLC, 2018. Available at https://www.splcenter.org/fighting-hate/extremist-files/ideology/male-supremacy.

7   Peter Baker, 'The Woman Who Accidentally Started the Incel Movement', *Elle*, 1 March 2016. Available at https://www.elle.com/culture/news/a34512/woman-who-started-incel-movement/.

8   Ben Zimmer, 'How Incel Got Hijacked', Politico, 8 May 2015. Available at https://www.politico.com/magazine/story/2018/05/08/intel-involuntary-celibate-movement-218324.

9   Alex Hern, 'Who are the "incels" and how do they relate to Toronto van attack?', *Guardian*, 25 April 2018. Available at https://www.theguardian.com/technology/2018/apr/25/what-is-incel-movement-toronto-van-attack-suspect.

10 Hadley Freeman, 'Elliot Rodger was a misogynist – but is that all he was?', *Guardian*, 27 May 2014. Available at https://www.theguardian.com/commentisfree/2014/may/27/elliot-rodger-was-misogynist-killing-spree.

11 G. Tyson et al., 'A First Look at User Activity on Tinder', Conference: 8th IEEE/ACM International Conference on Advances in Social Networks Analysis and Mining (ASONAM), 2016. Available at http://qmro.qmul.ac.uk/xmlui/handle/123456789/15100.

12 Elizabeth E. Bruch and M. E. J. Newman, 'Aspirational pursuit of mates in online dating markets', *Science Advances* 4(8), 8 August 2018. Available at http://advances.sciencemag.org/content/4/8/eaap9815.

13 See for example https://equalitycanada.com/wp-content/uploads/2012/09/Mens-Issues-Awareness-Newsletter1.pdf.

14 'Suicides in the United Kingdom: 2012 Registrations', Office for National Statistics, 18 February 2014. Available at https://webarchive.nationalarchives.gov.uk/20160107060820/http://www.ons.gov.uk/ons/dcp171778_351100.pdf, and 'Suicide statistics', Center for Disease Control and Prevention, 2015. Available at https://www.cdc.gov/violenceprevention/pdf/Suicide-DataSheet-a.pdf.

15 Jon Anthony on Masculine Development. Available at https://www.masculinedevelopment.com/lauren-southern-red-pill-women/.

16 Annie Kelly, 'The House Wives of White Supremacy', New York Times, 1 June 2018. Available at https://www.nytimes.com/2018/06/01/opinion/sunday/tradwives-women-alt-right.html. For other research by Annie Kelly see, for example, Annie Kelly, 'The alt-right: reactionary rehabilitation for white masculinity', *Soundings*, Number 66, Summer 2017, pp. 68-78(11).

17 'Extremists' "Unite the Right" Rally: A Possible Historic Alt-Right Showcase?', SPLC, 7 August 2017. Available at https://www.splcenter.org/hatewatch/2017/08/07/extremists-unite-right-rally-possible-historic-alt-right-showcase.

18 The livestream was accessible here: https://www.youtube. com/watch?v=esdZcvjITeA.

19 See for example A Domestic Discipline Society: https:// adomesticdisciplinesociety.blogspot.com/2013/04/taken-in-hand-head-of-household-tih-hoh-role-domestic-discipline.html.

20 Cf. Bruch and Newman, 'Aspirational pursuit of mates in online dating markets'.

21 'Tinder: Swiping Self Esteem?', 2016. Available at https:// www.apa.org/news/press/releases/2016/08/tinder-self-esteem.aspx.

22 Francesca Friday, 'More Americans are single than ever before', *Observer*, 1 August 2018. Available at https:// observer.com/2018/01/more-americans-are-single-than-ever-before-and-theyre-healthier-too/.

23 Bill Chappell, 'U.S. Births Dip to 30-Year Low; Fertility Rate Sinks Further Below Replacement Level', NPR, 17 May 2018. Available at https://www.npr.org/sections/ thetwo-way/2018/05/17/611898421/u-s-births-falls-to-30-year-low-sending-fertility-rate-to-a-record-low.

24 'Old at heart? Quiet life of the average 20 something in 2017', Nationwide Building Society, 23 February 2017. Available at https://www.nationwide.co.uk/ about/media-centre-and-specialist-areas/media-centre/ press-releases/archive/2017/2/23-british-20-something.

25 'Results of UK sex survey published', NHS, November 2013. Available at https://www.nhs.uk/news/lifestyle-and-exercise/results-of-uk-sex-survey-published/.

26 For an overview of cognitive behavioural therapy by the NHS see: https://www.nhs.uk/conditions/cognitive-behavioural-therapy-cbt/.

4: SISTERS ONLY

1 David Lipson, 'Surabaya bombings: neighbours say family responsible seemed like "ordinary" people', ABC, 14 May 2017. Available at http://www.abc.net.

au/news/2018-05-14/indonesia-church-attacks-joko-widodo-orders-investigation/9757512.

2   Ibid.

3   Cameron Sumpter, 'Extremism in Indonesia is a family affair', East Asia Forum, May 2017. Available at http://www.eastasiaforum.org/2018/05/18/extremism-in-indonesia-is-a-family-affair/, and Kirsten Schulze, 'The Surabaya Bombings and the Evolution of the Jihadi Threat in Indonesia', *CTC Sentinel* 11(6), June/July 2018. Available at https://ctc.usma.edu/surabaya-bombings-evolution-jihadi-threat-indonesia/.

4   For more information about socialisation into extremist groups see, for example, Diego Muro, 'What Does Radicalisation Look Like? Four Visualisations of Socialisation into Violent Extremism', University of St Andrews and Barcelona Centre of International Studies, 2016.

5   See Kumar Ramakrishna, *Islamist Terrorism and Militancy in Indonesia: The Power of the Manichean Mindset* (Singapore: Springer, 2015), and Kumar Ramakrishna, 'Radical Pathways: Understanding Radicalisation in Indonesia', *Contemporary Southeast Asia* 32(1), April 2010, pp. 102–4.

6   Beh Lih Yi and Luke Harding, 'ISIS claims responsibility for Jakarta gun and bomb attacks', *Guardian*, 14 January 2016. Available at https://www.theguardian.com/world/2016/jan/14/jakarta-bombings-multiple-casualties-after-indonesian-capital-hit-by-suicide-attacks. And Gayatri Suroyo and Stefanno Reinard, 'Indonesia makes arrests as Islamic State claims Jakarta attacks', Reuters, 26 May 2017. Available at https://www.reuters.com/article/us-indonesia-blast-arrests/indonesia-makes-arrests-as-islamic-state-claims-jakarta-attacks-idUSKBN18M0F3.

7   Euan McKirdy, 'Fleeing ISIS in the Philippines: "I will never go back to Marawi"', CNN, 27 June 2017. Available

at https://edition.cnn.com/2017/06/25/asia/isis-siege-marawi/index.html.

8 Francis Chan, 'Batam militants behind foiled Marina Bay plot jailed for terrorism conspiracy', *Straits Times*, 7 June 2017. Available at https://www.straitstimes.com/asia/se-asia/members-of-batam-terror-cell-behind-foiled-mbs-rocket-attack-plot-found-guilty-of. And Wahyudi Soeriaatmadja, 'Foiled rocket attack's Batam rocket site was 18km away from MBS', Asia One, 27 September 2016. Available at http://www.asiaone.com/singapore/foiled-rocket-attacks-batam-launch-site-was-18km-mbs.

9 Statista, 'Internet Usage in Indonesia', 2016. Available at https://www.statista.com/topics/2431/internet-usage-in-indonesia/. And JakPat, 'Indonesia Social Media Habit Report Q1 2017', May 2017. Available at http://www.emarketer.com/Chart/Social-Networks-Used-by-Smartphone-Users-Indonesia-April-2017-of-respondents/208536.

10 J. M. Berger, 'The Evolution of Terrorist Propaganda: The Paris Attack and Social Media', Brookings, 27 January 2015. Available at https://www.brookings.edu/testimonies/the-evolution-of-terrorist-propaganda-the-paris-attack-and-social-media/.

11 National Consortium for the Study of Terrorism and Responses to Terrorism, 'The Use of Social Media by United States Extremists', Research Brief, 2018. This research is based on the PIRUS database, which can be accessed at http://www.start.umd.edu/data-tools/profiles-individual-radicalization-united-states-pirus.

12 Public Intelligence, 'DHS Terrorist Use of Social Networking Facebook Case Study'. Available at http://publicintelligence.net/ufouoles-dhs-terrorist-use-of-social-networking-facebook- case-study/.

13 This post was written in broken English; for enhanced reader-friendliness, its grammar and spelling have been corrected.

14 Malcolm Nance and Chris Sampson, *Hacking ISIS: How to Destroy the Cyber Jihad* (New York: Skyhorse Publishing, 2017), pp. 60–78.

15 Jennifer T. Roberts, *Herodotus: A Very Short Introduction* (Oxford: Oxford University Press, 2011), p. 92.

16 Jack Kelly, 'Terror groups hide behind web encryption', *USA Today*, 5 May 2001. Available at https://usatoday30.usatoday.com/life/cyber/tech/2001-02-05-binladen.htm.

17 https://securityaffairs.co/wordpress/42581/intelligence/isis-mobile-app.html; https://www.ibtimes.co.uk/isis-app-islamic-state-launches-android-app-news-recruitment-1514055.

18 Cf. Schulze, 'The Surabaya Bombings and the Evolution of the Jihadi Threat in Indonesia'.

19 Charlie Winter, '1. Big news: the latest issue of #IS's newspaper features an unambiguous call to arms directed at female supporters', Twitter, 5 October 2017.

20 US Department of Justice, 'Wisconsin Woman Charged With Attempting to Provide Material Support to ISIS', 13 June 2018. Available at https://www.justice.gov/opa/pr/wisconsin-woman-charged-attempting-provide-material-support-isis.

21 'US woman charged with IS support had "virtual library" on bomb-making', BBC, 14 June. Available at https://www.bbc.com/news/world-us-canada-44485682.

5: INFO WARS

1 Julia Ebner, 'The far right thrives on global networks. They must be fought online and off', *Guardian*, 1 May 2017. Available at https://www.theguardian.com/commentisfree/2017/may/01/far-right-networks-nationalists-hate-social-media-companies.

2 Raheem Kassam, 'Tommy Robinson vs. Quilliam Show How the Establishment's Grip on Political Narratives is Slipping', Breitbart, 5 May 2017. Available at https://www.breitbart.com/europe/2017/05/07/

kassam-tommy-robinson-vs-quilliam-shows-how-the-establishments-grip-on-political-narratives-is-slipping/.

3   Ibid.

4   The 2011 census is available at https://www.ons.gov.uk/census/2011census.

5   Jamie Grierson, 'Four far-right plots thwarted last year, says counter-terrorism chief Mark Rowley', *Guardian*, 26 February 2018. Available at https://www.theguardian.com/uk-news/2018/feb/26/four-far-right-plots-thwarted-last-year-says-counter-terrorism-chief-mark-rowley.

6   Lizzie Dearden, 'Finsbury Park trial as it happened: Messages sent by Tommy Robinson to terror suspect Darren Osborne revealed in court', *Independent*, 23 January 2018. Available at https://www.independent.co.uk/news/uk/crime/finsbury-park-attack-trial-live-darren-osborne-court-muslims-mosque-van-latest-news-updates-a8173496.html.

7   Lizzie Dearden, 'Tommy Robinson supporters perform Nazi salutes at violent London protest, amid warnings of return to racist street movement', *Independent*, 11 June 2018. Available at https://www.independent.co.uk/news/uk/crime/tommy-robinson-free-protest-nazi-salutes-london-violence-police-arrests-attacks-prison-a8393566.html.

8   Lizzie Dearden, 'Man who taught girlfriend's pet pug dog to perform Nazi salutes fined £800', *Independent*, 23 April 2018. Available at https://www.independent.co.uk/news/uk/crime/count-dankula-nazi-pug-salutes-mark-meechan-fine-sentenced-a8317751.html.

9   Jake Ryan, 'Tommy Robinson to cash in on his notoriety by launching UK media company', *Sun*, 7 January 2019. Available at https://www.thesun.co.uk/news/8113022/tommy-robinson-to-cash-in-on-his-notoriety-by-launching-uk-media-company/.

10 'Tommy Robinson holds Salford protest against BBC Panorama', BBC, 23 February 2019. Available at https://www.bbc.com/news/uk-england-manchester-47335414.

11 'Trump supporter attacks BBC cameraman at El Paso rally', BBC, 12 February 2019. Available at https://www.bbc.com/news/world-us-canada-47208909.

12 See for example Sophie McBain, 'What Steve Bannon Really Believes In', *New Statesman*, 12 September 2018. Available at https://www.newstatesman.com/world/north-america/2018/09/what-steve-bannon-really-believes.

13 Betsy Woodruff, 'The Secret Heiress Funding the Right-Wing Media', Daily Beast, 13 September 2016. Available at https://www.thedailybeast.com/the-secret-heiress-funding-the-right-wing-media.

14 Paul P. Murphy, Kaya Yurieff and Gianluca Mezzofiore, 'Exclusive: YouTube ran ads from hundreds of brands on extremist channels', CNN, 20 April 2018. Available at https://money.cnn.com/2018/04/19/technology/youtube-ads-extreme-content-investigation/index.html.

15 'This is where internet memes come from', *MIT Technology Review*, 11 June 2018. Available at https://www.technologyreview.com/s/611332/this-is-where-internet-memes-come- from/.

16 Henryk M. Broder, 'Der Denunziant von Scholz & Friends', Achse des Guten, 7 December 2016. Available at https://www.achgut.com/artikel/der_denunziant_von_scholz_und_friends.

17 Anya Kamenetz, 'Professors are Targets in Online Culture Wars; Some Fight Back', National Public Radio, 4 April 2018. Available at https://www.npr.org/sections/ed/2018/04/04/590928008/professor-harassment.

18 Joshua Cuevas, 'A New Reality? The Far Right's Use of Cyberharassment Against Academics', American Association of University Professors. Retrieved from https://www.aaup.org/article/new-reality-

far-rights-use-cyberharassment-against-academics#.
WoGsdS-BofN.

19 Lizzie Dearden, 'Tommy Robinson case: why EDL founder could be jailed again for contempt of court', *Independent*, 26 September. Available at https://www. independent.co.uk/news/uk/crime/tommy-robinson-prison-jailed-why-contempt-court-grooming-gangs-muslim-protest-a8472566.html.

20 https://www.economist.com/the-economist-explains/2014/03/10/what-doxxing-is-and-why-it-matters.

21 Crash Override, 'Preventing Doxing: A primer on removing your personal information from the most commonly exploited places', 2018. Available at http://www. crashoverridenetwork.com/preventingdoxing.html.

22 Mat Honan, 'What is Doxing?', Wired, 3 June 2014. Available at https://www.wired.com/2014/03/doxing/.

23 Zoe Quinn, 'What happened after Gamergate hacked me', *Time*, 11 September 2017. Available at http://time.com/4927076/zoe-quinn-gamergate-doxxing-crash-override-excerpt/.

24 Bruce Schneier, '2015: The year "doxing" will hit home', BetaBoston, 31 December 2014. Available at http://www.betaboston.com/news/2014/12/31/2015-the-year-doxing-will-hit-home/.

25 Crash Override, 'Preventing Doxing: A primer on removing your personal information from the most commonly exploited places'.

26 See https://www.peoplelookup.com/privacy-policy.

27 Becky Gardiner et al., 'The dark side of Guardian comments', *Guardian*, 12 April 2017. Available at https:// www.theguardian.com/technology/2016/apr/12/ the-dark-side-of-guardian-comments.

28 'IFJ Survey, 'Two-thirds of women journalists suffered gender-based online attacks', IFJ, 7 December 2018. Available at https://www.ifj.org/media-centre/news/

detail/category/press-releases/article/ifj-survey-two-thirds-of-women-journalists-suffered-gender-based-online-attacks.

29 Caroline Jack, 'Lexicon of Lies: Terms for Problematic Information', Data and Society Research Institute, 2017.

30 Peter Pomerantsev, *Nothing Is True and Everything Is Possible* (Public Affairs, 2014), and John Pollock, 'Russian Disinformation Technology', *MIT Technology Review*, 13 April 2017. Available at https://www.technologyreview.com/s/604084/russian-disinformation-technology/.

31 David Robarge, 'Moles, Defectors, and Deceptions: James Angleton and CIA Counterintelligence', *Journal of Intelligence History* 3(2), Winter 2003, p. 31.

32 Interview with Donara Barojan, deputy director of the NATO Digital Forensic Research Lab.

33 Jon White, 'Dismiss, Distort, Distract, and Dismay: Continuity and Change in Russian Disinformation', *IES Policy Brief*, Issue 2016/13, May 2016. Available at https://www.ies.be/files/Policy%20Brief_Jon%20White.pdf.

34 Chloe Colliver et al., 'Smearing Sweden: International Influence Campaigns in the 2018 Swedish Election', ISD, October 2018. Available at http://www.lse.ac.uk/iga/assets/documents/arena/2018/Sweden-Report-October-2018.pdf.

35 Paris Martineau, 'How Alt-Right Twitter Tricks the Media into Panicking', Outline, 13 June 2018. Available at https://theoutline.com/post/4918/how-alt-right-twitter-tricks-the-media-into-panicking?zd=6&zi=csitrt27.

36 Samantha Bradshaw and Philip N. Howard, 'Challenging Truth and Trust: A Global Inventory of Organized Social Media Manipulation', Working Paper 2018.1, Oxford, UK, Project on Computational Propaganda. Available at comprop.oii.ox.ac.uk.

37 Jennifer Kavanagh and Michael D. Rich, 'Truth Decay: An Initial Exploration of the Diminishing Role of Facts and Analysis in American Public Life', RAND Corporation.

Available at https://www.rand.org/pubs/research_reports/RR2314.html.

38 Public Policy Polling, April 2013. The press release and summary are available at https://www.publicpolicypolling.com/wp-content/uploads/2017/09/PPP_Release_National_ConspiracyTheories_040213.pdf.

39 Kavanagh and Rich, 'Truth Decay: An Initial Exploration of the Diminishing Role of Facts and Analysis in American Public Life'.

40 Fabian Klask, 'Die Stille nach der lauten Nacht', *Die Zeit*, 29 December 2017. Available at https://www.zeit.de/2018/01/silvesternacht-koeln-sexuelle-belaestigung-schweigen-medien.

41 Reinhold Anton, *Die Lügenpresse* (Leipzig: Zehrfeld, 1914).

42 Bethan Bell, 'Child sexual exploitation: how the system failed', BBC, 16 March 2018. Available at https://www.bbc.com/news/uk-england-43400336.

43 David Neiwert, *Alt-America: The Rise of the Radical Right in the Age of Trump* (New York: Verso, 2017).

44 Angela Moon, 'Two-thirds of American adults get news from social media: survey', BBC, 8 September 2017. Available at https://www.reuters.com/article/us-usa-internet-socialmedia/two-thirds-of-american-adults-get-news-from-social-media-survey-idUSKCN1BJ2A8.

45 The term was coined by Data & Society researcher Joan Donovan; see for example Craig Timberg and Drew Harwell, 'We studied thousands of anonymous posts about the Parkland attack – and found a conspiracy in the making', *Washington Post*, 27 February 2018. Available at https://www.washingtonpost.com/business/economy/we-studied-thousands-of-anonymous-posts-about-the-parkland-attack---and-found-a-conspiracy-in-the-making/2018/02/27/04a856be-1b20-11e8-b2d9-08e74-8f892c0_story.html.

46 Ullrich Fichtner, 'Der SPIEGEL reveals internal fraud', *Spiegel*, 20 December 2018. Available at http://www.

spiegel.de/international/zeitgeist/claas-relotius-reporter-forgery-scandal-a-1244755.html.

47 'Claas Relotius und der Spiegel haben uns alle belogen', 19 December 2018. Available at https://www.youtube.com/watch?v=bpZEoAYDv2c.

48 'Rechtsextremisten greifen Medienhäuser und Parteien an', *TAZ*, 14 January 2019. Available at https://www.tagesspiegel.de/berlin/polizei-justiz/bundesweite-aktion-der-identitaeren-rechtsextremisten-greifen-medienhaeuser-und-parteien-an/23862586.html.

49 Chloe Colliver et al., 'The Battle for Bavaria: An Analysis of Online Information and Influence Campaigns in the 2018 Bavarian State Election', ISD, February 2019.

50 Colliver et al., 'Smearing Sweden: International Influence Campaigns in the 2018 Sweden Election'.

51 Yascha Mounk, *The People vs. Democracy: Why Our Freedom is in Danger and How We Save It* (Cambridge, Mass.: Harvard University Press, 2018).

52 T. Woodson, 'EDL's Tommy Robinson at a Luton BNP Meeting?', Three Counties Unity blog, 1 November 2010. Available at http://threecountiesunity.blogspot.com/2010/11/edls-tommyrobinson-at-luton-bnp.html.

53 The Twitter statistics are available at https://www.internetlivestats.com/twitter-statistics/.

6: MEME WARS

1 The current 'Alt-Right Leaks' account on Twitter is an American account and not associated with the original Europe-focused 'Alt Right Leaks' account.

2 Raphael Ottoni et al., 'Analyzing Right-wing YouTube Channels: Hate, Violence and Discrimination', in *Proceedings of the 10th ACM Conference on Web Science* (New York: ACM, 2018). Available at https://arxiv.org/pdf/1804.04096.pdf.

3 Ben Gilbert, 'YouTube now has over 1.8 billion users every month, within spitting distance of Facebook's

2 billion', *Business Insider*, 4 May 2018. Available at http:// uk.businessinsider.com/youtube-user-statistics-2018-5.

4 Jonas Kaiser, The Harvard Berkman Klein Center for Internet & Society. Available at http://cyber.harvard.edu/ events/2018/luncheon/01/Kaiser, https://www.youtube. com/watch?v=bhiA6pg4ohs.

5 Zeynep Tufekci, 'YouTube, the Great Radicalizer', *New York Times*, 10 March 2018. Available at https://www. nytimes.com/2018/03/10/opinion/sunday/youtube-politics-radical.html.

6 Ibid.

7 Angela Nagle, *Kill All Normies: Online Culture Wars from 4chan and Tumblr to Trump and the Alt-Right* (London: Zero Books, 2017).

8 Darren L. Linvill and Patrick L. Warren, 'Troll Factories: The Internet Research Agency and State-Sponsored Agenda Building', July 2018. Available at http://pwarren.people.clemson.edu/Linvill_Warren_TrollFactory.pdf.

9 Gabriele Thoß and Franz-Helmut Richter, *Ayatollah Khomeini: Zur Biographie und Hagiographie eines islamischen Revolutionsführers* (Münster: WurfVerlag, 1991), pp. 156–7.

10 Cf. Ervand Abrahamian, *Khomeinism: Essays on the Islamic Republic* (Berkeley: University of California Press, 1993), p. 2.

11 'The Oxymoron of "Illiberal Democracy"', Brookings, 2004, online: http://www.brookings.edu/research/opinions/2004/08/14islamicworld-abdulhamid, last accessed on 30 January 2015.

12 Caroline Jack, 'Lexicon of Lies: Terms for Problematic Information', Data & Society Research Institute, 2017. Available at https://datasociety.net/pubs/oh/DataAndSociety_LexiconofLies.pdf.

13 Jacob Davey and Julia Ebner, 'The Fringe Insurgency: Connectivity, Convergence and Mainstreaming of the Extreme Right', ISD, October 2017. Available at https://

www.isdglobal.org/wp-content/uploads/2017/10/The-Fringe-Insurgency-221017.pdf.

14 Sheila Johnston, 'The Wave: the experiment that turned a school into a police state', *Telegraph*, 5 September 2018. Available at https://www.telegraph.co.uk/culture/film/3559727/The-Wave-the-experiment-that-turned-a-school-into-a-police-state.html.

15 Michael Sailer et al., 'How gamification motivates: An experimental study of the effects of specific game design elements on psychological need satisfaction', *Computers in Human Behavior*, 69, April 2017, pp. 371–80. Available at https://www.sciencedirect.com/science/article/pii/S074756321630855X.

16 Jarret Brachman and Alix Levine, 'The World of Holy Warcraft: How Al Qaida is using online game theory to recruit the masses', *Foreign Policy*, 13 April 2011. Available at https://foreignpolicy.com/2011/04/13/the-world-of-holy-warcraft/.

17 Linda Schlegel, 'Playing jihad: The gamification of radicalization', *Defense Post*, 5 July 2018. Available at https://thedefensepost.com/2018/07/05/gamification-of-radicalization-opinion/.

18 See https://www.moddb.com/mods/stormer-doom/videos.

19 See https://yuki.la/pol/114837006.

20 Julia Ebner and Jacob Davey, 'Mainstreaming Mussolini: How the Extreme Right Attempted to "Make Italy Great Again" in the 2018 Italian Election', ISD, 2018. Available at https://www.isdglobal.org/wp-content/uploads/2018/03/Mainstreaming-Mussolini-Report-28.03.18.pdf.

21 Ahmed Al-Rawi, 'Video games, terrorism, and ISIS's Jihad 3.0', *Terrorism and Political Violence* 30(4), 2018, pp. 740–60. Available at https://www.tandfonline.com/doi/pdf/10.1080/09546553.2016.1207633.

22 Davey and Ebner, 'The Fringe Insurgency: Connectivity, Convergence and Mainstreaming of the Extreme Right'.

23 'Konstruktive Kritik', uploaded by Nerkur Xenus on 17 March 2018, https://www.youtube.com/watch?reload=9&v=nP5xZQaYgas&feature=youtu.be

24 The manual is available at https://www.hogesatzbau.de/wp-content/uploads/2018/01/HANDBUCH-FÜR-MEDIENGUERILLAS.pdf.

25 The original 'redpilling' manual was available at http://d-gen.de/2017/10/art-of-redpilling/; all contents were saved by Hogesatzbau and can be accessed at https://www.hogesatzbau.de/wp-content/uploads/2018/01/HANDBUCH-FÜR-MEDIENGUERILLAS.pdf.

26 Nagle, *Kill All Normies: Online Culture Wars from 4chan and Tumblr to Trump and the Alt-Right*.

27 Jeff Giesea, 'It's time to embrace memetic warfare', *Defense Strategic Communications Journal*, NATO Stratcom COE, 2017. Available at https://www.stratcomcoe.org/jeff-giesea-its-time-embrace-memetic-warfare.

28 Benite Heiskanen, 'Meme-ing Electoral Participation', *European Journal of American Studies* 12 (2), Summer 2017. Available at https://journals.openedition.org/ejas/12158.

29 Jack Phillips, '"Great Meme War" Could Hit the Media', *Epoch Times*, 11 November 2016. Available at https://www.theepochtimes.com/4chan-reddits-the_donald-may-take-great-meme-war-to-the-media_2184823.html.

30 Joseph Bernstein, 'This Man Helped to Build the Trump Meme Army – Now He Wants to Reform It', *BuzzFeed*, 18 January 2017. Available at https://www.buzzfeednews.com/article/josephbernstein/this-man-helped-build-the-trump-meme-army-and-now-he-wants-t.

31 Savvas Zannettou et al., 'On the Origins of Memes by Means of Fringe Web Communities', IMC '18, Proceedings of the Internet Measurement Conference 2018, pp. 188–202. Available at https://dl.acm.org/citation.cfm?id=3278550.

32 Matthew Costello and James Hawdon, 'Who Are the Online Extremists Among Us? Sociodemographic Characteristics, Social Networking, and Online Experiences of Those Who Produce Online Hate Materials', *Violence and Gender* 5(1), 2018, pp. 55–60.

33 Nelli Ferenczi, 'Are sex differences in antisocial and pro-social Facebook use explained by narcissism and relational self-construal?', *Computers in Human Behavior* 77, December 2017, pp. 25–31. Available at https://www.sciencedirect.com/science/article/pii/S0747563217305010.

34 'Online Harassment', Pew Research Center, 2014. Available at http://www.pewinternet.org/2014/10/22/online-harassment/.

35 'Toxic Twitter: A Toxic Place for Women', Amnesty International and Element AI, 2018. Available at https://www.amnesty.org/en/latest/research/2018/03/online-violence-against-women-chapter-1/.

36 See endnote 25.

37 Harriet Agerholm, 'Lily Allen gives up Twitter account after she is taunted over stillbirth of her son', *Independent*, 26 February 2017. Available at https://www.independent.co.uk/news/people/lily-allen-stillbirth-twitter-trolls-abuse-online-bullying-a7600416.html.

38 The ITV documentary which features ISD research is available at https://www.itv.com/news/2019-03-04/itv-investigation-reveals-extent-of-online-abuse-and-death-threats-aimed-at-mps-in-exposure-brexit-online-uncovered/.

39 'Online Harassment', Pew Research Center.

40 Philip Kreißel, Julia Ebner, Alex Urban and Jakob Guhl, 'Hass auf Knopfdruck: Rechtsextreme Trollfabriken und das Ökosystem koordinierter Hasskampagnen im Netz', ISD/#ichbinhier, July 2018.

41 Interview with the initiator of Alt Right Leaks.

42 Alt-Right Open Intelligence Initiative, 'Mapping the Alt-Right: The US Alternative Right across the Atlantic', July 2017. Available at https://wiki.digitalmethods.net/Dmi/AltRightOpenIntelligenceInitiative.

43 Ebner and Davey, 'Mainstreaming Mussolini: How the Extreme Right Attempted to "Make Italy Great Again" in the 2018 Italian Election'.

44 Kreißel, Ebner, Urban and Guhl, 'Hass auf Knopfdruck: Rechtsextreme Trollfabriken und das Ökosystem koordinierter Hasskampagnen im Netz'.

45 'When is the "OK" gesture not OK?', BBC, 16 May 2019. Available at https://www.bbc.co.uk/news/world-europe-48293817.

46 Julia Alexander, 'The NPC meme went viral when the media gave it oxygen', Verge, 23 October 2018. Available at https://www.theverge.com/2018/10/23/17991274/npc-meme-4chan-press-coverage-viral.

47 Whitney Phillips, 'Oxygen of Amplification: Better Practices for Reporting on Extremists, Antagonists, and Manipulators Online', Data & Society Research Institute, 2018. Available at https://datasociety.net/wp-content/uploads/2018/05/0-EXEC-SUMMARY_Oxygen_of_Amplification_DS.pdf.

48 Ibid.

7: ALT–TECH

1 The Quiverfull is a Christian fundamentalist movement that opposes all forms of birth control.

2 The app was promoted on Richard Spencer's AltRight.com platform, which can be accessed at https://altright.com/2017/02/16/patriot-peer-connecting-the-silent-majority/.

3 The thread on 4chan's /pol board can be accessed at https://archive.4plebs.org/pol/thread/112316443/.

4   Martin Sellner, 'Patriot Peer – Connnecting the Silent Majority', AltRight, 2017. Available at https://altright.com/2017/02/16/patriot-peer-connecting-the-silent-majority/.

5   Gab, 'Announcing the Free Spech Tech Alliance', Medium, 11 August 2017. Available at https://medium.com/@getongab/announcing-the-alt-tech-alliance-18bebe89c60a.

6   Ibid.

7   Ibid.

8   'Zuckerberg: Facebook "certainly doesn't feel like a monopoly to me"', *Washington Post*, 10 April 2018. Available at https://www.youtube.com/watch?v=zcFAvuWULiI.

9   Tony Romm, 'Congress wants to drag Google and Twitter into Facebook's privacy crisis', *Washington Post*, 26 March 2018. Available at https://www.washingtonpost.com/news/the-switch/wp/2018/03/26/facebooks-stock-falls-as-the-federal-trade-commission-confirms-its-investigating-the-company/?utm_term=.cd081f9c55b0.

10 Billy Bambrough, 'Bitcoin donations to neo-Nazis are climbing ahead of this weekend's Unite the Right rally', Forbes, 6 August 2018. Available at https://www.forbes.com/sites/billybambrough/2018/08/06/bitcoin-donations-to-neo-nazis-are-climbing-ahead-of-this-weekends-unite-the-right-rally/#3e1fb0c769ac.

11 Nikita Malik, 'Terror in the Dark: How Terrorists Use Encryption, the Dark Net and Cryptocurrencies', Henry Jackson Society, April 2018. Available at https://henryjacksonsociety.org/publications/terror-in-the-dark-how-terrorists-use-encryption-the-darknet-and-cryptocurrencies/. And David Carlisle, 'Cryptocurrencies and Terrorist Financing: A Risk, But Hold the Panic', RUSI, March 2017. Available at https://rusi.org/commentary/cryptocurrencies-and-terrorist-financing-risk-hold-panic.

12 Ibid.

8: FOLLOW Q

1   In this chapter, my conversations with roughly a dozen QAnon adherents were synthesised into a just few characters for better readability.

2   For more information about these classic conspiracy theories see C. Stempel, T. Hargrove and G.H. Stempel III, 'Media use, social structure, and belief in 9/11 conspiracy theories', *Journalism & Mass Communication Quarterly* 84(2), 2007, pp. 353–72. M. J. Wood, K. M. Douglas and R. M. Sutton, 'Dead and alive: beliefs in contradictory conspiracy theories', Social Psychological and Personality Science 3, 2012, pp. 767–73. J. W. McHoskey, 'Case closed? On the John F. Kennedy assassination: biased assimilation of evidence and attitude polarization', Basic and Applied Social Psychology 17, 1995, pp. 395–409.

3   J. T. Jost, A. Ledgerwood and C. D. Hardin, 'Shared reality, system justification, and the relational basis of ideological beliefs', *Social & Personality Psychology Compass* 2, 2008, pp. 171–86, and Karen M. Douglas et al., 'The Psychology of Conspiracy Theories', *Current Directions in Psychological Science* 26(6), 2017, pp. 538–42.

4   Jan-Willem van Prooijen and Karen M. Douglas, 'Conspiracy theories as part of history: The role of societal crisis situations', *Memory Studies* 10(3), 2017, pp. 323–33. Available at https://www.ncbi.nlm.nih.gov/pmc/articles/PMC5646574/.

5   Michael J. G. Gray-Fow, 'Why the Christians? Nero and the Great Fire', *Latomus* 57(3), 1998, pp. 595–616. Available at http://www.jstor.org/stable/41538370.

6   'Brexit and Trump voters more likely to believe in conspiracy theories, survey study shows', YouGov-Cambridge Centre, 23 November 2018. Available at https://www.cam.ac.uk/research/news/brexit-and-trump-voters-more-likely-to-believe-in-conspiracy-theories-survey-study-shows.

7   'Brain fills gaps to produce a likely picture', *Science Daily*, 27 June 2014. Available at https://www.sciencedaily.com/ releases/2014/06/140627094551.htm.

8   See for example D. R. Ballinger, 'Conspiratoria – the Internet and the Logic of Conspiracy Theory', University of Waikato, 2011. Available at https://hdl.handle. net/10289/5786.

9   The original post can be found at https://io.kym-cdn. com/photos/images/newsfeed/001/322/344/860.jpg.

10 Jerry S. Piven (ed.), *Terror and Apocalypse: Psychological Undercurrents of History Volume II* (Bloomington, Indiana: Universe, 2002).

11 Norman Cohn, *The Pursuit of the Millennium: Revolutionary Millenarians and Mystical Anarchists of the Middle Ages* (London: Pimlico, 1993).

12 See etymological source of 'apocalypse' in the Merriam Webster Dictionary, https://www.merriam-webster. com/dictionary/apocalypse.

13 Michael Barkun, 'Failed Prophecies Won't Stop Trump's True Believers', Foreign Policy, 8 November 2018. Available at https://foreignpolicy.com/2018/11/08/failed-prophecies-wont-stop-trumps-true-believers/.

14 Leon Festinger, Henry Riecken and Stanley Schacter, *When Prophecy Fails* (New York: Harper & Row, 1956), and Lorne L. Dawson, 'The Failure of Prophecy and the Future of IS', ICCT Policy Brief, September 2017. Available at https://icct.nl/wp-content/uploads/2017/09/ICCT-Dawson-The-Failure-of-Prophecy-and-The-Future-of-ISIS-Sept-2017.pdf.

15 Hayley Peterson, 'Amazon and Costco are selling emergency kits that can feed a family for a year – and it reveals a disturbing new normal in America', Business Insider, 9 March 2018. Available at https://www.businessinsider. com/costco-amazon-emergency-kits-2018-3. And Kylie Mohr, 'Apocalypse Chow: We Tried Televangelist Jim Bakker's "Survival Food"', NPR, 3 December

2015. Available at https://www.npr.org/sections/thesalt/2015/12/03/456677535/apocalypse-chow-we-tried-televangelist-jim-bakkers-survival-food.

16 See for example https://www.emergencyfoodstorage.co.uk/products/brexit-box.

17 'Terrorism suspect makes reference to extremist conspiracies', SPLC, 20 July 2018. Available at https://www.splcenter.org/hatewatch/2018/07/20/terrorism-suspect-makes-reference-extremist-conspiracies.

18 Mark Fisher, John W. Cox and Peter Herman, 'From rumor to hashtag to gunfire in D.C.', *Washington Post*, 6 December 2016. Available at https://www.washingtonpost.com/local/pizzagate-from-rumor-to-hashtag-to-gunfire-in-dc/2016/12/06/4c7def50-bbd4-11e6-94ac-3d324840106c_story.html?utm_term=.30b166abe2bf.

19 Blake Montgomery, 'A Man Allegedly Killed His Brother with a 4-Foot Sword Because He Thought He Was A Lizard Person', BuzzFeed, 10 January 2019. Available at https://www.buzzfeednews.com/article/blakemontgomery/man-brother-murder-charge-sword.

20 'The Book of Q: The biggest drop ever', 20 November 2017. Available at https://drive.google.com/file/d/1G6guY_q-PzZfdJM4ItzmQIF9gfPrOQxk/view.

21 See for example https://www.buzzfeednews.com/article/ryanhatesthis/its-looking-extremely-likely-that-qanon-is-probably-a and https://twitter.com/wikileaks/status/1001139404805738498.

22 Ryan Broderick, 'People Think This Whole QAnon Conspiracy Theory is A Prank on Trump Supporters', Buzzfeed, 8 August 2018. Available at https://web.archive.org/web/20180806121403/.

23 See the Anonymous tweet: https://twitter.com/YourAnonNews/status/1025454095228985349.

24 Stewart Home, *Mind Invaders: A Reader in Psychic Warfare, Cultural Sabotage and Semiotic Terrorism* (London: Serpent's Tail, 1997).

25 Will Sommer, 'Why a Red "X" is the New Symbol of Conservative Twitter', Daily Beast, 8 October 2018. Available at https://www.thedailybeast.com/why-a-red-x-is-the-new-symbol-of-conservative-twitter and https://emojipedia.org/cross-mark/.

26 Michael J. Wood, Karen Douglas and Robbie M. Sutton, 'Dead and alive: Belief in contradictory conspiracy theories', *Social Psychology and Personality Science* 3, 2012, pp. 767–73.

27 S. Moscovici, 'The conspiracy mentality', in C. F. Graumann and S. Moscovici (eds), *Changing Conceptions of Conspiracy* (New York: Springer, 1987), pp. 151–69.

28 David Dunning, 'Chapter Five: The Dunning–Kruger Effect: On Being Ignorant of One's Own Ignorance', *Advances in Experimental Social Psychology* 44, 2011, pp. 247–96. Available at https://www.sciencedirect.com/science/article/pii/B9780123855220000056.

29 See https://twitter.com/danieleganser/status/824953776280854528?lang=en.

30 See https://8ch.net//qresearch//res/4279775.html#4280231.

31 See https://www.qanon.pub.

32 Kyle Feldscher, 'QAnon-believing "conspiracy analyst" meets Trump in the White House', CNN, 25 August 2018. Available at https://edition.cnn.com/2018/08/25/politics/donald-trump-qanon-white-house/index.html.

33 Will Sommer, 'What is QAnon? The Craziest Theory of the Trump Era Explained', Daily Beast, 7 June 2018. Available at https://www.thedailybeast.com/what-is-qanon-the-craziest-theory-of-the-trump-era-explained.

34 Fruzsina Eordogh, 'What is QAnon, the Conspiracy Theory Attracting Alex Jones, Roseanne Barr and … a Guy from "Vanderpump Rules"', *Elle*, 7 August 2018. Available at https://www.elle.com/culture/career-politics/a22665744/qanon-conspiracy-theory-explainer/.

35 Emma Grey Ellis, 'Win or Lose, the Alex Jones Lawsuit Will Help Redefine Free Speech',

Wired, 16 August 2018. Available at https://www.
wired.com/story/alex-jones-lawsuit-will-help-
redefine-free-speech?mbid=nl_080618_daily_list1_
p4&CNDID=50329017.

36 The ITV documentary which features ISD research is
available at https://www.itv.com/news/2019-03-04/
itv-investigation-reveals-extent-of-online-abuse-and-
death-threats-aimed-at-mps-in-exposure-brexit-online-
uncovered/.

37 Joel Rogers de Waal, 'Brexit and Trump voters more
likely to believe in conspiracy theories, survey study
shows' International YouGov–Cambridge Centre, 14
December 2018. Available at: https://yougov.co.uk/
topics/international/articles-reports/2018/12/14/
brexit-and-trump-voters-are-more-likely-to-believe-co.

38 Michael Butter, *Nichts ist, wie es scheint* (Berlin:
Suhrkamp, 2018).

39 Richard Hofstadter, 'The Paranoid Style in American
Politics', *Harper's Magazine*, November 1964. Available
at https://harpers.org/archive/1964/11/the-paranoid-
style-in-american-politics/.

40 Butter, *Nichts ist, wie es scheint*.

41 Andrew F. Wilson, '#whitegenocide, the Alt-right
and Conspiracy Theory: How Secrecy and Suspicion
Contributed to the Mainstreaming of Hate', *Secrecy and
Society* 1(2), 2018. Available at https://core.ac.uk/down-
load/pdf/153389078.pdf.

9: UNITE THE RIGHT

1 Andrew Anglin, 'PSA: When the Alt-Right Hits the
Street, You Wanna Be Ready', Daily Stormer, 9 August
2017. Available at https://dailystormer.name/psa-when-
the-internet-becomes-real-life-and-the-alt-right-hits-
the-street-you-wanna-be-ready/.

2 Ibid.

3   Cynthia Miller Idris, *The Extreme Gone Mainstream: Commercialization and Far Right Youth Culture in Germany* (Princeton, NJ: Princeton University Press, 2018).

4   Bernhard Forchtner and Christoffer Kolvraa, 'Extreme right images of radical authenticity: Multimodal aesthetics of history, nature, and gender roles in social media', *European Journal of Cultural and Political Sociology* 4(3), 2017. Available at https://www.tandfonline.com/doi/abs/10.1 080/23254823.2017.1322910?src=recsys&journalCode=r ecp20.

5   Miller Idris, *The Extreme Gone Mainstream: Commercialization and Far Right Youth Culture in Germany*.

6   Artur Beifuss and Francesco Trivini Bellini, *Branding Terror: The Logotypes and Iconography of Insurgent Groups and Terrorist Organizations* (London; New York: Merrell Publishers, 2013).

7   Patrick Hanlon, *Primalbranding: Create Zealots for Your Brand, Your Company, and Your Future* (New York: Free Press, 2011).

8   Jacob Davey and Julia Ebner, 'The Fringe Insurgency: Connectivity, Convergence and Mainstreaming of the Extreme Right', ISD, October 2017. Available at https:// www.isdglobal.org/wp-content/uploads/2017/10/The-Fringe-Insurgency-221017.pdf.

9   Hunter Wallace, 'Why we should #UniteTheRight', *Occidental Dissent*, 4 August 2017. Available at http://www.occidentaldissent.com/2017/08/04/ why-we-should-unitetheright/.

10   Lee Rogers, 'Join Daily Stormer Staff at the "Unite the Right" Rally in Charlottesville, Virginia', Daily Stormer, 30 July 2017.

11   Cf. Davey and Ebner, 'The Fringe Insurgency: Connectivity, Convergence and Mainstreaming of the Extreme Right'.

12   Ibid.

13   Mark Bray, *Antifa: The Anti-Fascist Handbook* (New York: Melville House, 2017).

14   Cf. Davey and Ebner, 'The Fringe Insurgency: Connectivity, Convergence and Mainstreaming of the Extreme Right'.

15   Harvey Whitehouse et al., 'The evolution of extreme cooperation via shared dysphoric experiences', *Scientific Reports* 7: 44292. DOI: 10.1038/srep44292.

16   Harvey Whitehouse, 'Dying for the group: Towards a general theory of extreme self-sacrifice', *Behavioral and Brain Sciences* 7, 2018, pp. 1–64. DOI: 10.1017/S0140525X18000249.

17   'Charlottesville Unite the Right Updates from TRS and Cantwell', Daily Stormer, 9 August 2017. Available at https://www.dailystormer.com/charlottesville-unite-the-right-updates-from-trs-and-cantwell/.

18   Paul P. Murphy, 'White nationalists use tiki torches to light up Charlottesville march', CNN, 14 August 2017. Available at http://money.cnn.com/2017/08/14/news/companies/tiki-torches-charlottesville/index.html.

19   Davey and Ebner, 'The Fringe Insurgency: Connectivity, Convergence and Mainstreaming of the Extreme Right'.

20   'Charlottesville: Who was Heather Heyer', BBC, 14 August 2017. Available at https://www.bbc.co.uk/news/world-us-canada-40924922.

21   Christine Hauser, 'DeAndre Harris, Beaten by White Supremacists in Charlottesville, Is Found Not Guilty of Assault', *New York Times*, 14 August 2017. Available at https://www.nytimes.com/2018/03/16/us/deandre-harris-charlottesville.html.

22   See https://boards.4chan.org/pol/thread/137112233.

23   'Political Event Calendar', Right Wing United, 2019. Available at https://rightwingunited.wordpress.com/political-event-calendar/.

24   'Guide to Attending Rallies', Right Wing United, 2019. Available at https://rightwingunited.wordpress.com/guide-to-attending-rallies/.

25   Joseph Cox, 'Leaked Documents Show Facebook's Post-Charlottesville Reckoning with American Nazis',

Motherboard, 25 May 2018. Available at https://mother-board.vice.com/en_us/article/mbkbbq/facebook-charlottesville-leaked-documents-american-nazis.

26 Kelly Weil, 'The Far-Right is Trying to Co-Opt the Yellow Vests', Daily Beast, 8 January 2019. Available at https://www.thedailybeast.com/the-far-right-is-trying-to-co-opt-the-yellow-vests.

27 Alexander Hurst, 'The Ugly, Illiberal, Anti-Semitic Heart of the Yellow Vest Movement', *New Republic*, 7 January 2019. Available at https://newrepublic.com/article/152853/ugly-illiberal-anti-semitic-heart-yellow-vest-movement.

28 The opinion poll carried out by Elabe for BFMTV on 5 December 2018 is available at https://elabe.fr/wp-content/uploads/2018/12/rapport_20181205_elabe_bfmtv_les-francais-les-gilets-jaunes-et-les-mesures-annoncees-par-edouard-philippe.pdf.

29 Lizzie Dearden, 'Yellow vest protests: who is the "far-right element" harassing MPs outside parliament?', *Independent*, 8 January 2019. Available at https://www.independent.co.uk/news/uk/politics/yellow-vest-protests-parliament-protest-anna-soubry-brexit-nazi-james-goddard-who-met-police-owen-a8716621.html.

30 Philip Kuhn, 'Die unheimliche Mobilisierung der Neonazis in Chemnitz', *Die Welt*, 28 August 2018. Available at https://www.welt.de/politik/deutschland/article181342196/Rechtsextreme-Ausschreitungen-Die-unheimliche-Mobilisierung-der-Neonazis-in-Chemnitz.html.

31 David Crossland, 'Germany: Migrant beaten with iron chain as far-right violence spreads', *The Times*, 30 August 2018. Available at https://www.thetimes.co.uk/article/germany-migrant-beaten-with-iron-chain-as-farright-violence-spreads-fkj6870tt.

32 Klaus Ott, Annette Ramelsberger, Nicolas Richter and Antonie Rietzschel, 'Revolution von rechts', *Süddeutsche*

Zeitung, 1 October 2018. Available at https://www.
sueddeutsche.de/politik/revolution-chemnitz-1.4152545.

33 Simone Rafael and Miro Dittrich, 'Online Mobilisierung für Chemnitz: Bewegtbild-Hetze sorgt für Reichweite', Belltower, 1 September 2018. Available at https://www.belltower.news/online-mobilisierung-fuer-chemnitz-bewegtbild-hetze-sorgt-fuer-reichweite-49176/.

34 Ibid.

10: SCHILD & SCHWERT

1 Samira Alshater, 'Die Rückkehr von "Blood & Honour" und dem bewaffneten Arm Combat 18', Belltower, 10 April 2018. Available at http://www.belltower.news/artikel/die-rueckkehr-von-blood-honour-und-dem-bewaffneten-arm-combat-18-13545.

2 Patrick Gensing, 'Rassistische Mordserie, staatliches Versagen', *ARD Tagesschau*, 27 August 2013. Available at https://www.tagesschau.de/inland/rechtsextrememord serie104.html.

3 See https://www.facebook.com/Terrorsph%C3%A 4ra-150707598416109/ and https://www.youtube.com/watch?v=iAGIOepeq8k.

4 'Nazi Hipster Patrick Schröder', Belltower, 16 April 2014. Available at http://www.belltower.news/artikel/nazi-hipster-patrick-schr%C3%B6der-macht-ansgar-aryan-fsn-tv-und-live-h8-9391.

5 Roman Lehberger, 'Nazi-Mode: Die Hintermänner der rechten Mode-Labels', Spiegel TV, 8 July 2018. Available at https://www.youtube.com/watch?v=GhJn2KJLaOk.

6 Karsten Schmehl and Marcus Engert, 'An diesem AfD-Stand war ein Mann mit "HKN KRZ" Shirt und die AfD So: Haben wir nicht gemerkt', BuzzFeed, 27 August 2017. Available at https://www.buzzfeed.com/de/karstenschmehl/der-interessierte-buerger-mit-hakenkreuz-tshirt.

7   Andreas Dieste and Roman Lehberger, 'Stil–Berater Patrick Schröder: Der nette Nazi', Spiegel TV. Available at https://www.spiegel.tv/videos/160827-der-nette-neonazi.

8   Lehberger, 'Nazi-Mode: Die Hintermänner der rechten Mode-Labels'.

9   His Twitter profile can be found at https://twitter.com/patricks_fsn?lang=en.

10 'Nazi Hipster Patrick Schröder', Belltower, 16 April 2014. Available at: https://www.belltower.news/nazi-hipster-patrick-schroeder-37300/.

11 Dieste and Lehberger, 'Stil-Berater Patrick Schröder: Der nette Nazi'.

12 Their website can be found at http://www.kampf-der-nibelungen.com/.

13 Simon Parkin, 'The rise of Russia's neo–Nazi football hooligans', Guardian, 24 April 2018. Available at https://www.theguardian.com/news/2018/apr/24/russia-neo-nazi-football-hooligans-world-cup.

14 Robert Claus, Hooligans: Eine Welt zwischen Fußball, Gewalt und Politik (Berlin: Die Werkstatt, 2017), and Christoph Ruf, 'Wie rechte Hooligans den Kampfsport erobern', Spiegel, 9 October 2017. Available at http://www.spiegel.de/sport/sonst/kampf-der-nibelungen-wie-hooligans-den-kampfsport-erobern-a-1170558.html.

15 See for example https://www.youtube.com/watch?v=Z46IpqjQs8M.

16 Tim Hume, 'A Russian Neo-Nazi Football Hooligan is Trying to Build an MMA Empire Across Europe', Vice, 26 July 2018. Available at https://news.vice.com/en_us/article/435mjw/a-russian-neo-nazi-football-hooligan-is-trying-to-build-an-mma-empire-across-europe.

11: BLACK HATS

1   Jenkins is an open-source server written in JavaScript and used to automate software development.

2   Ms Smith, 'Hackers exploit Jenkins servers, make 3$ million by mining Monero', CSO Online, 20 February 2018. Available at https://www.csoonline.com/article/3256314/security/hackers-exploit-jenkins-servers-make-3-million-by-mining-monero.html.

3   Malcolm Nance and Chris Sampson, *Hacking ISIS: How to Destroy the Cyber Jihad* (New York: Skyhorse Publishing, 2017), pp. 23–6.

4   Ibid.

5   Jessica Mazzola, 'Pro-ISIS group hacks N.J. school website, posts recruitment video', NJ, 7 November 2017. Available at http://www.nj.com/essex/index.ssf/2017/11/hack_posts_isis_recruitment_video_on_nj_school_web.html.

6   'Prince Albert Police Service website hacked, pro-ISIS message left', CBC News, 8 November 2017. Available at http://www.cbc.ca/news/canada/saskatchewan/prince-albert-police-website-hacked-isis-1.4392568.

7   Dawn Chmielewski, 'Cyber Security Expert Mikko Hyppönen Worries About Extremists with Computers', Recode, 20 October 2015. Available at https://www.recode.net/2015/10/20/11619776/cybersecurity-expert-mikko-hyppnen-worries-about-extremists-with.

8   Nance and Sampson, *Hacking ISIS: How to Destroy the Cyber Jihad*, p. 31.

9   Yonah Jeremy Bob, 'Exclusive: Islamic Cyber Terrorists Trying to Target Infrastructure', *Jerusalem Post*, 9 July 2018. Available at https://www.jpost.com/Arab-Israeli-Conflict/Exclusive-Islamic-cyber-terrorists-trying-to-target-infrastructure-562052.

10 J. R. Raphael, 'Hacker Claims Credit for Amazon Gay-Themed Book "Glitch"', *PC World*, 13 April 2009. Available at https://www.pcworld.com/article/163024/hacker_claims_credit_for_amazons_gay_themed_book_glitch.html.

11 Karen McVeigh, 'US hacker Andrew Auernheimer given three years jail term for AT&T breach', *Guardian*, 18 March 2013. Available at https://www.

theguardian.com/technology/2013/mar/18/us-hacker-andrew-auernheimer-at-t.

12   Kim Zetter, 'AT&T Hacker "Weev" Sentenced to 3.5 Years in Prison', Wired, 3 August 2013. Available at https://www.wired.com/2013/03/att-hacker-gets-3-years/.

13   Archived on Reddit: http://www.reddit.com/r/IAmA/comments/1ahkgc/i_am_weev_i_may_be_going_to_prison_under_the/c8xgqq9.

14   Weev, 'What I Learned from My Time in Prison', Daily Stormer, October 2014.

15   From Weev's blog: https://weev.livejournal.com.

16   Ibid.

17   Ibid.

18   Weev's Hatreon page can be found at https://hatreon.net/weev/.

19   The post can be found in the archived 4chan thread: https://archive.4plebs.org/pol/thread/157481867/.

20   Rachel Gutmann, 'Who is Weev, and Why Did He Derail a Journalist's Career?', Atlantic, 14 February 2018. Available at https://www.theatlantic.com/technology/archive/2018/02/who-is-weev/553295/. The court case materials can be found at https://www.splcenter.org/sites/default/files/whitefish_complaint_final.pdf.

21   Dylan Matthews, 'Who is Saul Alinsky, and why does the right hate him so much?', Vox, 6 October 2014. Available at https://www.vox.com/2014/10/6/6829675/saul-alinsky-explain-obama-hillary-clinton-rodham-organizing.

22   C is a general-purpose, machine-independent programming language that was used to write a range of well-known applications – from Windows operating systems to Oracle databases.

23   x86 assembler is programming language used for time-sensitive applications and detailed software systems.

24   Jon Erickson, Hacking: The Art of Exploitation (San Francisco, CA: No Starch Press, 2008).

25   A 0-day is a form of cyberattack that exploits a vulnerable spot in software that is unknown or unaddressed by the software vendors

26   A skiptracer is a person whose main job it is to geolocate and track down individuals.

27   A git pull is a command used to download and change content from a remote repository.

28   Bridget Johnson, 'Cyber Caliphate Vows to Kill Anonymous Hackers Who Have Been Taking Down ISIS', PJ Media, 15 August 2018. Available at https://pjmedia. com/homeland-security/cyber-caliphate-vows-to-kill-anonymous-hackers-who-have-been-taking-down-isis/.

29   See Techopedia definition at https://www.techopedia. com/definition/26361/hacking.

30   'Guardians of the New World', 6 February. Available at https://www.youtube.com/watch?v=jUFEeuWqFPE.

31   Oliver Holmes, 'Israel: Hamas created fake dating app to hack soldiers' phones', Guardian, 3 July 2018. Available at https://www.theguardian.com/world/2018/jul/03/israel-hamas-created-fake-dating-apps-to-hack-soldiers-phones.

32   'Russia "was behind German parliament hack"', BBC, 13 May 2016. Available at https://www.bbc.com/news/technology-36284447.

33   Raphael Satter, 'Inside Story: How Russians Hacked the Democrats' Emails', Associated Press, 4 November 2017. Available at https://www.apnews.com/dea73efc01594839 957c3c9a6c962b8a.

34   Megha Mohan, 'Macron Leaks: anatomy of a hack', BBC Trending, 9 May 2017. Available at https://www.bbc. co.uk/news/blogs-trending-39845105.

35   'NHS "could have prevented" Wannacry ransomware attack', BBC, 27 October 2017. Available at https://www. bbc.co.uk/news/technology-41753022.

36   Chris Ratcliffe, 'Hacker who stopped WannaCry charged with writing banking malware', Wired, 3 August

2017. Available at https://www.wired.com/story/wannacry-malwaretech-arrest.

37 Greg Otto, 'Marcus Hutchins pleads guilty to two counts related to Kronos banking malware', Cyber-scoop, 19 April 2010. Available at https://www.cyberscoop.com/marcus-hutchins-malwaretech-guilty-plea-kronos/

38 Valeria C. Moreno et al., 'Analysis of physical and cyber security-related events in the chemical and process industry', *Process Safety and Environmental Protection* 116, May 2018, pp. 621–31. Available at https://www.sciencedirect.com/science/article/pii/S095758201830079X.

39 Alix Langone, '11-Year-Old Hacked into a U.S. Voting System Replica in 10 Minutes This Weekend', *Time*, 14 August 2018. Available at http://time.com/5366171/11-year-old-hacked-into-us-voting-system-10-minutes/.

40 Stefan Nicola, 'Hackers Dump Data on Merkel, Politicians in Giant German Leak', Bloomberg, 4 January 2019. Available at https://www.bloomberg.com/news/articles/2019-01-04/hackers-release-personal-data-of-hundreds-of-german-politicians.

41 'German politicians targeted in mass data attack', BBC, 4 January, 2019. Available at https://www.bbc.co.uk/news/world-europe-46757009.

42 Patrick Beuth et al., 'Merkel and the Fancy Bear', *Die Zeit*, 12 May 2015. Available at https://www.zeit.de/digital/2017-05/cyberattack-bundestag-angela-merkel-fancy-bear-hacker-russia.

12: GAMIFIED TERRORISM

1 Jason Wilson, 'Christchurch shooter's links to Austrian far-right "more extensive than thought"', *Guardian*, 16 May 2019. Available at https://www.theguardian.com/world/2019/may/16/christchurch-shooters-links-to-austrian-far-right-more-extensive-than-thought.

2 J. M. Berger, *Extremism* (Cambridge, Mass.: MIT Press, 2018).

3 Home Office, 'Individuals referred to and supported through the Prevent programme, April 2017 to March 2018', 13 December 2018. Available at https://assets. publishing.service.gov.uk/government/uploads/system/uploads/attachment_data/file/763254/individuals-referred-supported-prevent-programme-apr2017-mar2018-hosb3118.pdf.

4 Bundesministerium des Innern, für Bau und Heimat, 'Verfassungsschutzbericht 2018', June 2019. Available at https://www.verfassungsschutz.de/de/oeffentlichkeitsarbeit/publikationen/verfassungss chutzberichte/vsbericht-2018.

5 Anti-Defamation League, 'Murder and Extremism in the United States in 2018', 2019. Available at https://www.adl. org/murder-and-extremism-2018.

6 Ty McCormick, 'Gamification: A Short History', Foreign Policy, 24 June 2013. Available at https://foreignpolicy. com/2013/06/24/gamification-a-short-history/.

7 The official Facebook newsroom announcement is available at https://twitter.com/fbnewsroom/status/1107117981358682112.

8 The entry is available at https://encyclopediadramatica. rs/Brenton_Tarrant.

9 Weiyi Cai and Simone Landon, 'Attacks by White Extremists Are Growing. So Are Their Connections', *New York Times*, 3 April 2019. Available at https://www. nytimes.com/interactive/2019/04/03/world/white-extremist-terrorism-christchurch.html.

10 Robert Evans, 'Ignore the Poway Synagogue Shooter's Manifesto: Pay Attention to 8chan's /pol/ Board', Bellingcat, 28 April 2019. Available at https://www. bellingcat.com/news/americas/2019/04/28/ignore-the-poway-synagogue-shooters-manifesto-pay-attention-to-8chans-pol-board/.

11 Andrew Marantz, 'The Poway Synagogue Shooting Follows an Unsettling New Script', *New Yorker*, 29 April

2019. Available at https://www.newyorker.com/news/
news-desk/the-poway-synagogue-shooting-follows-an-
unsettling-new-script.

12 The archived post on 8chan can be found at https://web.
archive.org/web/20190803162950/https:/8ch.net/pol/
res/13561044.html.

13 Steve Almasy, Dave Alsup and Madeline Holcombe,
'Dozens of people have been arrested over threats to
commit mass attacks since the El Paso and Dayton
shootings', CCN, 20 August 2019. Available at https://
edition.cnn.com/2019/08/21/us/mass-shooting-threats-
tuesday/index.html?no-st=1566483067.

14 'Gab and 8chan: Home to Terrorist Plots Hiding in
Plain Sight', ADL, n.d. Available at https://www.adl.org/
resources/reports/gab-and-8chan-home-to-terrorist-
plots-hiding-in-plain-sight#_ftn1.

15 M. Bilewicz et al., 'Harmful Ideas: The Structure and
Consequences of Anti-Semitic Beliefs in Poland', *Political
Psychology* 34(6), 2013, pp. 821–39.

16 Joel Finkelstein et al., 'A Quantitative Approach to
Understanding Anti-Semitism', Cornell University,
5 September 2018. Available at https://arxiv.org/
abs/1809.01644.

17 Evans, 'Ignore the Poway Synagogue Shooter's
Manifesto: Pay Attention to 8chan's /pol/ Board'.

18 J. M. Berger, 'The Alt-Right Twitter Census: Defining and
Describing the Audience for Alt-Right Twitter Content
on Twitter', VOX-Pol Network of Excellence, 2018.
Available at https://www.voxpol.eu/download/vox-pol_
publication/AltRightTwitterCensus.pdf.

19 Jacob Davey and Julia Ebner, '"The Great Replacement":
The Violent Consequences of Mainstreamed Extremism',
ISD, June 2019. Available at https://www.isdglobal.org/
wp-content/uploads/2019/07/The-Great-Replacement-
The-Violent-Consequences-of-Mainstreamed-
Extremism-by-ISD.pdf.

20 Ibid.

21 'Europe's Far-Right Parties Hunt Down the Youth Vote', Associated Press, 16 May 2019. Available at https://www.apnews.com/7f177b0cf15b4e87a53fe4382d6884ca.

22 Ibid.

23 'Wann hört das endlich auf, Herr Strache?', *Kronen Zeitung*, 28 April 2019. Available at https://www.krone.at/1911848.

24 Author's translation of the original posts in Flemish: Available at https://www.facebook.com/ KiesDries/posts/2102641296693640?comment_ id=2102646506693119&comment_tracking=%7B%2 2tn%22%3A%22R%22%7D and https://twitter.com/ DVanLangenhove/status/1118153920508039170.

25 Laurens Cerulus, 'Inside the far right's Flemish victory', Politico, 27 May 2019. Available at https://www.politico. eu/article/inside-the-far-rights-flemish-victory/. Van Langenhove denied all allegations and said the investigation misrepresented him.

26 'Européennes: pourquoi Renaud Camus retire sa liste', *Le Parisien*, 22 May 2019. Available at http://www. leparisien.fr/elections/europeennes/europeennes-renaud-camus-annonce-le-retrait-de-sa-liste-la-ligne-claire-22-05-2019-8077329.php.

27 Alex Ward, 'The New Zealand shooter called immigrants "invaders". Hours later, so did Trump', Vox, 15 March 2019. Available at https://www.vox.com/2019/3/15/18267745/ new-zealand-mosque-attack-invade-trump.

28 Davey and Ebner, '"The Great Replacement": The Violent Consequences of Mainstreamed Extremism'.

29 AfD Berlin, 8 April 2019. Available at https://www. facebook.com/afdberlin/photos/a.153594904822650/114 9164865265644/?type=3&theater.

13: IT ALL STARTED SO WELL

1 Abu Musab Al-Suri, 'The Call for a Global Islamic Resistance', 2004 (English translation). Available at

https://archive.org/stream/TheCallForAGlobalIslamic
Resistance-EnglishTranslationOfSomeKeyPartsAbuMusa
bAsSuri/TheCallForAGlobalIslamicResistanceSomeKey
Parts_djvu.txt.

2 Alex Hern, 'New AI fake text generator may be
too dangerous to release, say creators', *Guardian*, 14
February 2019. Available at https://www.theguardian.
com/technology/2019/feb/14/elon-musk-
backed-ai-writes-convincing-news-fiction.

3 Paige Leskin, 'The AI tech behind scare real celebrity
"deepfakes" is being used to create completely ficti-
tious faces, cats, and Airbnb listings', Business Insider, 21
February 2019. Available at https://www.businessinsider.
de/deepfake-tech-create-fictitious-faces-cats-airbnb-
listings-2019-2?r=US&IR=T.

4 Lizzie Plaugic, 'Watch a man manipulate George Bush's
face in real time', Verge, 21 March 2016. Available at
https://www.theverge.com/2016/3/21/11275462/
facial-transfer-donald-trump-george-bush-video.

5 Hern, 'New AI fake text generator may be too dangerous
to release, say creators'.

6 Friedrich Nietzsche, *Beyond Good and Evil: Prelude to
a Philosophy of the Future* (Mineola; New York: Dover
Publications, unabridged edn, 1997).

7 Amy Chua, *Political Tribes: Group Instinct and the Fate of
Nations* (London: Bloomsbury, 2018).

8 Ibid., p. 164.

9 David Goodhart, *The Road to Somewhere: The Populist
Revolt and the Future of Politics* (London: Hurst, 2017).

10 Hamza Shaban, 'Google for the first time outspent
every other company to influence Washington in
2017', *Washington Post*, 23 January 2018. Available at
https://www.washingtonpost.com/news/the-switch/
wp/2018/01/23/google-outspent-every-other-company-
on-federal-lobbying-in-2017/?noredirect=on&utm_
term=.9ef88d34f4d2.

11 'Bundestag nimmt umstrittenes Facebook-Gesetz an', *Handelsblatt*, 30 June 2017. Available at http://www.handelsblatt.com/politik/deutschland/hass-im-netz-bundestag-nimmt-umstrittenes-facebook-gesetz-an/20002292.html.

12 Article 19, 'Germany: Act to Improve Enforcement of the Law on Social Networks undermines free expression', 1 September 2017. Available at https://www.article19.org/resources/germany-act-to-improve-enforcement-of-the-law-on-social-networks-undermines-free-expression/.

13 More information about the Global Internet Forum to Counter Terrorism (GIFCT) is available at https://gifct.org/about/.

14 Michael Scheppe, 'NetzDG – das umstrittene Gesetz', *Handelsblatt*, 1 April 2018. Available at https://www.handelsblatt.com/politik/deutschland/fragen-und-antworten-netzdg-das-umstrittene-gesetz/20812704.html.

15 'Regulating social media: we need a new model that protects free expression', Article 19, 25 April 2018. Available at https://www.article19.org/resources/regulating-social-media-need-new-model-protects-free-expression/.

16 James B. Comey, 'Going Dark: Are Technology, Privacy, and Public Safety on a Collusion Course?', Federal Bureau of Investigation, 16 October 2014. Available at https://www.fbi.gov/news/speeches/going-dark-are-technology-privacy-and-public-safety-on-a-collision-course.

15: TEN SOLUTIONS FOR 2020

1 More information about the Tech Against Terrorism initiative can be found at https://www.techagainstterrorism.org.

2   More information about Hate Aid can be found at https://
    fearlessdemocracy.org/hate-aid/.

3   Jacob Davey, Jonathan Birdwell and Rebecca Skellett,
    'Counter Conversations: A Model for Direct Engagement
    with Individuals Showing Signs of Radicalisation Online',
    ISD, 2018. Available at https://www.isdglobal.org/
    wp-content/uploads/2018/03/Counter-Conversations_
    FINAL.pdf.

4   Interview with Donara Barojan and https://www.
    thedailybeast.com/the-baltic-elves-taking-on-
    pro-russian-trolls.

5   Adam Boult, 'Hackers flood ISIS social media accounts
    with gay porn', *Telegraph*, 25 April 2017. Available at
    https://www.telegraph.co.uk/news/2017/04/25/
    hackers-flood-isis-social-media-accounts-gay-porn/.

6   Simon Parkin, 'Operation Troll "ISIS": Inside
    Anonymous'War to Take Down Daesh', Wired, 6 October
    2016. Available at https://www.wired.co.uk/article/
    anonymous-war-to-undermine-daesh.

7   Joshua Stewart, 'Isis has been trolled with mountains of
    porn – and it's been far more effective than imams telling
    young Muslims off', *Independent*, 8 June 2016. Available
    at https://www.independent.co.uk/voices/isis-has-been-
    trolled-with-mountains-of-porn-and-its-been-far-more-
    effective-than-imams-telling-a7070881.html.

8   More information about the Hate Library can be found at
    https://www.nickthurston.info/Hate-Library.

9   More information about #ichbinhier can be found at
    https://ichbinhier.eu.

Index

Abdurrahman, Aman 79
abortion 29–30, 139, 185
Accelarationism 245, 287
Accurint 226
Achse des Guten 100
Adonis, Lord (Andrew) 168
advertising 99–101
Akademikierball 26
al-Adnani, Abu Muhammad 244
aliens 153, 164
Alinsky, Saul 222
Allen, Lily 128
Al-Qaeda 80, 91, 124, 149, 213, 215, 246, 254
Al-Rawi, Ahmed 125
al-Sadaqa 149
al-Suri, Aby Musab 254
Alt Right Leaks 130
Alternative for Germany (AfD) 121, 190, 202, 205
Altman, Mitch 227
Alt-Tech Alliance 146
alt-tech platforms, types of 145
Amadeu Antonio Foundation 191
'Amara, Umm 87
Amazon 218, 231

Ames, Aldrich 11
Amnesty International 128
Andelin, Helen 60
anger-management 69
Angern, Eva von 231
Angleton, James Jesus 105
Anglin, Andrew 174, 194, 222, 287
Anonymous 115, 160, 215, 217, 223, 227, 246, 278
Anschluss 198
Ansgar Aryan 200–1, 205
Antaios publishing house 27
Anthony, Jon 64
Anti-Defamation League 244
Antifa (anti-fascists) 173–4, 178, 184, 195
Anti-Racist Action 178
anti-Semitism 14–15, 18–19, 30, 43, 45, 100, 127, 207, 248, 289
  and Charlottesville rally 173–4, 176–7, 180–1, 220
  hackers and 216–17, 220, 222
  rising under Trump 244
  and terrorist attacks 242–4
  Tommy Robinson denies 98

and Yellow Vests 189
see also Jews; ZOG
Anton, Reinhold 108
'apocalypse' (the word) 157
apophenia 155
APT28 ('Fancy Bear') unit 232
AQ Electronic Jihad
    Organisation 215
Arendt, Hannah 34
Ares, Chris 191
Article 19, 260
artists 279
assault rifles, availability of 268
Association for Retired Persons
    of Austria 27
AT&T 218
Atomwaffen 245
Auernheimer, Andrew, *see* Weev
Auschwitz 16

Bakker, Jim 158
Bali bombing 76
Balliet, Stephan 244–5
Baltic Elves 277
Bambenek, John 148–9
Bannon, Steve 12, 99
Bantown 223
Barley, Katarina 233
Barojan, Donara 106–7
Barr, Roseanne 166
Bataclan attack 292
Batam Island 79
Bateman, Hannibal 41–2
BBC 94, 98, 231, 259
BDSM 68–9
Beiler, Ronald 34
Benjamin, Carl (Sargon of
    Akkad) 63, 146
Benjamin, Walter 4

Benotman, Noman 91
Berger, J. M. 247, 269
b4bo 223
bin Laden, Osama 84, 153, 164
birthrates 30, 235
Bissonnette, Alexandre 236, 238
BitChute 145
bitcoin 148–9, 212, 223
Blissett, Luther 160
Bloc Identitaire 28
blockchain technology 149
bloggers 217
Blood & Honour 195
Bloom, Mia 267
Bloomberg, Michael 218
Böhmermann, Jan 277
Bowers, Robert 243–5
Breed Them Out 139
Breitbart 43–4, 94, 99–100
Breivik, Anders Behring
    236, 238
'Brentonettes' 240
Brewer, Emmett 230
Brexit 168, 257
Britain First 85
British National Party (BNP)
    98, 111, 185
Broken Heart operation 229
Brown, Dan 167
Bubba Media 98
Bumble 70, 137
Bundestag hack 229, 232
BuzzFeed 160

C Star 31, 39
'Call of Duty' 124, 239
Cambridge Analytica 147, 254
Camus, Renaud 248
Carroll, Lewis 155

CBS 162
Channel programme 238
Charleston church shooting 20
Charlie Hebdo 191
Charlottesville rally 3–4, 17–18,
    145–6, 173–84, 187, 190,
    192, 220, 243
Chemnitz protests 190, 192
Choudary, Anjem 97
Christchurch terror attacks 23,
    235–42, 245, 247–8
Christian identity 139
Chua, Amy 257
CIA 105, 164–5, 213
Clinton, Bill and Hillary 114,
    154, 160, 162–3, 168,
    222, 229
Cohn, Norman 157
Collett, Mark 37
Cologne rape crisis 108
Combat 18, 195
Comey, James 262
Comvo 186
concentration camps 15–16
Conrad, Klaus 155
Conservative Political Action
    Conference 187
Constitution for the
    Ethno-State 19
Corem, Yochai 229
counter-extremism
    legislation 258–60
counter-trolling 277–8
Covington, Harold 19
Crash Override Network 102
Crusius, Patrick 243–5
cryptocurrencies 148–50, 207,
    212, 223
Cuevas, Joshua 101

Cyberbit 228–9
Cyborgology blog 240

'Daily Shoah' podcast 173
Daily Stormer 124, 145, 148–9,
    174–5, 177, 180, 216,
    227, 287
  Weev and 219–20
Damore, James 146
Dark Net 148–9
Data and Society Research
    Institute 132
Davey, Jacob 270
Dawkins, Richard 99, 288
De La Rosa, Veronique 167
de Turris, Gianfranco 12
Dearden, Lizzie 101–4
deep fakes 255–6, 271
DefCon 226–7, 230
Der Spiegel 110
Deutsche Bahn 229
Diana, Princess of Wales 153, 164
Die Linke 231
Die Rechte 199
'digital dualism' 240
digital education 280–1
disinformation 105–11,
    254–6, 276–7
Disney 162
Domestic Discipline 58, 69
Donovan, Joan 14
Doomsday preppers 158
doubling 16
Dox Squad 102, 104
doxxing 102–4, 116, 241,
    284, 287–8
Doyle, Laura 57, 68
Draugiem 106
DTube 145

Dugin, Alexander 34
Dunning–Kruger Effect 165
Dutch Leaks 169–70
Dylan, Bob 161

Earnest, John 242–5
8chan 110, 131, 145, 157, 165–7,
    235–7, 242–4, 246
EKRE (Estonian fascist
    party) 268
El Paso shooting 243–4
Element AI 128
Emanuel, Rahm 218
encryption and
    steganography 83–4
Encyclopedia Dramatica 239
English Defence League 46,
    91–2, 95, 189
Enoch, Mike 173
environmentalism 266, 269–70
ethno-pluralism 28–9, 35
'Eurabia' 248–9, 288
'European Israel' 140
European National 189
European Parliament
    elections 187–8
European Spring 189
Evola, Julius 11–12
executions 262

Facebook friends 258
fashions and lifestyles
    175–6, 200–1
Fawcett, Farah 217
Faye, Guillaume 29
FBI 87, 214, 218–19, 242, 262
Fearless Democracy 101, 275
FedEx 229
Feldman, Matthew 279

Ferdinand II, King of
    Aragon 116
Fiamengo, Janice 64
Fields, James Alex 182
Fight Club 41–2
Finkelstein, Robert 127
Finsbury Mosque attack 97,
    102, 104
Fisher, Robert 56
Foley, James 81
Follin, Marcus 64
football hooligans 22, 203–4
Football Lads Alliance (FLA) 40
For Britain party 36
Fortnite 255
4chan 115, 124, 127, 131–2, 160,
    166, 177, 244, 271
FPÖ (Austrian Freedom Party)
    26–8, 32–3, 38, 64, 248
Frankfurt School 66
Fransen, Jayda 85
Fraternal Order of
    Alt-Knights 180
Freedom Fighters, The 161
freedom of speech 18, 177,
    249, 260
F-Secure 215
FSN TV 201

Gab 98, 145, 167, 186, 244, 288
Gamergate controversy 102
GamerGate Veterans 139
gamification 31, 49, 70, 123–5,
    144, 238–9, 247, 263
Ganser, Daniele 165
Gates of Vienna 94
Gateway Pundit 180–1
Gawker 218
GCHQ 125

GE 162
GellerReport 94
Generation Identity (GI) 3–4,
    25–50, 110, 128, 144, 202,
    235, 247
Generation Islam 131
genetic testing 13–15, 50
German elections 120–1, 126
German Institute on
    Radicalization and
    De-Radicalization
    Studies 265–6
German National Cyber
    Defence Centre 230
Gervais, Ricky 34
Ghost Security 84
Giesea, Jeff 127
Gigih Rahmat Dewa 79
Gionet, Tim 181
gladiators 262
Global Cabal of the New World
    Order 162
global financial crisis 18, 108
global warming 270
GNAA 223
Goatse Security 218
GOBBLES 223
Goebbels, Joseph 204
GoFundMe 149
Goldy, Faith 180
Goodhart, David 257
'Google's Ideological Echo
    Chamber' 146
Gorbachev, Mikhail 206
Graham, Senator Lindsey 147
Gratipay 219
Great Awakening 154–5, 168
Great Replacement theory 29–
    30, 168, 235–6, 244, 247–8

'Grievance Studies' 110
grooming gangs 97–8, 109
Guardian 94–5, 105

H., Daniel 190
Habeck, Robert 232
HackerOne 227
hackers and hacking 211–34
    'capture the flag' operations
        215, 217
    denial of service
        operations 217
    ethical hacking 227
    memory-corruption
        operations 226
    political hacking 230–4
    'qwning' 227
    SQL injections 213–14
    techniques 224–5
Halle shooting 244
Hamas 5, 229
Hanks, Tom 166
Happn 137
Harris, DeAndre 183
'hashtag stuffing' 131
Hate Library 279
HateAid 101, 275–6
Hatreon 145, 149, 219
Heidegger, Martin 33–4
Heise, Thorsten 193, 195
Hensel, Gerald 99–101, 275
Herzliya International Institute
    for Counter-Terrorism 216
Heyer, Heather 17–18, 183, 220
Himmler, Heinrich 12
Hintsteiner, Edwin 25–36
Histiaeus 83
Hitler, Adolf 10, 26, 34, 124, 193
    Mein Kampf 118, 174

Hitler salutes 22, 98, 189–90, 200
Hitler Youth 268
HIV 153
Hizb ut-Tahrir 48, 91, 131
Höcker, Karl-Friedrich 15–16
Hofstadter, Richard 169
Hollywood 164
Holocaust 26
Holocaust denial 18, 29, 114,
        122, 145
Holy War Hackers Team
        215–16
Home Office 241
homophobia 18, 28–30,
        189
Hooton Plan 30
Hoover Dam 158
Hope Not Hate 38–9, 48, 270
Horgan, John 268
Horowitz Foundation 99
Hot or Not 54
House of Saud 162
Huda, Noor 80
human trafficking 163, 168
Hussein, Saddam 124, 214
Hutchins, Marcus 230
Hyppönen, Mikko 215

Identity Evropa 45, 180
iFrames 218
Illuminati 164
Incels (Involuntary Celibacy)
        56, 61–3
Independent 48
Inkster, Nigel 266
Institute for Strategic Dialogue
        (ISD) 1, 32, 129–30, 132,
        166, 247, 270, 276
Intelius 103

International Business Times 214
International Centre for the
        Study of Radicalisation
        (ICSR) 269
International Federation of
        Journalists 105
International Holocaust
        Memorial Day 26
International Institute for
        Strategic Studies 266
Internet Research Agency
        (IRA) 115
iPads 218
iPhones 254
iProphet 217
Iranian revolution 118–19
Isabella I, Queen of Castile 116
ISIS 3, 72, 75–87, 91, 124,
        149, 176, 179, 239, 244,
        259, 266–7
    hackers and 211, 213–16, 226–
        7, 233, 278
Islamophobia 14, 18, 36, 40, 48,
        115, 189
    Tommy Robinson and 91, 97
    see also Finsbury
        Mosque attack
Israel 42, 87, 140, 180, 228–9
Israel Defense Forces 5, 229

Jackson, Michael 217
jahiliyya 45
Jakarta attacks 79
Jamaah Ansharud Daulah
        (JAD) 76
Japanese anime 21
Jemaah Islamiyah 78
Jesus Christ 13
Jewish numerology 110

Jews 13–16, 26, 34, 98, 116, 139, 145, 148, 166
    see also anti-Semitism; ZOG
JFG World 241
jihadi brides 4, 75–88
JihadWatch 94
Jobs, Steve 253
Johnson, Boris 165
Jones, Alex 166–7
Jones, Ron 123
Junge Freiheit 100
Jurgenson, Nathan 240
JustPasteIt 145

Kafka, Franz 42
Kampf der Niebelungen 193, 203
Kapustin, Denis 'Nikitin' 204
Kassam, Raheem 94
Kellogg's 238–9
Kennedy, John F. 153, 165
Kennedy family 162
Kessler, Jason 173, 179
Khomeini, Ayataollah 119
Kim Jong-un 13
Kohl, Helmut 206
Köhler, Daniel 265
Kronen Zeitung 248
Kronos banking Trojan 230
Ku Klux Klan 175, 180
Küssel, Gottfried 29

Lane, David 289
Le Loop 227
Le Pen, Marine 189
LeBretton, Matthew 194
Lebron, Michael 166
Lee, Robert E. 173
Li, Sean 118

Li family 162
Libyan Fighting Group 91
LifeOfWat 23
Lifton, Robert 16
Littman, Gisele 288
live action role play (LARP) 116, 123, 160, 174, 237, 288
lobbying 258
Lokteff, Lana 57
loneliness 16, 62, 86, 140, 179, 220, 263
Lorraine, DeAnna 65–6
Lügenpresse 108

McDonald's 162
McInnes, Gavin 177
McMahon, Ed 217
Macron, Emmanuel 157, 189, 229, 258
MAGA (Make America Great Again) 127
'mainstream media' 92–3, 109, 133
'Millennium Dawn' 124
Manosphere 56–7, 59, 64
March for Life 187
Maria Theresa statue 44, 47
Marighella, Carlos 246
Marina Bay Sands Hotel (Singapore) 79
Marx, Karl 125
    Das Kapital 118
Masculine Development 64
Mason, James 245
MAtR (Men Among the Ruins) 9–24, 243
Matrix, The 20–1, 41, 155, 289
May, Theresa 92, 165, 258
Meechan, Mark 98

Meme Warfare 161
memes 99–100, 127–8,
    271, 288–9
and terrorist attacks 239–43
Men's Rights Activists
    (MRA) 56
Menlo Park 253–4
Mercer Family Foundation 99
Merkel, Angela 100, 120–1,
    230–1, 258
MGTOW (Men Going Their
    Own Way) 53–6, 61, 71
MI6, 158, 164
migration 28–30, 40, 42, 66, 97,
    108, 216, 248, 289
    see also refugees
millenarianism 157
Millennial Woes 130
millennials 70
Minassian, Alek 63
Mindanao 79
Minds 145, 186
misogyny 102, 105, 115, 256, 270
    see also Incels
mixed martial arts (MMA) 193,
    200, 202–5, 207
Morgan, Nicky 129
Mounk, Yascha 111
Movement, The 99
Mueller, Robert 154, 165
Muhammad, Prophet 77, 87, 162
mujahidat 87
Mulhall, Joe 270
MuslimCrypt 81
MuslimTec 211–12, 215
Mussolini, Benito 12

Naim, Bahrun 79, 149
Nance, Malcolm 213

Nasher App 84
National Action 148
National Bolshevism 28
National Democratic Party
    (NPD) 193, 199–200,
    202, 205
National Health Service
    (NHS) 229
National Policy Institute 29, 173
National Socialism group 139
National Socialist
    Movement 180
National Socialist
    Underground 196
NATO DFR Lab 106–7
Naturalnews 161
Nawaz, Maajid 91
Nazi symbols 43, 122, 175, 180,
    187, 196, 200–1
    see also Hitler salutes;
    swastikas
Nazi women 175
N-count 55
Neiwert, David 109
Nero, Emperor 154
Netflix 181
Network Contagion Research
    Institute 244
NetzDG legislation 259, 275
Neumann, Peter 269
New Balance shoes 194
New York Times 242
News Corp 162
Newsnight 41
Nietzsche, Friedrich 33–4, 257
Nikolai Alexander, Supreme
    Commander 116, 119–20,
    122–3, 125, 133, 221
9/11 attacks 109, 153

'nipsters' 32–3, 201
No Agenda 161
Northwest Front (NWF)
    19–20, 23
Nouvelle Droite 29, 288–9
NPC meme 132
NSDAP 10, 34, 155

Obama, Barack and Michelle
    99, 109, 154, 163, 165
Omas gegen Rechts 26
online harassment, gender
    and 128–9
OpenAI 256
open-source intelligence
    (OSINT) 103, 241
Operation Name and
    Shame 161
Orbán, Viktor 154, 248
organised crime 266
Orwell, George 41, 256
Osborne, Darren 97, 102
Oxford Internet Institute 107

Page, Larry 253
Panofsky, Aaron 14
Panorama 98
Parkland high-school
    shooting 110
Patreon 39, 145, 149, 219
Patriot Peer 31–2, 144
PayPal 219
PeopleLookup 103
Periscope 169
Peterson, Jordan 63
Pettibone, Brittany 41, 45, 69
Pew Research Center 109, 128
PewDiePie 237
PewTube 145

Phillips, Whitney 44
Photofeeler 54
Phrack High Council 223
Pink Floyd 161
Pipl 103
Pittsburgh synagogue
    shooting 243
Pizzagate 158
Podesta, John 154, 229
political propaganda 274–5
Popper, Karl 165
populist politicians 247–9
pornography 213, 278
Poway synagogue shooting
    242–3, 248
Pozner, Lenny 167
Presley, Elvis 161
Prideaux, Sue 34
Prince Albert Police 215
Pro Chemnitz 190
'pseudo-conservatives' 169
Putin, Vladimir 144

Q Britannia 167–8
QAnon 5, 153–70, 189, 243
Quebec mosque shooting 236
Quilliam Foundation 91,
    94–6, 111
Quinn, Zoë 102
Quran 115

racist slurs (n-word) 244
Radio 3Fourteen 57
Radix Journal 42
Rafiq, Haras 94–5
Ramakrishna, Kumar 78
RAND Corporation 108
Rasmussen, Tore 37–8, 41,
    43, 46–7

Raymond, Jolynn 68
Rebel Media 40, 92, 180
Reconquista Germanica 115–23, 125, 129–30, 200, 221, 243, 277
Reconquista Internet 277
Red Pill Women 53–62, 64, 67, 72, 88
Reddit 53, 55–6, 61–2, 131, 166–7, 177, 186, 189, 218, 289
redpilling 20–1, 40, 44–5, 289
refugees 31, 104, 154, 190, 231
Relotius, Claas 110
'Remove Kebab' 237
Renault 229
Revolution Chemnitz 190
Rigby, Lee 98
Right Wing Terror Center 245
Right Wing United (RWU) 184–9
RMV (Relationship Market Value) 59
Robertson, Caolan 91
Robinson, Tommy 46, 91–8, 101–2, 104, 109, 111, 133, 168
Rockefeller family 162
Rodger, Elliot 63
Roof, Dylann 20, 245
Rosenberg, Alfred 10
Rothschilds 162, 164
Rowley, Mark 97
Roy, Donald F. 239
Royal Family 162
Russia Today 106, 132

S., Johannes 231
St Kilda Beach meeting 186
Salafi Media 124

Saltman, Erin 260–1
Salvini, Matteo 248–9
Sampson, Chris 213, 266
Sandy Hook school shooting 166–7
Sargon of Akkad, see Benjamin, Carl
Schild & Schwert rock festival (Ostritz) 4, 193–208, 243
Schilling, Curt 166
Schlessinger, Laura C. 58
Scholz & Friends 101
SchoolDesk 214
Schröder, Patrick 200–2
Sellner, Martin 27, 29–30, 33–6, 38, 41, 43–8, 110, 144, 202, 235
Serrano, Francisco 249
'sexual economics' 54
SGT Report 161
Shodan 212, 217
Siege-posting 245
Sleeping Giants 100
SMV (Sexual Market Value) 53–5, 58, 71
Social Justice Warriors (SJW) 144, 184
Solahütte 16
Soros, George 154, 162
Sotloff, Steven 81
Southern, Lauren 45
Southfront 161
Spencer, Richard 34, 45, 144, 148, 173–4, 201
Spiegel TV 201–2
spoofing technology 271
Sputnik 106, 132
SS 11, 15
Stadtwerke Borken 215

Star Wars 42
Steinmeier, Frank-Walter 232
Stewart, Ayla 65
STFU (Shut the Fuck Up) 58
Stormfront 22, 124, 148–9
Strache, H. C. 248
Süddestsche Zeitung 255
suicide gender paradox 64
Sunday Times 49
Suomenuskos 10
Surabaya bombing 75–6, 78
Survival Food 158
swastikas 17, 29, 174, 201, 216, 219
Swift, Taylor 21

Taken in Hand (TiH) 68–9
Tarrant, Brenton 236–42, 244–5, 248
Taylor, Jared 130
TAZ 110
Team System DZ 214–15
Tech Against Terrorism 274
tech firms, business models 262–3
Terror Agency Sisters 75, 77–9, 85–8
terrorist instruction manuals 246, 266
Terrorsphära 193–4, 198
The Red Pill (TRP) 56, 61, 67, 70–1
Thompson, Kevin 22
Thunberg, Greta 191
Thurston, Nick 279
Tichys Einblick 100
Time Warner 162
Tinder 63, 70, 137, 139
Törvény, Fehér 205

Trad Wives 4, 53–73, 78, 86, 207
Traditional Britain
    Conference 37
Traditionalist Worker Party 180
Traini, Luca 124
tribalism 257–8, 263
'trigger' (the word) 201
Troll Watch 92, 94
trolls, rise of 114–15
True Lies QNN 169–70
Trump, Donald 13, 42, 59, 98, 100, 107, 109, 114, 241, 244, 257, 271
    Charlottesville rally and 173, 176
    and Great Replacement theory 247–9
    hackers and 222–3
    New Balance shoes and 194
    pro-Trump memes 127–8
    QAnon and 153–4, 156, 160, 166, 168
    retweets Britain First videos 85
    RWU and 185–6
Trump Singles 143
Truth Decay 107
Tufecki, Zeynep 114
Twitch 186

Uhud, Battle of 87
UKIP 36–7, 63, 185
Unite the Right 173–6, 187, 202
United Cyber Caliphate 216, 227
urban environment, and extremism 267
US House Intelligence Committee 115

US National Security
Agency 154
Uyghurs 267

vaccines 166
van den Bruck, Arthur
Moeller 118
Van Langenhove, Dries 248
Vanguard America 180
Vatican, the 164
Verma, Sajal 212
Viacom 162
Vietnam War 158
Vigrid 37
violence, against women 58,
67–9, 231
virtual private networks (VPNs)
83, 115, 148, 211
visual illusions 155
VK 145
Vlaams Belang 248
Voat 62
VoIP apps 221–2
Vox party 166, 249
VOX-Pol 269

Wachowski, Lana and Lilly
20, 155
Wallace, Hunter 176
WannaCry attack 229–30
WASP Love 137–43, 145, 243
Waters, Anne Marie 36

'Wave, The' 122–3
Weev (Andrew Auernheimer)
149, 217–26
Weiss, Michael 267
Welsh, Edgar 158
Westminster Bridge, GI
banner on 48
White Date 143
'white genocide' 29, 138, 177,
244, 289
White Rex 204, 206
Whitesingles 148
Wiebe, Ed 217
Wikileaks 160
Willinger, Markus 39
Wilson, Andrew 169
Wintrich, Lucian 180
Wolfsangel 17
Wolves of Odin 189
Women's March 187
women's voting rights 66
Wright, Matthew P. 158

Yellow Vests (Gilets Jaunes) 157,
168, 189
YouTube, prioritises
extremism 113–14

Zerohedge 161
ZOG (Zionist Occupied
Government) 15, 219, 289
Zuckerberg, Mark 147, 253

A Note on the Author

Julia Ebner is a Research Fellow at the Institute for Strategic Dialogue, where she leads projects on online extremism, disinformation and hate speech. She has given evidence to numerous governments and parliamentary working groups, and has acted as a consultant for the UN, NATO and the World Bank. Her journalism has appeared in the *Guardian, Independent, Prospect* and *Newsweek*, among many other publications, and she was a key contributor to a documentary for ITV on militant responses to Brexit, and a BBC Radio 4 piece on women in the far right. Her first book, *The Rage: The Vicious Circle of Islamist and Far-Right Extremism*, was a *Spiegel* bestseller, shortlisted for the NDR Kultur Sachbuchpreis and won the 2018 Bruno Kreisky award. She lives in London.

@julie_renbe

A Note on the Type

The text of this book is set in Bembo, which was first used in 1495 by the Venetian printer Aldus Manutius for Cardinal Bembo's *De Aetna*. The original types were cut for Manutius by Francesco Griffo. Bembo was one of the types used by Claude Garamond (1480–1561) as a model for his Romain de l'Université, and so it was a forerunner of what became the standard European type for the following two centuries. Its modern form follows the original types and was designed for Monotype in 1929.